Alaa al-Deeb by Adel El-Siwi

The Forum for Arab and International Relations

CALL FOR PAPERS

THE CONFERENCE ON
TRANSLATION
AND THE PROBLEMATICS
OF CROSSCULTURAL UNDERSTANDING (4)

(13-14 December 2017)
Doha, Qatar

The Forum for Arab and International Relations cordially invites you to participate in its fourth international conference on

Translation and the Problematics of Crosscultural Understanding

(to be held in Doha, Qatar, 13-14 December 2017)

The conference coincides with the third prize winning ceremony of
Sheikh Hamad Award for Translation and International Understanding

The topics of interest include:
- The challenges of idiom rendering
- Literary translation (translating poetry)
- Critiquing, assessing and editing sample translations
- News (political, economic, etc.,) translations
- The problematics of Arabic/Eastern Languages (Chinese, Japanese, Persian, Urdu, Malay) translations
- The problematics of Arabic/French translations
- Interpreting and legal translation in international organizations: nature & challenges
- Audio-visual translation

Translators, academics, researchers and interested people are welcome to apply.

Please send an abstract/proposal (maximum 1000 words (in Arabic) or, if absolutely impossible, in English), summarizing the problem and the methodology of your paper by 30 September 2017.

The Conference Reading Committee selects the approved abstracts/proposals and notifies the concerned participant(s).

It is preferable to receive the approved paper in full at least a fortnight before the start of the conference. However, it is possible to submit the paper in its final form after the conference (but not later than 30 December 2017).

Arabic is the language of the conference (with English translation)

The Paper accepted for publication in the conference proceedings book is given a token reward (US$600).

The conference provides return tickets and full board accommodation.

All submissions must be made by e-mail to the following address: translation@fairforum.org

For further details please visit our website at (www.fairforum.org) or contact the conference secretariat at (00974) 4408-0462.

Wasafiri

The Magazine of International Contemporary Writing

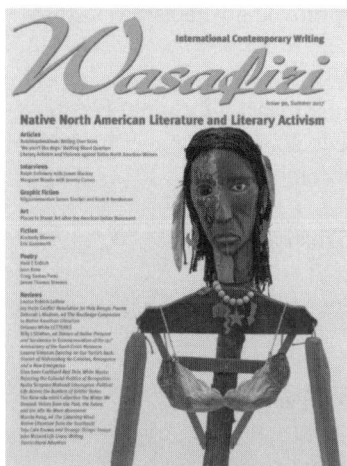

Wasafiri encourages readers and writers to travel the world via the word. For over three decades, we have created a dynamic platform for mapping new landscapes in contemporary international writing featuring a diverse range of voices from across the UK and beyond.

www.wasafiri.org @Wasafiri1

⋔NYU PRESS
THE LIBRARY OF ARABIC LITERATURE

NEW IN PAPERBACK

A Hundred and One Nights
Foreword by ROBERT IRWIN
Translated by BRUCE FUDGE
£12.99 | $15.00

Consorts of the Caliphs
Women and the Court of Baghdad
IBN AL-SAʿI
Translated by SHAWKAT M. TOORAWA
and the editors of the
LIBRARY OF ARABIC LITERATURE
Introduction by JULIA BRAY
and foreword by MARINA WARNER
£11.99 | $14.00

Disagreements of the Jurists
A Manual of Islamic Legal Theory
AL-QADI AL-NUʿMAN
Translated by DEVIN STEWART
Foreword by JOHN COUGHLIN and
JOHN SEXTON
£12.99 | $15.00

"The entire series, promises to be an invaluable mine of knowledge for scholars and general readers who need an introduction to the universal appeal and validity of the enlightening and enlightened literary heritage of the Arabic-Islamic intellectual tradition."
—*Journal of Islamic Studies*

Accounts of China and India
ABU ZAYD AL-SIRAFI
Translated by
TIM MACKINTOSH-SMITH
Foreword by ZVI BEN-DOR BENITE
£12.99 | $15.00

The Expeditions
An Early Biography of Muḥammad
MAʿMAR IBN RĀSHID
Translated by SEAN W. ANTHONY
Foreword by M.A.S. ABDEL HALEEM
£12.99 | $15.00

The Principles of Sufism
ʿĀʾISHAH AL-BĀʿŪNIYYAH
Translated by T. EMIL HOMERIN
Foreword by ROS BALLASTER
£12.99 | $15.00

Mission to the Volga
AHMAD IBN FADLAN
Translated by
JAMES MONTGOMERY
Foreword by TIM SEVERIN
£12.99 | $15.00

A Treasury of Virtues
Sayings, Sermons, and Teaching of
ʿAli, with the one Hundred Proverbs,
attributed to al-Jāḥiẓ
AL-QĀḌĪ AL-QUDĀʿĪ
Translated by TAHERA QUTBUDDIN
Foreword by ROWAN WILLIAMS
£12.99 | $15.00

The Epistle of Forgiveness
Volumes One and Two
ABŪ L-ʿALĀʾ AL-MAʿARRĪ
Translated by
GEERT JAN VAN GELDER and
GREGOR SCHOELER
Foreword by MATTHEW REYNOLDS
£13.99 | $16.00

Winner of the 2016 Sheikh Hamad Award for
Translation and International Understanding
(First Prize, Arabic to English)

The Life of Ibn Hanbal
IBN AL-JAWZI
Translated by
MICHAEL COOPERSON
Foreword by GARTH FOWDEN
£14.99 | $17.00

Leg over Leg
Volumes One and Two
AHMAD FĀRIS AL-SHIDYĀQ
Translated by HUMPHREY DAVIES
£14.99 | $17.00

Leg over Leg
Volumes Three and Four
AHMAD FĀRIS AL-SHIDYĀQ
Translated by HUMPHREY DAVIES
£14.99 | $17.00

All books are available as e-books
Supported by a grant from New York University Abu Dhabi the Library of Arabic Literature publishes significant works of pre-modern Arabic literature,
in both parallel-text editions and English-only paperbacks.
FOR MORE TITLES AND TO ORDER ONLINE:
WWW.LIBRARYOFARABICLITERATURE.ORG • WWW.NYUPRESS.ORG • WWW.COMBINEDACADEMIC.CO.UK (EUROPE/UK)

DIGITAL BANIPAL
Complete archive now available for Institutions and individuals

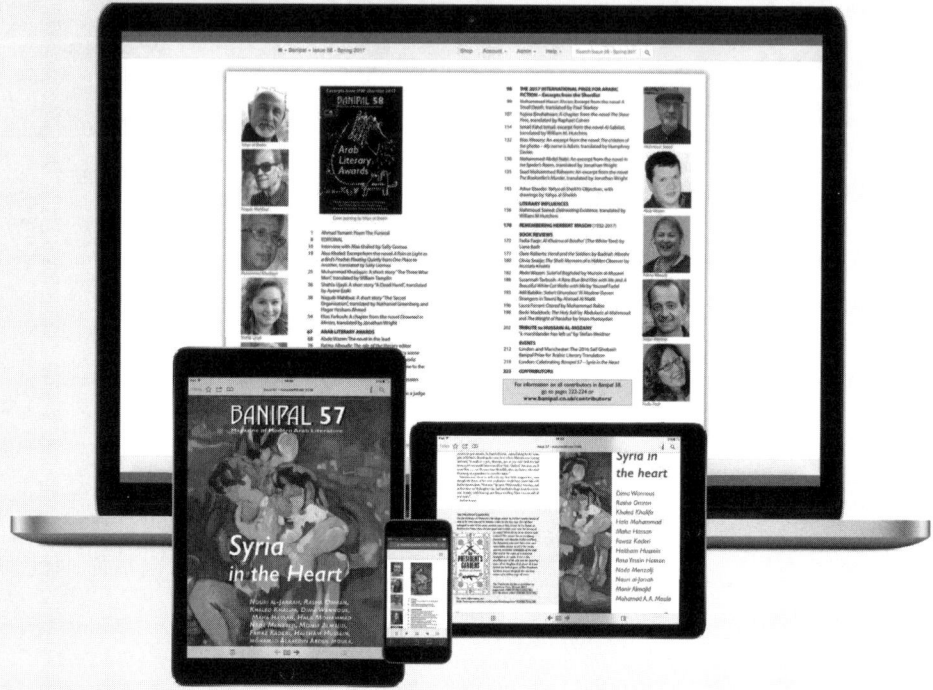

Banipal's digital edition offers readers all over the world the chance to flip open the magazine on their computers, iPads, iPhones or android smartphones, wherever they are, check out the current issue, search through the back issues and sync as desired.

A year's digital subscription comes with full access to the full digital archive, back to Banipal No 1, February 1998 – for individuals (£49.99) and for institutions (starting at USD450.00 and based on FTE). Print and digital subscriptions are still separate for the moment.

Download the free iTunes App or get it on an Android smartphone.

Preview the digital archive, preview the current issue or check out the Free Trial issue: *Banipal 53 – The Short Stories of Zakaria Tamer*

For more information, go to:
www.banipal.co.uk/subscribe/digital/

Trial issue

Subscribe Directly to Digital Banipal
Individual: exacteditions.com/banipal
Libraries: institutions.exacteditions.com/banipal

Banipal's digital partner

BANIPAL — Magazine of Modern Arab Literature

PUBLISHER: Margaret Obank

EDITOR: Samuel Shimon

CONTRIBUTING EDITORS
Fadhil al-Azzawi, Issa J Boullata, Peter Clark,
Raphael Cohen, Bassam Frangieh, Camilo Gómez-Rivas,
Marilyn Hacker, William M Hutchins, Adil Babikir,
Imad Khachan, Khaled Mattawa, Anton Shammas,
Paul Starkey, Mona Zaki

CONSULTING EDITORS
Etel Adnan, Roger Allen, Mohammed Bennis,
Isabella Camera d'Afflitto, Humphrey Davies,
Hartmut Fähndrich, Saif al-Rahbi, Naomi Shihab Nye,
Yasir Suleiman, Susannah Tarbush, Stephen Watts

EDITORIAL ASSISTANTS: Annamaria Basile, Rosie Maxton

ADDITIONAL TRANSLATION: Ben Koerber, Adil Babikir,
Jonathan Wright, Raphael Cohen

COVER PHOTOGRAPH: Randa Shaath

LAYOUT: Banipal Publishing

WEBSITE: www.banipal.co.uk

EDITOR: editor@banipal.co.uk

PUBLISHER: margaret@banipal.co.uk

INQUIRIES: info@banipal.co.uk

SUBSCRIPTIONS: subscribe@banipal.co.uk

ADDRESS: 1 Gough Square, London EC4A 3DE

PRINTED BY Short Run Press Ltd
Bittern Road, Sowton Ind. Est. EXETER EX2 7LW

Photographs not accredited have been donated, photographers unknown.

Copyright: *Banipal 60 – Alaa al-Deeb, A writer apart*
This selection © Banipal Publishing.
All rights reserved.
This issue is ISBN 978-0-9956369-3-4. RRP £9, €12, USD15

No reproduction or copy, in whole or in part, in the print or the digital edition, may be made without the written permission of the publisher.

BANIPAL, ISSN 1461-5363, is published three times a year by Banipal Publishing, 1 Gough Square, London EC4A 3DE

Banipal magazine, founded in 1998, takes its name from Ashurbanipal (668–627 BC), the last great king of Assyria and patron of the arts, whose outstanding achievement was to assemble in his capital Nineveh, Mesopotamia, from all over his empire, the first systematically organised library in the ancient Middle East. The thousands of clay tablets of Sumerian, Babylonian and Assyrian writings included the famous Mesopotamian epics of the Creation, the Flood, and Gilgamesh, many folk tales, fables, proverbs, prayers and omen texts.
Source: *Encyclopaedia Britannica*

Supported using public funding by
ARTS COUNCIL ENGLAND

www.banipal.co.uk

Widad Nabi

Safi Said

Lina Hawyan Alhassan

Abdallah Uld Mohamadi Bah

Lamia Makaddam

10	**EDITORIAL**
12	Safi Said: A chapter from the novel *Kitsch 2011*, translated by Jonathan Wright
36	Abdallah Uld Mohamadi Bah: A chapter from the novel *Birds of al-Nab'a*, translated by Julia Ihnatowicz
48	Lamia Makaddam: Four poems, translated by Karen McNeil & Miled Faiza
53	Abdelaziz Baraka Sakin: A short story, *My Mother, the Other Women and I*, translated by Adel Babikir
59	Widad Nabi: Five poems, translated by Jonathan Wright
68	**ALAA AL-DEEB, A WRITER APART**
70	Chapters from Alaa al-Deeb's novel *Lemon Blossom*, translated by Jonathan Wright
88	Mahmoud el-Wardany: *The Trans-generational Alaa al-Deeb*
92	Yasser Abdel Latif: *A Lofty Eucalyptus Tree in Maadi*
100	Mansoura Ez-Eldin: *The Defeated Leftist Intellectual*
103	Alaa al-Deeb: An excerpt from the novella *Al-Qahira*, translated by Raphael Cohen
108	Alaa al-Deeb: A chapter from the novel *Children without Tears*, translated by Raphael Cohen
119	Alaa al-Deeb: An excerpt from the novel *Moon over the Swamp*, translated by Paul Starkey
130	Ibrahim Farghali: *Observing the Distortion of Intellectual Identity*
133	Youssef Rakha: *Five Memories of Alaa al-Deeb*

136   Alaa Khaled: *Alaa al-Deeb's Cairo*, translated by Suneela Mubayi
141   Ben Koerber reviews Alaa al-Deeb's novel *Lemon Blossom*
144   Alaa al-Deeb: A short story *The River beneath the Rocks*, translated by Nariman Youssef
146   Alaa al-Deeb: Chapters from his memoir *Pause before the Decline*, translated by Sally Gomaa & Jonathan Wright

A TRAVELLING TALE
162   Lina Hawyan Alhassan: Chapters from the novel *Wolves Do Not Forget*, translated by Samira Kawar

BOOK REVIEWS
178   Paul Starkey: *No Road to Paradise* by Hassan Daoud
181   Laura Ferreri: *The American Quarter* by Jabbour Douaihy
184   Susannah Tarbush: *Him, Me, Mohammad Ali* by Randa Jarrar
188   Margaret Obank: *Farewell, Damascus* by Ghada Samman
192   Paul Blezard: *The Book of Safety* by Yasser Abdel Hafez
195   Hassouna Mosbahi: *Birds of al-Nab'a* by Abdallah Uld Mohamadi Bah
198   Becki Maddock: *Maryam, Keeper of Stories* by Alawiya Sobh
202   Clare Roberts: *The Baghdad Eucharist* by Sinan Antoon

BOOKS IN BRIEF
204   *The Scent of Jasmine: Coming of Age in Jerusalem and Damascus* by Anan Ameri
205   *Codename: Butterfly* by Ahlam Bsharat

TRIBUTE
206   Denys Johnson-Davies (1922-2017)

EVENTS
210   LONDON: Sheikh Zayed Book Award Seminar
212   BERLIN: Banipal at the International Literature Festival
214   FRANKFURT: ICORN-Banipal panel discussion
215   ASSILAH: Banipal Symposium marking 20 years

222   **CONTRIBUTORS**

Mahmoud el-Wardany

Mansoura Ez-Eldin

Yasser Abdel Latif

Ibrahim Farghali

Abdelaziz Baraka Sakin

Youssef Rakha

Alaa Khaled

EDITORIAL

Opening the ICORN-Banipal panel at the Frankfurt Book Fair, moderator Peter Ripken started by mentioning the old saying "Cairo writes, Beirut prints and Baghdad reads". Certainly it was true in the past, but not today. I think that Iraqis were known as readers and writers. I remember reading an interview with Naguib Mahfouz years ago in which he said his books sold more in Iraq than in other Arab countries. When I was a teenager, even though my main interest was cinema, literature was very important for me. It seems it was part of Iraqi life, and this is how one day I bought a small book, *Al-Qahira*, by an Egyptian author called Alaa al-Deeb. I did not know that this was a first book written by a young author, unlike the many Egyptian authors I already knew – Naguib Mahfouz, Ihsan Abdel Quddous, Tewfiq al-Hakim, Taha Hussein, Yusuf Idris, Mohamed Abdel Halim Abdullah, Youssef al-Sebai and others. It is very true to say that Egyptian authors were influential in Iraq, and in Arabic literature in general.

I don't remember that I read any more of Alaa al-Deeb's works until the 1990s when a friend of mine in Paris lent me a book of stories, long ones, by Alaa al-Deeb and told me that the best for him was *Zahr el-Laymoon* (Lemon Blossom) which I read and admired. Years later, when I reread it in a new edition by Dar el-Shorouk, I liked it even more than the first time, particularly as it reminded me of the friend who had lent it to me, and who had died in Paris very early; I remember his character was very similar to Abdel Khaliq al-Messiri, the hero of *Zahr el-Laymoon*, the good, the defeated dreamer.

Between 1964 and 1974 Alaa al-Deeb published many long stories and novellas; and since 1987 changed his style to what seems to be a different outlook on Egyptian society, writing *Zahr el-Laymoon* (1987), *Children without Tears* (1989), *Moon over the Swamp* (1993), *Violet Eyes* (1999) and *Rosy Days* (2002).

I first had the idea to present a feature on **Alaa al-Deeb** a couple of years ago, when he was alive, but tragically he died in February 2016 before it could happen. However, in this issue we devote 93 pages to him and his simple yet profound works, none of which have ever been translated into English before. I have always questioned, without having any answers, why he never attracted the attention that other authors of his generation did, with a number of them having their works translated into English, but not him. The feature includes articles and testimonies about his life and works by six talented Egyptian writers from the younger generations who followed him in the '80s and later as well as a number of translated excerpts from his works.

Mahmoud El-Wardany relives the moment in 1969 when, as a 19-year-old, he came across a collection of stories by Alaa al-Deeb – it was a "different type of writing, creating a "veritable storm", knocking conventionality aside and departing from the style of just telling a tale.

Yasser Abdel Latif describes Alaa al-Deeb as "the most genuine recluse", an "eternal citizen of Maadi" (the Cairo suburb where he lived), writing and reading without stop, commenting in a new way on the "disillusionment and deceit", the isolation, alienation and defeat felt by a middle-class intellectual during the troubled times for the Arab world of the '60s and '70s.

When interviewing the late Ibrahim Aslan, **Mansoura Ez-Eldin** discovered that he regarded Alaa al-Deeb almost as a mentor of the '60s generation of Egyptian authors rather than one of the '60s writers that they both were: al-Deeb was up there with Yahya Haqqi and Abdel Fatah el-Gamal. Referring to two of al-Deeb's works she discusses how the defeated identities of his leftist intellectual protagonists echo the author's own existential anxieties, how the humiliating debacle of the Six-Day War in 1976 embodied "an incurable disease".

Ibrahim Farghali loved Alaa al-Deeb the novelist – "I like his style; the short sentences loaded with literary charges and emotions" – and he explains how the realist Deeb was preoccupied "with the psychological changes in the Egyptian character, particularly among the intellectuals", due to the massive social and political changes going on in the '60s.

Youssef Rakha gives us five beautiful memories of meeting and knowing Alaa al-Deeb, tramping down to Maadi to call at his house, and holding an image of him that "is part of how I know who I am in this world".

Alaa Khaled writes about Alaa al-Deeb's Cairo, both the city, and his novella, (which was written in 1961); the main character of the novella, an ordinary young man old before his time, is slowly being suffocated by the pressure of the totalitarian regime on the city that was the opposite of the old paternalism of the '50s and also at odds with the iconic images of '60s Cairo.

* * *

Banipal 60 opens with a chapter from *Kitsch 2011*, the latest novel of Tunisian politician, journalist and author **Safi Said**, who writes that it is "a mongrel text *par excellence*: exuberant, effusive, unsettling, frightening, with tense rhythms and sudden outbursts . . ." Its narrator is Stephanie, a western journalist charged with getting an interview with Islamic State's Caliph.

In the novel of Mauritanian author **Abdallah Uld Mohamadi Bah** the narrator comes to life in his memories, being back in the desert until his next trip, with nothing to do except read poetry (he should be so lucky!), and recalls living in Madrid, where his work was also boring until he met a young Brazilian woman whom he thought about marrying but knew it would be impossible in his conservative village back home.

Tunisian poet **Lamia Makaddam** writes personal poems about her relationship to the world, while Syrian poet **Widad Nabi** writes of places painfully left behind and memories that won't leave her. In the short story by Sudanese author **Abdelaziz Baraka Sakin** the unnamed narrator recounts how he's become obsessed with remembering his mother and finds her coming to visit him every night now he is living alone.

* * *

Reports on highly successful events in Morocco and Germany to mark Banipal magazine's 20th year of publishing this year fill the issue's final pages. The day of discussions at the 39th Assilah Forum Festival prompted some participants to make suggestions for the future: Robert Irwin suggested attention is turned to genre fiction with special issues of Banipal primarily devoted to crime, humour, romance or science fiction. Walid Hamarneh and Jonathan Wright both thought Banipal might consider publishing occasional articles on the theory, practice and technique of translation by academics and practitioners. Great suggestions that Banipal will certainly be looking at introducing next year.

SAMUEL SHIMON

SAFI SAID

Meeting Abu Omar al-Adnani

CHAPTER FROM THE NOVEL *KITSCH 2011*,
TRANSLATED BY JONATHAN WRIGHT

About three weeks after I started work in Istanbul, I had to travel to Mosul. I felt as if I were heading for ruination yet unable to resist. But really I wanted to go on the trip, even if it would be exhausting and highly risky. It was Mus'ab who chose the members of the team that would go to Mosul. He told me only two days before we were due to leave. When he visited me in my apartment, he said, "Bashkir Agha will be the team leader. You'll go with Maram Hassan, Habib Roodbari as reporter and Sufyan al-Tunsi as cameraman. You'll find everything ready, and I'm sure you'll do a magnificent job. I'm relying on your intelligence and courage." He paused a moment, then added: "What you're going to do will make you a star in the media world and it'll provide valuable historical material for your memoirs in the future. It's the raw material of history."

At that moment I could have resisted the offer of the assignment. But since I wanted to do it, I asked just one question: "Was this your idea, or Sheikh Rushdi al-Attar's?"

"At the end of the day, you've been chosen. It doesn't matter whether it was my idea or Sheikh al-Attar's," he replied. "In any case we have to respect the hierarchy set by the company's

human resources department. As you know, Sheikh al-Attar is the chairman of the board and I'm the chief executive, and Karim Karaouan is a member of the board and deputy chief executive. I think that's clear."

That's how the conversation between me and Mus'ab ended. I didn't think much had changed in recent times until we reached Mosul. Although I followed Arab politics closely, the accession of a

I WARN READERS OF THIS BOOK to put behind them the ready-made ideas that have been typical of most Arabic novels. I also warn them not to trust the information, numbers, theories, dates, events or names that appear in the text.

It's a mongrel text *par excellence*: exuberant, effusive, unsettling, frightening, with tense rhythms and sudden outbursts, often illogical, sometimes dressed up to look wise but not endowed with finesse or decorum. It's not real and it's not pure fiction. It takes readers to places where they might lose their way, feel confused, or have their intelligence challenged. Reality and imagination will overlap, with characters flying from one country to another, driven unwittingly from one adventure to the next, ranting at length sometimes and trying to control their weaknesses at other times.

We have Shahi Shahbar, Mus'ab al-Sarraf, Sheikh Attar, Murad Abbas, Karim Karaouan Beg, Yahya Alwan, Jose Plantiro, Maha Zaafarani, Sandra, Murad Shaman, Stephanie Nicolas, Bashkir Agha, Maram Hassan from Aleppo, Sama Abdel Samad, Abbas Farshkhay and Eliahu Daniel on a trip from Granada to Mosul by way of Tangier, Tunis and Istanbul, where the strings of the Middle East game are pulled in the house of the Ushaki family, the house where Kemal Ataturk's divorced wife Latife Hanim once lived. Ownership of the house passed from Karim to Mus'ab al-Sarraf, and then to Sheikh Rushdi al-Attar, who launched a new phase by removing Mus'ab al-Sarraf and eliminating the Caliph, Abu Omar al-Adnani. Eco and Nietzsche also lived with all these. Lorca meets Salvador Dali, Tagore debates with Einstein, Marx has a discussion with Nehru, King Hassan of Morocco vies with Mitterrand, and they all drink a toast to this wretched age or this false spring, without any of them noticing that Maram the free, Maram the Aleppan, Maram the Yezidi, that white swan, has moved out of the novel.

SAFI SAID

new king in Saudi Arabia about three months earlier had led to a change in the company hierarchy and in the way jobs and assignments were given out. Since the start of the Arab Spring, some had believed that Qatar would play a long game and would ride a wave of Arab nationalism as the leader of the Arab Spring. But in the end Saudi Arabia would inherit everything. It struck me that my ex-husband, Murad Abbas, was right when he used the casino metaphor. "Mark my words," he once told me, "I don't want you to get it wrong. There are many players, but in the end it's always the casino that wins."

We reached Diyarbakir airport in the evening and found two Toyota four-wheel-drive vehicles waiting for us. Each vehicle had a driver and a guard. Bashkir and Sufyan got into one vehicle, while Maram, Habib and I got in the other one. We had to leave Diyarbakir for Mardin and spend the night there. The three hours we spent on the road were tiring, because our impatience to reach Mardin was not matched by the speed we travelled. That was because the weather was cold and stormy and the road that wound through the mountains was excruciating. On top of that, sometimes we had to stop in the middle of the road so that cows could pass. I was going to ask Habib whether the cowherds weren't afraid that wolves might attack at such a late hour, but he volunteered an explanation: "These cows have been stolen and they're going to the slaughterhouse. They'll reach Syria before us."

After spending what was left of the night in Mardin, in a hotel built on the top of a hill, we set off early for Qamishli and the border between Turkey and Syria. At that stage the driver said reassuringly: "Now we're going into Syrian territory. We'll be going along a mountain road that's controlled by the Nusra Front. There's nothing to endanger our journey. If all goes well we'll be in Mosul in less than three hours."

After about two very long hours we reached the town of Sinjar, which isn't far from Mosul. We had left Hasaka to the west, then descended east towards Sinjar. We pushed on further to the east and Mosul loomed in the distance as if it were awaiting Haroun al-Rashid's cortège from afar. Sometimes we kept our fears at bay with idle gossip or raucous laughter, but it wasn't only fear that brought us together. It must be said that, as we drove across territory held by Islamic State, which the combined armies of sixty countries had failed to defeat, it was our sense of pride and prestige that united us and dispelled any fear. The more checkpoints we stopped at, the prouder we felt. As soon as the escort showed his ID card and gave the password, they opened the road for us. It certainly wasn't divine intervention, but we definitely had a form of international protection that it would take more than one tiring journey for us to decipher.

Mosul is not just a big sprawling city that is heavily populated and rich in resources, trade and traditions. It stands at the crossroads between Arabs, Persians and Turks and has been lying on the banks of the Tigris for thousands of years. About three thousand years ago and more, it was the Assyrians' capital. Then the Chaldeans seized it, seven centuries before the birth of Christ. During those centuries many castles were built there, and when the Islamic age began many fortified caravanserais were added. In none of the major wars between the peoples of the region did Mosul escape destruction. Everyone wanted to control it because it was where roads, trade and water converged. Persians and Greeks ruled the city. It surrendered to the Arabs long ago but it still manoeuvred to find an elusive peace whenever frictions arose. The Mosul that loomed in front of us as we came down from the hills to the plains was the Mosul that the Arabs had built, on the right bank of the Tigris. Ancient Mosul, which lay on the eastern bank of the river, was known as Nineveh. It is said that the Akkadians gave it this name, which means fertility and "connection". I believe that the Arabs translated the word, because fertility and connectedness are the main features of the land around Mosul. The Arab Muslims came to the city from Tikrit and the Taghlib and Nimr tribes arrived from the south of the Anbar region. The city expanded in Umayyad times and recovered its old historic grandeur. In Abbasid times unforgettable wars raged over the city. After that it returned to peace. It was annexed to the principality of Aleppo in the time of Abu Firas al-Hamdani and became the most important source of food for Baghdad. The Seljuk Turks took control of it for a while and it spent a third of a century living in ruin and in fear. It helped to push back the Crusaders, however, and in the time of Imad ad-Din Zengi order was restored, along with trade, agriculture and learning. But when the Mongols attacked from the north and the east they inflicted all kinds of torment and humiliation on the city. The most horrendous wars took place in that period; what is happening now might well be just a carbon copy of that grim era. The Mongols ravaged the city, killed its inhabitants, and drove them out to the mountains and the deserts. The Yezidis of Sinjar were not spared their violent oppression. After about two centuries of Mongol rule, two states appeared in the Mosul area. The first was known as the Black Sheep state and the other as the White Sheep state. At the time none of the inhabitants understood the terminology. They thought it was a fanciful distinction invented by the Mongols when their leaders fell out in the fourth generation of rulers. Some people said the black sheep represented the Mongols who originally came from southern China and the White Sheep state was the term chosen by the Tatars, who were Mongolians from the northern region. Towards the end of the history of those two states, it became clear that the war between the sheep was really between Persia and the Turks, or between the Shi'ites of Persia, the sayyeds of the Prophet's family (the black turban) and the Sunni Turks. As soon as the Safavids took control of Iraq, the history of the two sheep that had long been jostling for power in Iraq came to an end. Even now the bloody history of Iraq is the history of Mosul, concentrated and gory. From the Assyrians to the Baathists and those who came after them in the age of the mullahs, the pashas, in their turbans or their hats. When Baghdad loses its power and its splendour, the country is torn between Basra and Mosul, and Baghdad might have been set up as a capital to resolve this ancient and recurring struggle. But when it became just the Green Zone for politicians who are conspiratorial, envious and constantly contentious, Basra and Mosul reverted to that accursed and bloody rivalry.

To be honest I didn't understand the Daesh story, or to be precise I began to break the Daesh code only about three days after I arrived in Mosul. A woman in a shop came up to me, smothered in a black garment with only her thin white face showing. She realised I wasn't from Mosul by what I was wearing (jeans, a long jacket that covered my bottom, sports shoes and then a pink scarf on my head). She was emboldened to speak with me. Bashkir, who was with me, moved away with the escort and she asked me: "Are you a tourist?"

"I'm a journalist," I said, "I've come to find out about your city."

She prayed that my assignment would be a success and said: "Will you be staying here long?"

"I've no idea."

"I'm sorry I can't invite you home," she said.

I felt embarrassed at what she said, so I thanked her and said:

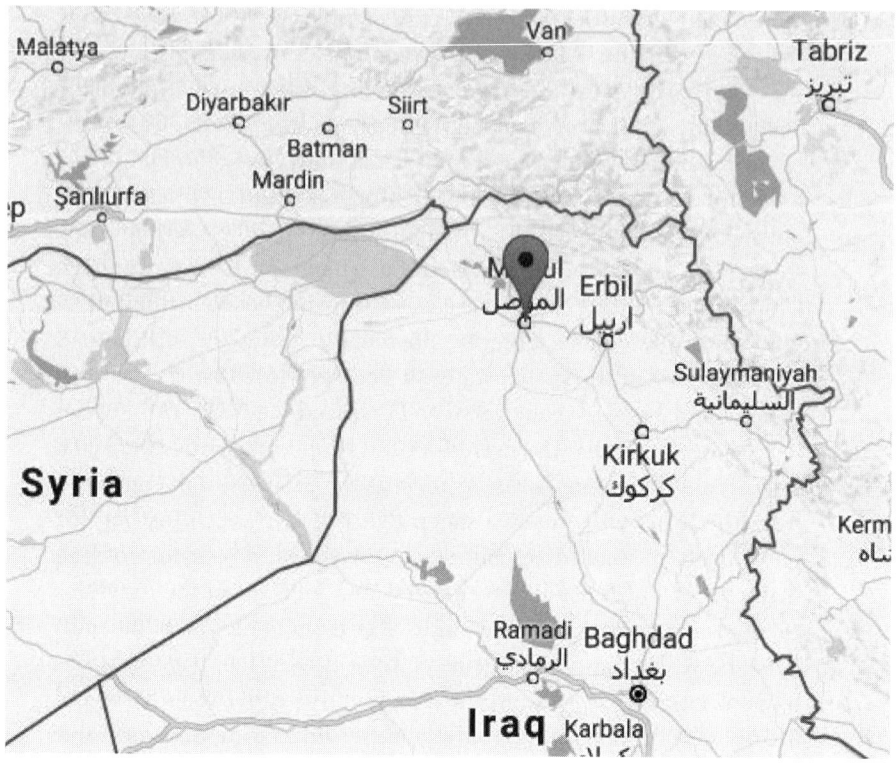

"Never mind. Things are bound to change . . ." I was about to say her name but of course I didn't know it.

"I'm Zainab, a paediatrician and a painter," she said. "My clinic was destroyed so I went to work at one of the camps far off. My studio was destroyed too and they burnt all my paintings. My punishment is to work without pay at a camp four days a week."

During our short conversation Zainab was looking in all directions in trepidation. When she saw a group of policewomen she left me and slipped into the crowd without explanation.

* * *

In every era the ruler of Baghdad has been like an accordion player. If he has mastered the score, can control the two ends of the instrument and can pump vigorously enough to generate the sounds and rhythms, then he can play the symphony of Iraq. If he can't do that, people won't hear a strong, coherent symphony. Instead they will listen to lamentations and sad discordant sounds. The player hangs the accordion on his chest with straps on his shoulders, then holds the instrument by the two ends, which move by means of bellows that the player pushes and pulls with his left hand, while his right hand moves the right keyboard, which plays the melody, and he also uses his left hand to play the bass notes on the other keyboard. Harmony is the result. This musical instrument is very recent compared with other instruments. It was invented two centuries ago but only became well known during the First World War. It seems to have been invented for the modern ruler of Iraq, because the country lies between two headstrong forces – Iran and Turkey – and its territory has long been a battleground for all the world's invaders, whether from the east or the west. Maybe the Abbasids set up their capital Baghdad in the central part of this territory only because they were aware the ruler of Baghdad had to play with both hands, towards the north and the south, so that Iraq could maintain its harmony. By this theory, what is happening now in Mosul is the result of a mistake made by the rulers of Baghdad while they were playing the music. The bass notes are too loud and the higher notes of the melody are too soft. While Basra, together with Kufa and Kerbala, have become more prominent, Mosul, Falluja and the Anbar region have started to fade away or become peripheral. The rulers in Baghdad did not notice this flaw in the harmony until Mosul slipped out of their control and they could see that the main keyboard was now completely out of action. Baghdad won't find harmony until it has restored the harmony between Basra and Mosul.

I was thinking of the musical balance that the accordion produces and that so enthralled me when I was young, listening to it in my grandfather's house, and also outside St Sylvester's church in our neighbourhood, and at school at end-of-term celebrations. And then Bashkir Agha came up to me looking very cheerful. "You have an appointment to meet the Caliph, Abu Bakr al-Adnani," he told me. "We'll be ready," he added quickly, before I had time to ask him when. "We won't leave the house until it's time. They'll send someone to take us to the Caliph's place."

I called Sufyan and Habib at once to tell them we had to be ready. Habib asked us to sit with him to prepare the main lines of questioning. We would share out the work between us. Before he started working on the questions to put to the Caliph, we had to have a quick look at the television channels. The most shocking news on all the news reports was the explosion in Ankara, close to the mausoleum of Kemal Ataturk, which had killed many soldiers. Two groups had been blamed for it: the PKK (the Kurdish Workers' Party) and Daesh. The other outrage was an explosion in the Baghdad vegetable market, with more than 150 dead and twice as many injured. The third piece of news was that the Russians had bombed some bases and command posts of the Nusra Front and Daesh in central, northern and coastal Syria. Obama was hinting at a ceasefire agreement with Putin, and Saudi Arabia was stepping up its air attacks on the Marib area of Yemen and the capital Sanaa.

Habib and Stephanie came back to the sitting room to prepare their questions. They discussed what to do if Abu Omar al-Adnani refused to let us film the interview. Stephanie thought he wouldn't refuse because he often appeared to give sermons at Friday prayers or on other religious occasions. Habib thought it best to prepare for surprises because someone might stand in for Abu Omar. "Put yourself in his position," he joked. "If I was in his position, for example, I'd send someone else to answer the questions."

"You mean he'd send a double – someone who looks like him and speaks like him."

"Let's assume that. How would we know if the person we're meeting is the real Abu Omar al-Adnani or a double?"

Indeed, we were going to meet a man about whom we knew only scraps. Mullah Omar, the leader of the Taliban, lived and died without meeting any journalists. It was even said that he was a figment of the imagination and that Mullah Omar was just another version of Bin Laden. Al-Qaeda gave the impression that there was an Afghan leader called Mullah Omar but some people were sceptical until US warplanes hunted him down in one of the Kandahar valleys. Bin Laden was gone, followed by Mullah Omar, because the Americans no longer needed them, and now there were plenty of rumours from time to time that Abu Omar al-Adnani had been killed. He may indeed have been killed in an air raid, but Daesh didn't want to announce it so that its prestige wouldn't collapse, or because the Americans couldn't or didn't want to provide definitive proof that he had been killed. It's true that he had appeared on numerous occasions but who could confirm that the person said to be Abu Omar was really Abu Omar?

According to Bashkir Agha, who had worked alongside him as a bodyguard for six months before being assigned other duties abroad, travelling between Mosul and Istanbul, Abu Omar was now more cautious than before, than a year earlier that is. He expected to be assassinated at any moment and changed his bodyguards every week or every two weeks. He also changed where he slept and worked constantly, and sometimes he even had to disguise himself in sports clothes or women's clothing. The people who knew where he was could be counted on the fingers of one hand and the only means of communication they had was a small device that connected them directly to the security unit.

I asked Habib about Maram, who had come with us from Istanbul to Mosul. He said he hadn't seen her for two days. Then he said he doubted Maram slept in the same house they slept in. "I think Maram leaves the house at night and comes back in the morning," he said.

"What makes you think that?" I asked in surprise.

He told me what he had seen with his own eyes when he was sitting in the sitting room reading a novel by Elif Shafak. "I saw her wearing a black abaya that covered even her face, but I could tell it was her by the way she walked. A man arrived with another veiled woman and they took her off with them. Then I heard the sound of a car driving off at speed. I stayed sitting in the sitting room till late at night but she didn't come back." Habib stopped, leaving many of my questions unanswered. At the time I believed what Mus'ab al-Sarraf said: that Maram Hassan knew Abu Omar al-Adnani well, that she had received plenty of training when she supervised a college that trained women to fight, and that she might have known Abu Omar since she was in Raqqa. But Mus'ab didn't tell me whether Maram had met Abu Omar and then come to Istanbul, or whether she had gone from Aleppo to Istanbul, and was then recruited and sent to Abu Omar in Mosul, and then gone back to Istanbul on other assignments.

"What do you make of that woman?" I asked Habib.

"When she's in Istanbul she's like a piano player. Now she looks like a spy. Like Mata Hari. Am I mistaken?" he replied.

I laughed at what Habib said, and at the same time I remembered what Mus'ab himself had said to me, based on what Maram had told him: "You're going to meet a man who has made the world eat out of his hand. He never sleeps in the same place or in the place where he lives. His food is prepared in various alternating places that are unconnected with each other, and he has many food tasters so that he doesn't get poisoned. He never goes out without a bulletproof jacket. With Mohamed Abdel Wahhab the musician, Howard Hughes the millionaire, Saddam Hussein and Joseph Stalin he shares the morbid obsession known as compulsive soap disorder: he washes his hands when he shakes someone's hand since he's worried he might be poisoned by substances carried on their fingers, as happened to Castro once, and also to Chavez more recently. And so that he's always ready whatever occasion arises, Abu Omar has people who look strangely similar and can take his place. Very few of those present can tell the difference between the real version and the fake. Stalin was always doing the same thing and would uncover his enemies in the politburo in this way. He managed to have them all executed, except for two of them. There was Khrushchev, who replaced him and was severely punished because he kept silent and thought that the person chairing the meetings was Stalin, even when it wasn't. The other person was Beria, the head of the KGB, who knew which was the real Stalin and which was the fake.

At first I convinced myself that this didn't matter. Even if we spoke to Abu Omar's double, people wouldn't know if the interview was with him or with his double. Then I tried to convince Habib. "Suppose we do talk to his double," I said, "what matters is what he has to say. It would be what the real Abu Omar would have said. Don't bother yourself over this problem. We didn't come here to assassinate him or to check his identity. We came here to interview him."

"Ataturk had doubles too," said Habib. "But after a while, when he became popular, he gave them up. Sometimes he disguised himself in old man's clothes, and when his house was attacked he left in a woman's gown after making his wife Latifa Hanim wear military uniform and cap. He had her stand at the window behind thin white curtains, on a crate of oranges he brought from the restaurant so that she looked tall and like him. And when he escaped from those who had come to arrest him, he attacked them from the rear after bringing a combat platoon from a military camp."

After that he told me what Saddam used to do with his doubles. When the doctors tried to force Saddam to exercise to reduce his weight because of severe pains in his back, he sent doubles to run daily so that they would lose weight. In the meantime he put himself on a strict diet. After a while he discovered he'd lost twelve kilos and now looked taller and younger. His doubles, however, had stayed the same weight. He then demanded that all his ministers and officers lose weight and said that this was the Age of Slimming. Nero liked to attend the Olympic Games and take part in the chariot race at the opening. But as soon as he turned up, all the other competitors would pretend to be ill and none of the other chariots were prepared to compete in case Nero came second and had the winner executed. He would race alone and win the first day's medals, and then the real races would begin."

Habib and I amused ourselves with such stories about the lives of dictators and tyrants in many countries in the East and the West. We could have talked about Ceausescu, who never took a plane or a train unless the head of the secret police, the army commander and half a dozen of his ministers were with him. They were his arsenal and the cloak that protected him from every act of treachery or revolution. The list would have been long, from Hitler to Bin Laden, had not Bashkir Agha suddenly burst in on us to say: "Your appointment is for afternoon prayers. Are you ready?"

I called Sufyan to tell him to come out of his room and check his camera and the battery for the lighting.

But Bashkir Agha quickly interjected. "There's no need," he said. "Everything's ready there. The filming will be done there. Then they hand you a copy on a CD."

"And the answers? Are they ready, too?" I asked him.

"The answers depend on your questions, Stephanie," he replied with a laugh. "No one speaks in place of the Caliph. Even his deputy, Abu Bishr al-Qahtani, can't speak on his behalf."

It was the first time I had heard the name Abu Bishr al-Qahtani as that of the Caliph's deputy, and I had a feeling that it might soon be time for a changing of the guard in Daesh, and maybe this meeting with Abu Omar was just a farewell meeting or a transition meeting. I had visions of flashing question marks. I said to myself that after the meeting I might have the dirty truth rather than elaborate speculation.

We quickly jumped into three black four-wheel-drive Range Rovers, each of us in a separate car. Then each car moved off in a different direction. We found ourselves arriving simultaneously outside a massive gate, well protected with machineguns, guards and sandbags.

* * *

The barriers soon went up and the three cars drove into a long underground room. A wide and very heavy door opened at the end of the basement. The cars drove on into another underground room. I felt we must be four or five floors underground. Then we left the cars and walked to a staircase to go down between forty and sixty steps. We ended up in a large hall that was well lit with powerful lights. Several people greeted us and we realised they were the camera crew and production people. A man in his thirties, who introduced himself as Michael the producer and who was clearly European, led us to where Habib and I would sit to do the interview. He asked us to sit down for them to arrange the set. "You two will sit facing the Caliph. There are five cameras that'll do the shooting," he added.

Then he spoke to the cameramen to set the framing. He called one of his assistants and told him to provide us with microphones.

Less than five minutes after we were ready and installed on the chairs, a deep silence fell. Then we heard some commotion at the back of the hall. We understood that the Caliph had arrived. We stood up to greet him. I was determined to put out my hand to him even if it hung unshaken, and that's what I did when Caliph Abu Omar al-Adnani appeared before us. He took hold of my hand and hung on to it as he smiled towards the camera. Then he gave a friendly greeting to Habib and kept looking at us until we sat down, so that he could sit down too.

I had to start with a question that was emotionally charged so that we could work our way into the depths of the man. My teacher at the faculty of journalism and communications, Regis Debray (yes, the very same who was friends with Che Guevara), always advised me to inject an emotional element at the start in order to win over the interviewee. And it would be best to wait till the end of the meeting to pose little questions about his personal life so that it would make an indelible impression on the reader or the viewer. Of course I'll never forget another piece of advice I had heard from General Badinter. When I asked him, "How can a shy person overcome his shyness in front of a president, a king, a leader or a general?", the general replied: "It's simple. You have to imagine him going to the toilet and sitting down to have a shit like anyone else."

After the greetings my first question was: "Judging by what we'd read and seen and heard about you and Daesh, we never expected you to be so friendly, informal and easy-going. After seeing the interview, people will wonder whether this friendliness is real or whether it is merely designed to promote a good image of yourselves."

Abu Omar smiled and slowly stroked his beard, muttering a prayer that God might preserve him from Satan and grant him success.

Then he started to speak: "The image people have of us is the one our enemies want to project. People will remain victims as long as they don't seek the truth for themselves. The way to the truth must go by way of justice. There is no truth without justice and no justice without truth. Here I am before you. What do you see? Am I a man or a devil? Anyway, when you are strong and a believer, you no longer need to beg for justice from the unjust. Our dream will not fail, because we will see it come true soon, and nor will our strong certainty fail, because it is the certainly of God Almighty. I always tell the mujahideen and the guerrillas that when we stick together, we're at one with God. The djinn and many human beings have joined forces against us, but they will not be able to shake us. The American rabble no longer frighten us, so how dare the other bastards wage war on us? We've told them: 'This is our land, this is our religion and we are free to set up a state based on truth and justice on this land.' "

The Caliph stopped and looked at Habib with sharp eyes, anticipating that the next question would come from him.

Habib began by extending thanks to the Caliph for receiving us and giving us a chance to interview him. Then he said: "Your state extends from the Euphrates to the Tigris. It controls enormous resources and vast amounts of territory. But most observers don't expect it to survive. They say it's a short-lived incursion from the deserts of Arabia. They describe it as a state based on knives and suicide belts or as the state of the new dervishes. Sometimes they go further and say it's a state of intercontinental gangsters. No doubt this upsets you and makes it hard for you to defend your principles. What do you think about this?"

Abu Omar listened attentively to Habib's question. He gave an earnest smile that showed his well-aligned teeth but didn't suggest informality. It was just a relaxation of his jaw. I think he was looking for a tone and a rhythm for what he was going to say, far removed from any levity. "Listen well, my friends," he said. "If everyone is against you, it's hard to win them over immediately. I'm fully aware that some people ridicule us and make jokes about us, but everyone stands in awe of us, takes every precaution against us and tries to negotiate with us. If we were merely a gang, why all these international alliances and all this fuss and bother about us, which starts from the seats at the United Nations and extends to the bedrooms of leaders and presidents? If we were a state based on knives and suicide belts, then how come Mosul enjoys electricity, when Baghdad does not? If we were new dervishes, how come we're running a state with more territory than the British state?"

Abu Omar paused, drew a deep breath, then resumed speaking with a steady cadence.

"Look, Mr Habib," he said. "We're an extraordinary phenomenon because we're not like those who try to analyse us or like those who fight us. We're a phenomenon that cannot be understood by comparing or contrasting us with others. We're not part of the Muslim Brotherhood and we're not a new version of the Assassins. We're not a political party like the other parties. We're a group of people that wants to assert the principles of God and His Prophet. This land, the land of Iraq and al-Sham, which is now called Daesh, is the land where Islam was first established, cathartic Islam, bursting with love and justice and receptive to everything good. I cannot reduce the exceptional nature of our state to the world of politics alone, and I would say that my admiration for science and mathematics doesn't make me an ascetic or a dervish. I tried experiencing beauty as a geometrical quality when I was young, but I am now fully convinced that all beauty, as a concept, as form and as content, has only one name – the name of the Living and Holy God.

"I tell you today, our idea has spread to all Arab countries and we have loyal followers and warriors. The truth is that for the first time in a thousand years the Arab world is open to an idea that is well-defined and distinctive – the idea of rebuilding the Islamic state. For a century since the fall of the Ottoman Caliphate Islamic groups as political parties have been dreaming of making this dream a reality but they haven't been able to do so because they chose the path of compromise, dependency, adaptation and consensus. There's something vital that these people haven't grasped: what I have called self-construction, based on a kind of unadulterated authenticity, experience, adventure and exceptionalism. I am Abu Omar al-Adnani and if I wanted to be like those people I would have to betray myself and betray the divine essence!"

I had agreed with Habib that he would leave the most sensitive questions to me on the chance that Abu Omar would be more forthcoming if the questions came from a woman, but I saw that with his first question Habib had encroached on the sensitive zone, and so I phrased my question thus: "Sheikh Omar, you promoted a slogan: 'Daesh is expanding'. But after a while it looked as though you were content to live between The Tigris and the Euphrates. You haven't expanded towards Damascus or Baghdad or even towards the south. Are these the borders of your state for the foreseeable future? In fact some people think it is no longer expanding but receding."

"Here I might answer you philosophically," he said. "There's a big difference between the real world and ideas. They're interconnected but they work against each other. We may now be engaged in a heroic struggle to survive, but our idea is bigger than our presence on the ground. Hence the tensions and the contradictions, even the divisions and disagreements. We have something that can never fall apart. What we yearn for is what hundreds of millions of people yearn for. Time must be the bridge between our lives as they are and our idea. A year ago we were at the gates of Baghdad and we could have gone inside, but our assessment was that the losses and the atrocities would be too great for our people.

"I said: 'Leave it. It will fall like a ripe fruit.' As for Damascus, it was our assessment that it would fall as soon as Aleppo fell, but Aleppo persists in its errant ways. There's no point in attacking Damascus. It has to be strangled in the north from Aleppo and in the east from Deir ez-Zor, and then you'll see how the Damascus regime falls apart. We've been able to close the Persian supply line that runs from Baghdad to Deir ez-Zor, and this was a strategic necessity to cut off what's known as the Shi'ite Crescent. In fact we didn't reckon on Moscow interfering so forcefully. The Russians may have stopped us reaching Damascus but that can only be temporary."

"And what about Turkey? It seems to be friendly towards you. Everything comes through Turkey: volunteers, goods, supplies, weapons and the oil trade. What the press says is that without Turkey Daesh wouldn't last three weeks, that it would hardly have time to withdraw without losses, while others say Daesh is in the pouch of the Turkish kangaroo. Is this analysis correct, Sheikh Omar?"

That question was posed by a Turkish man, a Turkish journalist no less. Abu Omar understood that well and concluded that the Turks were not united in how they saw Daesh or Erdogan's policy. "Turkey is a country that could be friendly," he replied. "But every state has to reconcile contradictory interests. Yes, we sell oil abroad but who said we sell it to the Turkish state? Besides, what would we do with the oil if we didn't sell it. Should we burn it when our people need food, clothing and medical care? Is there any state that doesn't sell its oil? Besides, there are many exaggerations about the volunteers and weapons that come through Turkey. Yes, there are Arab and Muslim volunteers from across the world, but most of our fighters are our own people, people from Iraq and Syria. As for weapons, I'm ready to sell to those who want weapons. We have a surplus. We don't need tanks or missile systems. Our warfare is unconventional warfare and we don't need weapons that would prove a burden. In the battles for Falluja and Mosul we seized enough weapons to arm three medium-sized armies. What would these weapons do if there wasn't someone to fight with them?"

Abu Omar gave us a sharp look when he had finished answering and I understood he was telling me to ask another question.

"There are also those who say you're neo-Wahhabis by other names," I said, "in other words that you're a Saudi-Qatari-Turkish joint creation."

Abu Omar interrupted me: "We're not a car factory, and we're not a car with parts made in many different places and then assembled somewhere else. If we were like that we would have been finished off a while ago. But do you think, my sister, that we could live cut off from the rest of the world, even if we were just a few people? We're a big project, a very big project that hasn't been completed yet. No one is able to contain us. We're a novice state and there are states that we cooperate with. There are other states that we negotiate with and cooperate with under the table and in secret. Then there are states that are frightened of us and try to win our favour. Of course we have friends and these friends provide different levels of cooperation and they have different assessments of our project. Some of them think there's a contradiction between our project and theirs. Some even expect conflict with us in the future. In the world of politics nothing is final. Those who think we are someone else's pawns or minions are mistaken. Abu Omar al-Adnani might die tonight or tomorrow night but there are millions who believe what Abu Omar believes."

"And Israel, Abu Omar, your relationship with Israel is confusing and unclear. Many of those who sympathise with you criticise you for what might be called a suspect relationship. How can an Islamic state that preaches justice and liberation from tyrants cooperate with a Zionist entity such as Israel? Is it an alliance of necessity, or is it an alliance based on faith: an Islamic state alongside a Judaic state?" (I was conveying to him what most people were thinking).

Abu Omar expressed his displeasure at the question initially by a simple knitting of his eyebrows. Then I knew he was displeased by his sharp tone.

"If my country's occupied, must I go and liberate some other country? In the past the Muslim Brotherhood thought that the task of liberating Jerusalem could start in Afghanistan. Even Palestinians went to Afghanistan because it was occupied by the Soviets. Should we leave Iraq to Iran and go to liberate Jerusalem, as the Persian propaganda says? A day may come when interests and territory lead to conflict but the priorities today compel us to protect our own Islamic state until it has built up its strength. We, and Israel, are going through what might be called the not-speaking stage. Things are bound to get clearer and the world will realise that we don't cooperate with Israel any more or less than others do. In fact, I should be straightforward with you: if Israel has relations with some of our friends, that doesn't mean we have Israeli weapons or trainers or officers."

"But you have commercial and non-military relations. Most of the medical drugs are said to come from there, and some of your officers have had medical treatment there."

"We don't know where the oil we sell goes. Even Iranian oil reaches Israel, but through other countries. The same with medicines. They come to us through companies that are mostly Arab, Turkish, Azerbaijani and even French. As for our officers going there for treatment, we don't know anything about that. I'm said to have visited Israel many times. Should we believe everything that's said? Yes, I went to Irbil for treatment about six months ago but I don't believe that the people treating me were Israelis, unless Israelis have started speaking Kurdish."

He paused a while, then resumed: "What's the point of discussing things that are not based on certainties? People say anything without thinking or knowing. This is an insult to people's intelligence. They seem to think they will be the saviours of Jerusalem. The question of Jerusalem is still attractive to these people. But I challenge them to be honest. Israel is present with America in Baghdad, and our relationship with America is no better than Baghdad's or Tehran's relationships with Israel and America. The cloak of Jerusalem will soon be torn to shreds and their supreme leader will appear with their ayatollah, both of them naked."

The caliph looked to Habib for the next question, giving him a chance to ask a very sensitive one.

Habib laid the groundwork for it well, then finally let it out like a stray bullet: "You are the leader and caliph of the Islamic State. You're well aware that the history of Islamic states has been full of tolerance and pluralism. Whatever setbacks or violent reverses may have occurred, the non-Muslim minorities lived in peace in Islamic states. The Abbasid state was inclusive, pluralistic and tolerant. Some people recently have even called it the first secular state. The Islamic state in Andalucía too. And the Ottoman state, despite its might, included pluralism and tolerance. I say all this in order to ask you: what have you done to the Yezidis? Does your state have no room for this ancient religion?"

Abu Omar looked into the distance and up at the ceiling. Then he launched into his response: "The Yezidis are there in their villages and their homes. Personally one of my bodyguards is a Yezidi. You might be even more surprised if I told you that Maram Hassan, who came here with you from Istanbul, is from the Yezidi sect. She's from Baashiqa, and then she moved with her family to Aleppo. The Yezidis mostly speak Kurmanji, one of the Kurdish languages, but some of them consider themselves to be Arabs. Their religion doesn't proselytise and it's close to Islam or a distorted form of Islam. They're monotheists but they worship the sun. Generally, it's a mixture of Islam, Zoroastrianism and Manichaeism. This doesn't bother the Islamic State at all. But for the Persians to use them to stir up trouble and to defame our state, we are not responsible for that. Over their history the Yezidis have been the targets of more than seventy attempts to exterminate them, by the Persians and others. They wanted to forget all these exterminations and blame our state for a crime that we did not commit. If the Yezidis have run off into the valleys and the hills, it's because other people want to use them to discredit the Islamic State. Go to Sinjar on your way back and you'll see the Yezidis living in peace. I tell you quite frankly, it's the Persians who created the Yezidi tragedy a long time ago, ever since they sent a man called Yezid bin Abi Anisa from Persia to Basra to claim that God would send a Persian prophet and reveal to him a book which would be written in a single sentence and would repeal Islamic sharia, God forbid."

When Abu Omar stopped, I thought the time had come for the emotionally charged question because the interview was about to end.

"Do you have any sons, Abu Omar?" I asked.

"Yes, three sons and a daughter, and I have one wife. You don't believe that."

I laughed and Habib laughed and then the laughter spread until the cameramen and bodyguards were laughing too.

* * *

As we were getting into the Range Rover, which was not where we had left it, to go back to the house, and as the sun began to set over the city of Mosul, Habib said, "We've got a very special scoop. There's been nothing like it since Suleymanoglu had his scoop with Kemal Ataturk when he was still at the Villa Cankaya in Izmir, awaiting the right moment to take power and destroy what remained of the Ottoman system."

"Damn Kemal Ataturk," I said to myself. "The Turks bring up Ataturk even when they're going to the bathroom, even when they sleep with their wives. Kemal Ataturk still has a grip on their souls and is by their side even when they are impregnating their wives." When we reached the house and were sitting alone in the sitting room, I said to Habib: "Yes, it's a massive scoop that will have serious repercussions."

In fact I was pleased with myself and at the same time angry, because we often notice some details only when it's too late, and then we discover there are some missing pieces. Then we start belittling the work we have done because it could have been better and we could have asked more questions to get more out of it. For a journalist, the question of when to be satisfied is very tricky. Very few journalists feel completely satisfied with their work. Whenever they finish they say to themselves: "It would have been better if I'd taken it slower or faster there or if I had inquired further there." That's what happened to me all that night. I felt as if the job I had done was incomplete or too compromised, although no one had dictated the questions to us and no one had asked us to submit written questions in advance, as some politicians do. No one had made us feel that time was short, and I, at least from my point of view, thought I should have asked many more questions. Had I forgotten them? Had I been wary of making Abu Omar angry? Had I been overawed by him? Had I compromised out of deference and complacency when I sat facing the most dangerous man in the world? There were more interesting questions that I hadn't tackled, such as the beheading of foreigners, burning prisoners, enslaving women, using children in suicide operations, recruiting teenagers, taking hallucinogenic drugs and destroying ancient ruins, or such as Daesh's relations with Jordan and Qatar and the other Daeshes in Libya and Sinai, or such as the terrifying propaganda films with the Hollywood plots that Daesh put out on the internet. I could also have asked about the system of government and the caliphate in Islamic states, about what they call consultative democracy, or about the caliphate and the internal conflicts between governors, commanders and judges, even between tribes and nationalities. The members of the big Arab tribes were divided, the supporters coming from abroad had disagreements and the commanders and the judges were at loggerheads. We hadn't taken on any of that in our interview with Abu Omar.

Sufyan came and joined us in the sitting-room. He had come out of his room in a bad mood, or rather he was angry because he hadn't been able to film the interview or even attend the meeting. He told us he had been put in a room with three of the bodyguards, who plied him with tea and questions and gave him odd looks. He also said that one of the guards was a Tunisian from the coastal region who introduced himself by the pseudonym Huda al-Mada'ini but wasn't prepared to discuss anything to do with Tunisia, and Sufyan didn't dare try to encourage him to change his mind. Trying to appease his anger, I said: "We'll watch the interview when we get it from the Caliph's office tomorrow."

"Did they keep the interview?" Sufyan asked. "They might keep it forever," he added, shocked by the thought.

"What do you mean?"

"I mean, they could change their minds about broadcasting it, or send it straight to Istanbul or broadcast it on YouTube through their own channels."

That was something I hadn't thought of, and Sufyan made so much of the possibility that I was worried and angry and I felt that my head was about to burst. "Stop, stop," I said to Sufyan. "Why are you being so pessimistic? Is it because you didn't film the interview?"

When he saw I was tense, Habib stepped in calmly. "Stephanie, tomorrow morning we'll find out everything," he said. "I don't think they'll put out the interview on YouTube. Why suggest horrible possibilities at such a time?"

I thought I'd go up to my room to look for a sleeping pill to fend off the ghosts and hallucinations I saw approaching. I didn't manage to sleep until dawn, when the minarets started to call people to prayers. The muezzin at the mosque of Abu Dharr al-Ghifari, only a few yards from where we were staying, might as well have been inside the room. I thought for the moment that the curtains were swaying from the vibrations from his voice, and when I got up to pull the curtains, I found that the window wasn't firmly closed and the dawn breeze was playing with the curtains. I closed the window tight and went back to bed. At that point I was about to forget everything, after I had settled on a theory that this interview might be a way to exacerbate the conflicts between Abu Omar and the other leading members of his state, or that they had sent us here to bring about a rapid resolution of the struggle underway between Abu Omar and his deputies, Abu Bishr al-Qahtani and Abu Yahya al-Qurashi, as well as with the governor of Raqqa, Abu Nasr al-Umawi. After about four hours of sleep, I dismissed my sad thoughts, then rushed into the bathroom to remove the powder left on my face. I looked fresher despite the wretched night I had had because of my damned speculations. At night conjectures grow larger, to become nightmares and phantoms. If Sufyan had suggested his thought during the day, no one would have thought about its plausibility. But since he suggested it by night, and late at night, it very soon seemed real because it was so devastating that we almost felt that disaster had struck.

After fetching a coffee and some cake from the kitchen, I took from my bag some magazines with articles about the caliphate and the conflicts inside the Islamic State organisation. I had read plenty about them in French and English newspapers and I had kept some clippings to refer to when I wrote a report on my visit to Mosul. I was certain that it was Abu Omar al-Adnani who had set up Jaysh al-Mujahideen in Iraq after the US invasion of Iraq in 2003. He had another patronymic, Abu Maryam al-Anbari, and at first he had joined the Muslim Brotherhood organisation, gone to Afghanistan and come back with radical ideas that focused on creating a state similar to the Taliban state. He left the Brotherhood and began to attack them, accusing them of compromise and intellectual blindness. He was living in hiding from the Saddam Hussein regime, but the Americans had known this man since he was in Afghanistan and then they found out he was in Iraq busy building his own organisation. Maybe it was on this basis that Bush accused Saddam Hussein of co-operating with Al-Qaeda. He had entered Iraq from Iran and disappeared, then reappeared at the time of the Sahawat, or Awakenings, the Sunni militias the Americans created to counter Al-Qaeda. He saw the Sahawat as an American plot to wipe out the resistance and push Iraq into a civil war along sectarian lines. He started to gain increasing popularity in resistance circles and among Sunni imams. At the time Mus'ab al-Zarqawi had achieved stardom in the resistance to the American invasion.

When Zarqawi was killed, the way was clear for Abu Maryam al-Anbari, who changed his name to Abu Omar al-Adnani. He faced many accusations: he was said to be arrogant, oversensitive, aggressive in his views, bloodthirsty, jealous, moody and unpredictable in his decisions. Then he was said to have been an officer in the secret police under Saddam and that he had been released from prison after an agreement with the Americans to strike at Zarqawi's bases. The two men cooperated at first and Abu Omar once said that Zarqawi was "a gift to the Iraqi people from God in Heaven". But they soon fell out over many matters, such as which Shi'ites and which people in government should qualify as infidels. Must all Shi'ites be called infidels, or only the leaders and their families? Must the whole government be denounced as infidel, or only the police and the army? When Zarqawi was killed, the rift between Zarqawi's followers and Adnani's followers reached its peak and Ayman al-Zawahiri was unable to resolve it. The declaration of the Islamic State of Iraq helped to turn this rivalry into a bloody conflict between the two groups. In the conflict two of Abu Omar al-Adnani's men who were more radical than him were killed: Abu Hamza and Abu Obeida. Abu Omar was accused of killing them to get rid of men who were competing with him for leadership. When war spread in Syria, Abu Omar favoured expanding relations with the Nusra Front, so he sent a friend, who was initially known as Abu Aws, to Syria to take control of the Nusra organisation through a merger or by infiltrating the organisation to get rid of those who wouldn't pledge allegiance to him and to the Islamic State organisation. Shortly afterwards, the Islamic State in Iraq and al-Sham (ISIS) was declared, which was just an ideological composite of the ideas of the old Al-Qaeda and the new Al-Qaeda, and a merger between the Islamic State in Iraq, which was promoted by Jaysh al-Mujahideen, and the Islamic State in Syria, which was promoted by Jabhat al-Nusra.

When I'd finished reading *The Guardian* report I found that the information, the names and dates, didn't match. But I emerged convinced that Daesh was full of intrigues, external interference and competing leaders, and that Abu Omar al-Adnani might only be the temporary caliph, until the time came for him to go.

I went downstairs from my bedroom to the sitting-room, where I found Bashkir Agha waiting for Habib and me. Moments later Habib arrived and then, from a little bag he was carrying under his arm, Bashkir pulled two little bundles of booklets and other publications.

Inside each bundle there was a CD. He gave us one each, saying: "I've brought each of you a copy of the interview. The original will be sent straight to Istanbul. Both Sheikh Mus'ab al-Sarraf and Sheikh Rushdi al-Attar have asked for it urgently."

Translated from *Kitsch 2011*, published by Bissan for Publishing and Distribution, Beirut, 2017

ABDALLAH ULD MOHAMADI BAH

In Teresa's Shadow

A CHAPTER FROM THE NOVEL *BIRDS OF AL-NAB'A*

TRANSLATED BY JULIA IHNATOWICZ

My days in the desert are sluggish and dull. There is nothing here to rouse my spirits except reading poetry, which helps me escape my current stagnation and keeps my mind clear. It seems I am still longing for Madrid, which I left behind. I'm still longing for my morning coffee with sandwiches stuffed with cream cheese, longing for the sight of the agile Colombian waitress, who would race to beat all her peers to bring me a glass of orange juice with ice, and a smile as wide as the broad sky.

In Madrid, I worked in accounting, but I have no real sway over numbers. I just checked expenses and made sure they complied with regulations. I collected receipts, sorted them, and passed them on to the ministry in the diplomatic pouch.

My work routine at the embassy was boring. The naked truth is that my only job was adding up the endless and insatiable expenses of His Excellency the Ambassador. He knew that the Foreign Office was always generous towards him, so whenever he needed more, he would add a new item to the budget and then simply have a word with the Secretary General at the Ministry of Foreign Affairs to make sure he approved it. Of course, the funds would then arrive at the appointed time, and never a moment later. Yet somehow at the end of each month, we would find that half the budget had not been spent. At that point, we would meet again and endeavour to spend what was left. His Excellency took the lion's share. I would look at him as he picked up his bundle of money without even blinking, without even a flicker of guilt in his fingertips, and I would apologise

for what had happened. And something inside me crumbled. That said, it gave me something to help combat the tedium of my flat in Madrid.

Inviting my friends, neighbours and compatriots over became a Sunday tradition. We enjoyed ourselves playing cards, laughing and trading witticisms well into the afternoon. Usually, we would lay out a roast Andalusian lamb on the table, straight from the barbecue and untouched by any of us. The delicious smell of the grill engulfed us as we turned our attention back to the cards. Meanwhile, my neighbour Teresa, whom I had instructed in the art of grilling and in our Saharan way of preparing spices, was singing a gypsy song of blood and betrayal, abandonment and who knows what else. She hovered around us like a moth drawn to the flame, while we occasionally glanced at her with admiring eyes, yearning for the fire concealed behind her song. She prepared the table and some appetisers for us, while flitting among us like a gentle breath of fresh air.

At first, Teresa thought it was unbearably extravagant. She came into my place while I was preparing to welcome my friends one Friday evening and she was wearing very little, just a scanty white shirt wrapped around her firm breasts that barely reached her smooth, pink belly button, and a pair of shorts that revealed her fleshy thighs and slipped down when she moved, not quite reaching her ivory knees. Teresa shook her head like a restless filly in heat. The fragrance of her long hair, hanging loose down her back, spread through the room so that every corner was filled with the scent of orange blossom pouring off her. At that time, I was almost knocked sideways by how alluring she was in that deserted apartment in the heart of lurid Madrid.

Teresa heard me that morning talking to the Spanish butcher, who was originally from North Africa. I was asking him to bring us a fat lamb and grill it on the barbecue for us, when she immediately intervened, saying firmly: "My God, what are you doing with all that meat? You must be some kind of carnivorous rodents . . ."

I replied: "Yes, we are, madam. We fight the wolves for scraps."

She laughed and said: "Try eating some fruit and vegetables . . ."

"Only animals eat grass," I said, and went on, "after this advice, you could help us prepare for the Sunday gathering."

She replied, kindly and politely: "Sure, I could. Let's get to work then."

Teresa had burst into my life with no prior warning. Everything aligned to pave the way for a relationship that started out as a mix of friendship, concealed infatuation, and true kinship. All these feelings mixed together like when the weather in some Spanish cities is sunny, rainy and snowy in the course of a single day.

I introduced her to the proper way of making tea. I got her used to buying mint from the Moroccan quarter, while each month I took in a supply of the green tea the Ambassador had recommended; they brought it for him specially from Nouakchott, putting it in a bag inside the diplomatic pouch. Teresa and I exchanged roles through this magical tea: she came closer to the desert, to its flavours and rituals, and her passion grew for preparing tea and grilled meats; I, in turn, took up residency under her genial auspices, in the stillness deep within her merry soul.

Since the North African merchants first brought green tea to parts of the desert in the eighteenth century, the drink has become our companion wherever we go. We know how to pick out the good stuff by its smell, and leave it in bags inside iron boxes to mature. We're addicted to drinking it at breakfast in the morning, after lunch, and in the afternoon like the English gentry. To maintain our harmony and camaraderie, I taught Teresa to make tea for us whenever possible. It was as if her heart no longer belonged to her, as if she had taken us into her clan. Or perhaps her Latin blood had turned into Saharan tea, flowing through her veins and guiding her through mazes to reach a heart of sand in the desert.

* * *

When I arrived in Madrid, I lived in a small hotel, not far from the Embassy headquarters. Spain was under the rule of General Franco and had not yet healed from the wounds of its civil war. Nevertheless, life in Madrid embraced everything new. The city released both hot and cold breaths from the same mouth, one after the other. It remembered the calamities and blazing fires of the war in its perturbed psyche, but as soon as the flames died down, people stayed up through the night, looking for pleasure and oblivion, as if running away would lead to salvation.

The hotel was run by an old married couple who seemed about to step off the train of life. However, they were resisting by snatching moments of stolen pleasure from the time they had left. They were assisted by their young and impetuous daughter, who went here and there devoid of purpose.

The moment I arrived – and after an initially weak smile had turned into an encouraging one following the first moments of our acquaintance – the old woman gave me the key to a room on the first floor. It was a spacious room overlooking a well-lit, narrow street, adorned with flowers and plants that hung from walls built in a bygone era. Generally, they treated me pleasantly.

I was their guest on Sundays for paella, which they say was invented by our Arab ancestors. Andalusian paella is a mix of fish, seafood, chicken, rice, and vegetables all infused with saffron and other spices and blended with olive oil. They would put the dining table in a courtyard opposite their room with the windows and doors open to let it bathe in the sun's rays as much as possible. The little faience-topped table was usually placed in the middle, with cups of cold water on it, plus fresh juice from oranges the old woman had brought from a farm not far from Madrid.

The old lady excelled in making this delicious food, which was devoured in copious quantities. That was how they used the proceeds from running the hotel, spending it liberally on themselves; and on Sundays that included me. It was enough for me to share gratefully in their happiness, offering words of thanks that gave them pleasure and cheered the hearts of that lovely old couple and their daughter.

They would set a place for me next to their rebellious, quarrelsome daughter, whose face glowed between frizzy ringlets. She was usually quieter in the mornings, but in the evening, when the sun disappeared over the horizon and darkness spread its wings over every nook and cranny of the hotel, then she was overcome by fits of hysterical laughter. This may have been due to the alcohol she so abundantly consumed in her private room, or it may have been the effect of the drugs she took in secret, without her father's knowledge.

I spent the whole of my first year at the Santa Mañana Inn. I knew that it had become a part of me. It resided in me, as much as I did in it, as if I were a jailer and it was a prisoner I found hard to release. Nevertheless, one autumn day, I bid the hotel owners farewell. I had learned to speak a little Spanish and what I couldn't communicate to them naturally, I tried to relay through gestures.

I addressed the old couple courteously, although my voice couldn't hide my feelings of embarrassment and unease: "This is the end of happy days, but now it is time to depart . . ."

The day I left the hotel was memorable. I felt their genuine affection for me as they said goodbye and the old lady cried passionately. The girl watched the scene without interest from a distance, as if she were free of the burden of my presence and could now relax in the absence of anyone who could tell on her. I left her to her indifference and juvenile fantasies, and turned away.

The old couple accompanied me to the outside door where a taxi was waiting for me. I had gathered up my few possessions and my private papers into a leather Samsonite bag I had bought from a fancy shop, and which I now placed in the boot. The car set off towards my new flat in the centre of Madrid.

Before I left, I turned back to wave to the old couple and to imprint on my memory a last image of the rite of farewell. I saw the couple hugging their daughter, who was deeply affected and streaming with tears. I hadn't expected that, and I didn't believe it. I was amazed at her attachment to the Saharan neighbour who hadn't paid her very much attention. There was nothing I could do. I waved and felt an emptiness beginning to fill my insides.

"Goodbye. I'm so sorry, little one, I didn't understand."

I found my new flat on Gran Vía thanks to a private estate agent. They call Gran Vía the Broadway of Madrid, in reference to New York's famous avenue of arts and entertainment. In contrast to the latter, however, Gran Vía (literally, the "Great Way") dates back to the nineteenth century, although it didn't take its final form until the 1920s. Its name has changed constantly with Spain's political upheavals. Its most provocative name was during the Civil War when the leftists called it "Soviet Union Avenue"; that was before it regained its older name with Franco's victory. Gran Vía remains one of the biggest and most important streets in Madrid, and its most lively. High-end shops stretch along it, as well as clubs, restaurants, and bars, so it's known as the only place in Madrid that never sleeps.

On my first night, what worried me was the nightclub right underneath my window. It's true that it sometimes played nice music, but it became irritating in the summer when the neighbouring plaza turned into an open-air dance floor and I, despite myself, was sucked into the racket.

In my third month, a single girl moved into the flat next door. She arrived at the entrance hall just as I was preparing to leave for work.

She said good morning and asked whether I was the "Moro" living at number four.

She was stammering and swaying, carrying a heavy bag on her back, and her eyes were red with tiredness from a long journey that had taken more than twenty hours – as she later told me. They had told her at the estate agent that her neighbour was a nice "Moro".

When I returned that evening, she was plunged in a deep sleep, judging by the regular snoring I could hear through the adjoining wall. I wanted to greet her, as dictated by the laws of neighbourliness in which my grandmother had instructed me.

The day after she arrived I was on my way to the Embassy when I came across my new neighbour sitting at a small café on the corner of our street. I said good morning. "First of all, buenos días," I said, taking to heart the idea of the nice Moro, as the agent had described me.

She replied amiably: "I'm Teresa. Have a seat." Then she asked me to join her for breakfast. We sat opposite each other at the table, face to face, her with her bitter black coffee, and me with my milky coffee mixture.

She kept chatting and talking, without any connecting thread, breaking off sometimes to talk to the waiters about the weather, poverty, music, military despotism. I liked how she drank her coffee with such relish, really taking her time to drain the cup of its contents. She sipped a drop of the black liquid like a bee sucking nectar, then nibbled on her full lips. Her manner reminded me of one of our desert women neighbours, and her great passion for tea. She would clasp the cup between her hands for minutes on end, which annoyed my grandmother, a woman quick to anger but also easily reconciled.

Teresa held her cup as if she were afraid it would escape from between her hands, drinking the black liquid with pleasure. It was as if she were saying "I'm drinking my coffee, but it's really you who's enjoying it". She told me her life story in less than half an hour: she had studied philosophy and recently completed her bachelor's degree, then returned to live in Spain from her own country of Brazil after one of her teachers had found her a job producing records in a music publishing company.

My neighbour's job seemed nice, as she spent most of her time listening to music by people of the various nations that were the company's speciality.

I said: "No doubt they look for unknown artists to buy the copyright for their work at low prices, then sell their records for double the price. Right?"

My neighbour smiled with a sly twinkle in her eye, and said conspiratorially: "Maybe what you say is true. Who knows . . ."

Teresa told me – and what a coincidence it was – that the last thing the company had produced was a record from a "Moro" country, but she didn't know whether it was Morocco or Mauritania. I, however, later identified this music, which drew Teresa closer to my country and made her tremble in joy and rapture with its beautiful melodies.

That evening, Teresa brought me a vinyl record in a colourful sleeve with pictures of women clad in black and apparently beating on drums. In the middle of a circle, there was a thin man in a baggy blue *jubbah*, raising his arm and holding a stick that was crooked at the top. The title in Spanish said "Songs of the Namadi".

We put the record on a new Sony record player. As I listened to the oscillating melody, it was mingled with trilling cries and women's voices. The girl asked me whether I knew who this band was, and I told her: "It's not a band in the general sense. It's a case of when desert people spontaneously turn a simple occasion into a great act of rejoicing. They can turn the smallest gathering into a singing ensemble."

"Who are they, the Namadi? Is it one of your big tribes?"

"No, they're a mix of tribes united in the art of hunting. They live in an expanse of desert in the border region between Morocco, Mauritania, and Algeria." Noticing the attentive and alert surprise in her eyes, I added: "They live by hunting gazelles with their saluki dogs. They value these dogs so highly that they consider them their real treasure, and even include them in marriage dowries."

The girl seemed amazed as she collected her thoughts around this jumble of hunting and music and rearing dogs. This is what awakened her appetite for knowing more about the desert dwellers.

We were reeling enraptured, our fingers touching, as we listened to that gambolling music, which spoke of love and dogs and dried gazelle meat. The whole time she was giving me a cryptic look that I didn't fully understand, and I looked back at her quizzically. And that was enough for us!

Later on, the tunes on that record, produced by the company in Madrid, became a sort of companion to me and I kept them with me while I was away from my native country. Through them and other music I was drawn to a world that stirred in me feelings of Sufi ecstasy known only to those whose spirits long for the great expanse of space and whose souls reside somewhere between doubt and certainty. Perhaps Teresa, with her merry soul, would live in that world with me.

Later Teresa gave me yoga lessons, explaining that they helped her to forget about hardship and exhaustion. I tried it for a bit before realising that I have my own spiritual exercises that don't require me to sit like a Buddha or delve into the teachings of Taoism.

As time went by, Teresa the Brazilian would be my helper in organising matters at home. I would teach her how to make tea, with all the details of its rituals and how to prepare it with greater depth and deliberation. This starts with three different glasses of tea each having varying concentrations of leaves and therefore different flavours. They say that the first is as strong as love, the second as sweet as life, and the third as wan as death. It was unthinkable to me that Teresa should drink from the third glass.

I also showed her how to choose good mint, but the most profound difficulty was in the meditation of making the tea.

Yoga was helpful for that. I made use of some pictures used to advertise tourism in Mauritania that I brought her from the office of a colleague charged with promoting a country that has only very occasional flights. I asked her to draw herself up straight, as if she had been reincarnated as a squatting Buddha, and to relax, turn her thoughts inwards, and think of herself as living in an endless void, to focus on making the tea as if it were her only task, her final task. Then she would achieve a level of Nirvana and ultimate happiness, that kind of heavenly happiness that only the pure-hearted can attain. Or at least, she would think of herself as if she were making paella, since it is a dish that combines different things, and elements of varied flavours and aromas, with the end purpose of coming to a moment of harmony and integration between opposites in order to reach the pinnacle of taste and intoxication. Lastly, I stressed that the most important thing with tea is the elegance of how it is made. I added, joking: "For some Moorish women, making tea is a method of seduction and a ritual of love."

With time, her practice bore fruit. Teresa was completely drawn to her new work as a domestic helper, a home-maker and an extraordinary, plenipotentiary friend. She made the tea, grilled the meat and cleaned the house, and in return I helped her to meet the monthly expenses, which her paltry wages couldn't cover.

On Sundays, Teresa took up her place in the reception room like a princess from the land of the Tuareg. I had brought her a wrap of such deep indigo it was almost black and she looked bewitching wearing her flowing robes. She would take the tea things in her expert hands and then pour the tea elegantly, ensuring the bubbles, as I had taught her, ended up forming a froth that looked like foam atop the strong liquid.

With her authoritative appearance, she sometimes looked like a girl from Tiris, that stretch of desert that reaches from northern Mauritania up to the edges of the river Draa in Morocco.

Who's to say that this Brazilian girl, with her gorgeous, lightly-tanned skin, wasn't related to those tribes, some of whom live off the coast of the Atlantic, who are experts in nomadic life, and who met the first Europeans who ever set foot on dry Mauritanian land? Did one of them travel in the opposite direction and dare marry a Portuguese woman? Anything's possible. Even she knows only that her father was of Portuguese extraction and that she was born in Brazil, like most of her compatriots.

She began to crave verification of this story that she had roots going back to this desert region. Being among those music samples with African rhythms had whetted her appetite for reading and discovery. She poured herself into devouring travel literature and the writings of the European explorers, especially the Portuguese, who were among the first to reach that region and write about it in the fourteenth century AD.

Through Teresa I first heard about the ship *La Mendes*, that was tossed by the violent currents of the Atlantic Ocean towards the coast of Mauritania. It was laden with wondrous goods and commodities, and was greeted by the Saharan tribes with great elation. They considered it a blessing sent to them by God: sugar, tea, cloth, and especially the white slaves, fit for plenty of forced labour.

"They were mostly Spanish and Portuguese, those white men who had been made into prisoners and slaves. It happened in the days when the European nations ruled the seas by violence and by trade, when they deployed all the mechanisms of power in their search for wealth and control." Her face came so close to mine that I was almost drowning in the colour of her eyes and her rapid breathing. She went on: "Did you know that the Portuguese kings encouraged piracy and spent a lot of money on building ships and enlisting troops? They were jealous of the Moorish tribes and took them captive as slaves, sending them to their colonies, especially in Brazil. Their only opportunity to rival the other European nations was by engaging in colonialism and trade. Perhaps it was with the help of those slaves that they made it as far as governing parts of Indonesia, Brazil and Macau . . . and many parts of Africa. Sadly, though, they left their bad habits behind them everywhere. They introduced the colonised peoples to drinking, gambling, and incest. Look at me, my dear. I'm a part of that callous history, like it or not, love it or loathe it."

Teresa hadn't told me much about her family in Brazil. There was something sketchy in her relationship with her father that she didn't want to speak about openly. Was it because she was born from an unlawful relationship between a Portuguese man and a dark-skinned native woman? I don't know. What I do know, however, is that she rarely spoke about her father and that her closest relationship was with her mother. For my part, I was outside this chaos that surrounded her life.

I reached out my arms to embrace her, and said: "Well, I accept you, Teresa, just as you are. Maybe your blood is mixed with that of my ancestors, maybe you are my cousin and I don't know it . . ." Our lips met for the first time and we lost ourselves in a long embrace.

**

My relationship with Teresa lasted for several years. I really loved her, and my love was almost entirely chaste, except for a few moments of weakness when the devil whispered in my ear, but I always emerged repentant. I told her many stories of passion about the great Arab lovers whose ardour drove them, at best, to madness or death. It occurred to me many times to marry her, but it was out of the question. The shackles of Bedouin society are harsh and inescapable, and often unseen.

I thought about the social repercussions waiting for me if I brought a Brazilian girl whose origins were shrouded in doubt to those conservative border regions of the desert; if I tried to insert her into a social environment that set such store by family relations, noble descent, and purity of the blood line. My uncle might censure me with his biting words and refuse to shake my hand, my father would probably slap me round the face and chase me out of the house. The only man who would stand by my side would be the teacher Rajeb, and that would be offensive and cruel to the people of al-Nab'a, and also he might try to make Teresa one of his many lovers.

As I was preparing to travel back to Nouakchott, and trying to make sense of the frustration that had overcome me in the centre of Madrid's tumultuous racket, Teresa came to ask my advice on her wedding to somebody new. Touching my arm, she said clearly: "Even though love sometimes seems limitless, I've still always been looking for it. And I found it. Can you believe it?"

I knew that we were both looking for love, and that together we had found it resting between us in a climate of companionship and friendship. So I told her, as if answering a question hanging in the air: "That's right. Sometimes love is limitless, and that sums up my state too."

I offered my blessings to Teresa on her marriage to a young Spaniard, who worked in the night club right under my balcony. He was tall and brawny, with huge limbs bearing tattoos of scorpions, snakes, and dinosaurs breathing fire. By contrast, I bore only Teresa's name, stamped on my heart and impossible to remove by either fire or water.

The last day we met, Teresa said to me: "Look at him. Fernando is such a nice guy. He wouldn't hurt a fly. I've put him to the test and I think he's right for me, but sadly he doesn't like drinking tea." She laughed, then leant towards him and lost herself in his embrace. She held on to his back and hugged him tight. He couldn't escape her grip. He went on looking around before he lowered his head towards her and looked at her infatuated. That was the last interaction I had with them, at the end of my time living in that Spanish city.

Translated from the author's novel *Tuyour al-Nab'a*
(Birds of al-Nab'a), published by Jadawel, Beirut, 2017

LAMIA MAKADDAM

Four Poems

TRANSLATED BY KAREN MCNEIL AND MILED FAIZA

THE BREAD SELLER

One harsh winter
I was working as a bread seller
in a very small village
Someone arrived
and he was hungry
so I gave him a loaf of bread
and took him to my house
There, on the threshold, he sat for years
feeding pigeons and cats from his hand, from the loaf
I gave him that harsh, dark winter
in a remote little village
For he was hungry
and I was a bread seller

*

I woke up one night and didn't find him,
didn't find the loaf or the threshold,
history or geography,
seasons or their memory
But the cats and dogs,
the rats, pigeons and worms
have never left my home since

IF I EVER WROTE POETRY

For some reason that's unclear
I wanted to talk to you about the ugliness of the cold
during the harsh winter night and
about my trembling fingers,
about the desolation of absence and silence,
about darkness hanging from the ceiling like dust bunnies
I touched my mouth and didn't find my lips
I didn't find my voice either
In the deep sleeps a warm happiness
Whose is this scar?
And who is speaking this silence?

*

If I ever wrote poetry
it was because one of them had to cry
and if I screamed with a violence that destroys everything
it was because a door was shut on the fingers
of a girl somewhere in this world
The only thing I can share with you is that leafy sadness . . .
It is something we can share with love, anyway

*

All winters are the same
whether here or on the other side of the planet
If your fingers tremble, don't write in this area
and if absence fills your heart
then at least you know that there's something
dwelling in it, so write from that darkness
about what makes life bearable

A SHORT SKIRT

If you keep me from wearing a short skirt
then what is there left for us to strive for?
You see my knobby knees as a source of seduction
and you don't see the affection in my feet
I made these knees from old tin
cans and from walking sticks my father left hanging
on the wall of his room.
My knees, for these reasons, do not seduce anyone
except the mountain, the ant, and the tree
when I ran and when I fell.
When I loved and when I cried
I hugged my knees like pieces torn from a small heart
I once ate my left knee
while watching the movie "Hunger" and standing on one foot with
   my back against the wall
If you looked closely
you wouldn't see seduction in my knees
and you would ask me to bare my shoulder too and my breast
and my belly button
until I was walking beside you in the street completely naked
like a laurel leaf.
The body is not what people think it is, but rather
the body is an idea.
If you looked closely
you would let me decorate my knees with colored ribbons
I drag the two of them behind me in nightclubs
From time to time I give them a piece of candy
and I scream when they are naughty or splash in puddles
At the end of the day I tie them to my neck
and I return crawling on my veins
You're right: love is rough journey
a never-ending crawl toward the other
If you reach out your hand and touch the soft skin
you will find two orphan stones
blocking the way and spreading misery

LAMIA MAKADDAM

SOMETHING MUST BREAK IN THE END

You will find me every morning, a waitress in a café,
my hair pulled back in a ponytail, giving you coffee with shaky hands and saying: "Good morning", or: "Wake up, it's nine o'clock", or: "Why are you spending all your time on your phone? Write an article or a poem instead."
You will find me at seven o'clock in a train station,
Waving to you from platform to platform, and running between the riders to put my foot on the threshold, so the train door won't close without you.
Do not forget to go, there is always something waiting for us on the other bank.
And every year
every year,
you will find me in a bar or a nightclub
wearing farmers' clothes and dancing until
the end of the harvest, until the pitchforks are laid down
and the full sacks are stored.
You will find me in every word you write
in every woman you love
in every tree overlooking a house you haven't lived in yet.
I will sing so much for you,
in spring and winter, while I am migrating from you and to you.
And when my wing breaks
do not be sad, something must break
in the end
so that we know we are alive.

Translated from a forthcoming collection

ABDELAZIZ BARAKA SAKIN

My Mother, the Other Woman and I

A SHORT STORY
TRANSLATED BY ADIL BABIKIR

I am fifty years old now, exactly the age of my mother when she died thirty years ago. But I am not talking about her now to commemorate the thirtieth anniversary of her departure, as others would tend to mark the passing of their beloved mothers. Of course, I too love my mother, but the reason I mention her now is because I have been completely obsessed with her as of late. When I say obsessed, I mean it. Although she died more than a quarter of a century ago, I never really felt she was dead. In fact, she isn't. She took a long, eternal leave from life's endless preoccupations, and particularly from me, her only son and companion in sorrow and joy. But it didn't take my mother long – only thirty years, to be precise – to call off her leave. And thirty years, as you know, is not really long by the standards of the dead; some believe that the state of death could last forever.

A few days ago, after a long day at the primary school, where I work as principal, and a boring evening spent at the teachers' club playing cards and chatting, I was really exhausted when I got home. I live alone: my eldest daughter having got married earlier this week and travelled abroad with her husband, just as her two younger sisters had done in the last two years. My wife too got married more than ten years ago to a man believed to be her first lover. She obtained a divorce verdict from the religious court, claiming that I was a useless man and husband and that she couldn't stand me any longer. But God only knows that I am by no means a despicable person. The proof: all my three daughters chose to stay with me and refused to accompany her to her father's house and then on to her new husband's abode. So who really is the despicable one here? But this is a subject that I don't like to get into. After all, she is the mother of my three daughters.

I was so exhausted that I hobbled to bed, throwing my body onto the mattress: my kind, softhearted mattress that was the last possession remaining with me after a mother, a wife and three girls, and my only source of compassion as it embraced my scrawny, emaciated body. My tiny, energy-efficient Chinese lamp with its faint light always remained on until the morning. I had barely closed my eyes when I heard the scraping of a chair on the floor. With the aid of the austere Chinese neon light, I saw a young woman dragging the chair towards me. She sat down on it close to my head and stared at me with unmistakable affection. Although this should have frightened me to death, I found myself saying in a welcoming tone:

"My God! My mother Amna?"

The softhearted, pretty young woman smiled. She then started to talk quietly, narrating endless anecdotes of my life since birth, minute by minute, second by second. I listened attentively, overwhelmed with astonishment, as if the subject of the story and the listener were but two aberrant parallels of me. I was discovering gradually that my entire life had been mired in sins; that I had indulged heavily in worldly pleasures, although some incidents clearly credited me with nobleness and kind-heartedness. I can't say exactly how long she remained by my head, narrating these accounts, but she surely stayed for quite some time. I don't know how many tales she narrated, but there were undoubtedly many. I don't even know when I eventually fell asleep, but that obviously happened quite late because I didn't wake up at the usual 4 am, as all school principals do. Rather, it was the school watchman who, somewhat astonished, woke me during the breakfast break – around 10:30 am. I understood from his mumblings that the staff were worried about my absence. Only one sentence from my mother's account still lingered in my head:

"I am with you day by day, minute by minute."

Fearing mockery and gloating, I refrained from telling anybody what had happened between me and my mother. I might be accused of insanity – and might well lose my job if the administration could prove me insane. Indeed, some would even rejoice at such circumstances.

So I kept it to myself.

I received a call from my eldest daughter, Amouna – I had named her after my mother – who enquired after my health and how I was coping with leading life alone. She suggested that I remarry ("she doesn't have to be a young lady," she explained). By her judgment, I needed a companion to overcome my loneliness. She even went as far as to recommend a particular lady: forty years old, pretty and divorced, mother of two children. I pretended that I didn't get the message, perhaps because I didn't feel like remarrying. To me, a woman is a beautiful creature who is good for anything but marriage!

In the evening I was ready for another meeting with my mother. She came, glitteringly beautiful and bursting with vitality, dressed in cheerfully-coloured clothes.

"You look ready tonight," she remarked.

A strange idea sprang into to my head and I set about acting on it right away. Typical of me, ideas always find their way straight to my fingers. I stretched them out towards her, groping about for her clothes. But all I felt was air. She disappeared; her voice came to me from the remotest corners of the room:

"I am but image and sound. Just image and sound," she said in a sweet tone that years under the ground had failed to distort.

"I hope I'm not hallucinating," I told her.

"I have always been close to you," said the same voice that I had known perfectly well since childhood.

My mother and I were close friends. We passed through years of great hardship and years of joy. I am also her only son, and, to this day, have never known of a father. Since the moment I entered this world, my eyes fell upon a tenderhearted, energetic creature which moved around as relentlessly as an ant in pursuit of a grain of food to share with me. She was able invariably to meet my demands, no matter how difficult they might seem. I remember having once asked her to buy me a bicycle, just like that of my schoolmate, Abbakar

NEXT ISSUE

FOCUS

NEW IRAQI NOVELS

Ishaq. I can still vividly recall how she reprimanded me and, in a blind fit of agony, hurled the object she was carrying at my face.

"Whose son do you think you are? Sadek El Mahdi's?" she shouted angrily.

Of course, I was not at all sure who Sadek El Mahdi was, but her question begat another: whose son am I?

In spite of this, I did not proceed to ask her that question, for it was not particularly pressing to me. Having never known the value, importance or even function of a father, I had never missed having one. And it's not as if any of the many fathers in our neighbourhood did anything extraordinary that was beyond my mother's capability. Conversely, it was my mother who did things that fathers couldn't do. She would build and mend our home with her own hands; construct earth dams to divert rainwater away from our hut, situated on the edge of a water stream. Not once did I see a father do this. To my bewilderment, they would even hire workers for the most trivial of jobs, such as making bed covers and mattresses for them and doing their laundry.

Beyond the confines of our home, my mother had another important job: selling tea and coffee by the prison gate. Everyone – including the commissioner himself – borrowed money from her. That was why I was confused. But now for the first time, I understand from my mother that one of the responsibilities of an ambiguous father named Sadek El Mahdi was to supply his children with bicycles.

The father question was ultimately put to rest about three months later, when my mother Amna managed to buy me a bicycle. Although it was second hand (not brand new like Abbakar Ishaq's), I was thrilled to have it – particularly after my friends assured me that it was beautiful, even better than Abbakar's.

My mother would make *zalabiya* doughnuts and at dawn I would go about selling them to the neighbours. After this, and having drunk a cup of tea, she would go to do janitorial work at the prison. Later on, once she had abandoned this latter job, she sold tea by the prison gate, effectively turning her old workmates into clients. Indeed, she actually became a serious competitor to Um Bakhout, who used to be one of my mother's customers when she worked as a janitor.

I, on the other hand, was one of those boys who, as a result of my constant attachment to my mother, earned the nickname 'mummy's boy'. After school, I would come straight to her workplace to assist her with washing teacups, delivering orders to clients who lived further out, buying her sugar and tea from the grocery store and, in the intermittent breaks between these errands, telling her all about my classmates, teachers and lessons. When I felt sleepy, she would lay out a carpet made of palm leaves in the space just behind her. Using my school bag as a pillow, I would stretch out my little body there, my beautiful bike standing by close to my legs, awaiting me.

I dared to ask her: "Where are you now? In Paradise? In Hell? In the earthly world? And where have you been all this time?"

"I am here," she said.

Sitting on the chair, like she did on the first day, she questioned me about my justifications for all the acts I had performed earlier in the day. I gave her truthful answers, on which she sometimes commented, but mostly she remained silent. Generally, however, she would assert that it didn't matter if what I did was good or not: what really mattered was whether or not I perceived any justification for my actions; whether or not they gave me self-satisfaction.

"How do you feel about your daughter Amouna's suggestion?"

"I am too old now to have a desire for women," I said. "Besides, I am able to take care of my own cooking and domestic needs. I have only one woman in my life: you! Only you. That's more than enough."

A wonderfully deep smile spread across her face, before she gradually dissolved into the emptiness of the room.

Early the next morning, my daughter Amouna called me once again, this time bluntly announcing that she would arrange for me to meet a forty-year-old lady, pretty and divorced, mother of two, and that it was fully up to me to decide whether or not I would ask for her hand in marriage.

"What have you got to lose?" I asked myself. "Just let it be."

She was pretty, and wore a permanent smile on her face. She didn't seem to need an excuse for laughing, as she was always laughing and could persuade anyone, even the most sullen, to reciprocate that lovely smile. But what was strange and astonishing, even frightening, about her was that she was wearing the exact same clothes worn by my mother Amna the previous night; she had the same pair of shoes, the same voice, the same accent, the same face, the same smile, and she was, I am quite able to say, the very same woman.

WIDAD NABI

Five Poems

TRANSLATED BY
JONATHAN WRIGHT

WIDAD NABI

A PLACE LIT BY MEMORY

1
Grief is
to visit the rubble of your house
and come back without a coat of its dust on your fingers

2
Kindness is
to water the wilting flowers
In your neighbours' garden
because the flowers in your own house died of thirst during the shelling

3
Distance is
a geography of oppression
that connects two cities thousands of miles apart.
In the first city you left your washing on the line
and in the second you reach up through the air
to bring in the washing from the balcony of the first.

4
Your finger holds down the doorbell of your old house
Who will tell it that
houses don't belong to those who have abandoned them?

5
Only the water
knows why the flowers weep
on the balconies of happy houses.

6
On the way to your new house
there's a long trail of nostalgia
that you will walk forever.

7
When you touch the harsh metallic parts of the bus here
and a daffodil grows on the metal door handle of your house there
that's how houses are loyal to owners forced to abandon them.

8
You always wake up in the middle of the night
and the tap's still dripping in your old kitchen.

9
Life won't be that bad.
It will give you a new house
but your soul will turn into a wolf
that howls every night
on the front steps of your old house.

10
Behind the old window
your picture watches the rain fall.
Drenched, the beech tree weeps,
and no one notices.

11
Darkness
grows in abandoned houses
like grass in April
and yet the place is lit by memory

IF I HAD A GARDEN'S HEART

If I had a garden's heart
I'd name the trees after you
I'd make the grass grow under your house,
and white flowers
would light the dark distance
between my heart and yours.

WIDAD NABI

If I had a garden's heart
I'd let crimson hibiscus flowers
grow under the boots of a soldier aiming
a bullet at the heart of a child.
I'd force him to see the beauty that grows on the ground
in the hope he might bend down to see the beauty beneath his feet
and forget how to open fire on living things.

If I had a garden's heart
I'd turn its trees into beds and seats for lovers.
I wouldn't let a lover wait without a seat
I wouldn't let a woman in love go without a bed for love
I wouldn't let the seats at the station go rusty waiting.

If I had a garden's heart
I'd have the roots of the beech trees in this town
reach out towards the olive trees in the garden of our house in the
    Kobani countryside
I'd water them with the water in my heart.
I'd link up with the orange tree next to my window in Aleppo
and tell it about a country where people do not kill each other.

About a country where children do not die under rubble
about a country where people grow up and grow old,
with people whose hair turns grey in the company of those they
    love
and who are buried in proper graves.

If I had a garden's heart
I would be the wood in your table
the wood in your bed
the wood in the chair you sit on at work
the wood in your kitchen spoons
the wood in the floors of your house
the wood in the hardness of your heart.

If I had a garden's heart
I'd love you with the heart of a thousand trees
and the heart of a thousand flowers

and the heart of a thousand shoots of wild grass
and this heart of mine.

If I had a garden's heart
I'd turn all the iron in the world into trees
and only gardens would not hurt the heart of any creature
and only gardens would stand against wars.

If I had a garden's heart
I'd turn my body into grass for your body
my breasts would be pomegranates for your hands,
my navel a glass of red wine for your mouth,
my ear a love bird for your poems
and my poems.
Flowers have been growing on the borders of our country
for a thousand years, and for a term in exile too.

IF YOU WERE A LOVER

You would want to be dust on the doorbell of your beloved's
    house,
the house where war lives.
If you were a lover,
you would want to be the dead cat
close to your beloved's head in the old picture,
you would want to be the book she reads on the train.
You would dream of turning into the festering wounds
on the hands of an old man in a Herta Müller novel,
just so that if she happened to read you her tears would fall on
    you.
If you were a lover
you would fight to be the headstone at your beloved's grave in
    exile
just to wake up before the nostalgia starts and whisper "I love
    you"
to the remains of her refugee bones
as if you were her faraway country.

LETTERS OF TWELVE GAZELLES

1

Sadness didn't have a home
so we welcomed it into our own homes
like one of the family

2

In the back garden
where there's no light
where there's no one,
there are delicate flowers that no one has seen

3

The rain falls and no one is listening
Listening is a job for the blind heart

4

The country that gave us dreary names
and anxious mothers
and a national anthem that glorifies murderers,
after a quarter century and a war,
will it give our coffins safe passage?

5

There must be some sorrow
to light the poet's house in a dark world

6

We've carried our suitcases many times
It's no longer frightening, you country.

7

Only the water
knows why the flowers weep
on the balconies of happy houses,

the ones we have abandoned.

8
I was a big shop for things
Only hatred didn't buy anything from me

9
I grow old by night
when the time doesn't notice
Without anyone seeing me
I grow a hundred years older
I turn the sadness that grows under my skin into poetry
and I stay as I am
the very image of the young gazelle at the waterhole

10
We love her, that country,
even in its latest state of ruin

A LITTLE BEFORE THIRTY HE KISSED ME

Like a bad faceless woman
who sells her body on the crowded streets of Berlin
I've dug a little hole
under a green beech tree
a little hole big enough to bury thirty years in
and a country in ruins
my old clothes
the shoes in the multiple closets at home
my old poems
And many miserable lovers

A little before thirty
I covered the hole with soil, properly and with great tenderness
as I did with my father's grave in another country's August.
"The dead don't come back,"
I whispered in the beech tree's ear
and I put lipstick on my dry lips.

WIDAD NABI

I sent a short love letter:
"Come on, more kisses, before the garden withers."
He and I,
we're well aware that the garden that bloomed this morning
knows nothing about towns that have tasted the salty sweat
of my little feet
the garden knows nothing of the war that has flattened the towns
   where I once lived
The garden that was in flower this morning smiles
at wrinkles that have not yet appeared on my face
and doesn't know that love is an anti-ageing serum.

A little before thirty
like a bad woman who sells her past to a drunk for a hundred
   euros
I sell those years for free
to the border guards in the countries I crossed as I ran from a war
   I didn't want
to the taxmen in capitalist Germany where I live
to the neo-Nazis as they chant We don't want refugees
to the men who clung to my coloured Kurdish caftan
like tulips at the moment of farewell
So I sent them smiling to hell
after burying their flowers, their letters, their names
the harshness of their voices, and their wounds under another
   green tree

A little before thirty
I laugh at the rigour my life has been through
A woman in love I am
a woman that doesn't grow old
a woman that doesn't hide the traces of love on her neck, her
   navel, her breasts
and that never regrets the sting of the viper between her legs.
A bad woman
that curses the world in the middle of a glass of vodka,
that attacks the regime in power in her country
when there's a checkpoint only a few yards away
from the front door of her house.

A bad woman
that smiles at strange men for no reason
just because someone once told her
that her smile was a gift from God, so don't begrudge it.
A woman that smiles at African refugees
at market traders
at her German neighbour's dog
at the bloody news reports
at the unfamiliar flowers under the green beech tree.

A very bad woman,
but when she takes a man she loves in her arms,
mist sets up its houses in her embrace.

A little before thirty
I bared my body for poetry to see
"Here are my old scars," I said,
pointing them out.
"The measles mark on my back,
the mark that small stone left on my knee,
the mark of a fresh love kiss on my neck,
and the mark of loneliness on my poem."

A little before thirty
I'm learning more rude expressions
I won't forget to eliminate the word war from language
and I don't care if someone whispers, "What a harsh woman!"
because I'm selling thirty years that are gone, with everything in
    them,
just to shout out in poetry:
"Kiss me, kiss me,
kiss me a little before thirty,
kiss me."

>Translated from her collection *al-Mawt kama law kana khurda*
>(Death as if it was Scrap), published by Bayt al-Mouwaten
>(Publications of the Syrian League for Citizenship), 2016

Alaa al-Deeb
A WRITER APART

INTRODUCED BY

YASSER ABDEL LATIF

MANSOURA EZ-ELDIN

IBRAHIM FARGHALI

MAHMOUD EL-WARDANY

YOUSSEF RAKHA

BEN KOERBER

ALAA KHALED

TRANSLATED BY

JONATHAN WRIGHT

SALLY GOMAA

RAPHAEL COHEN

NARIMAN YOUSSEF

ADIL BABIKIR

SUNEELA MUBAYI

PAUL STARKEY

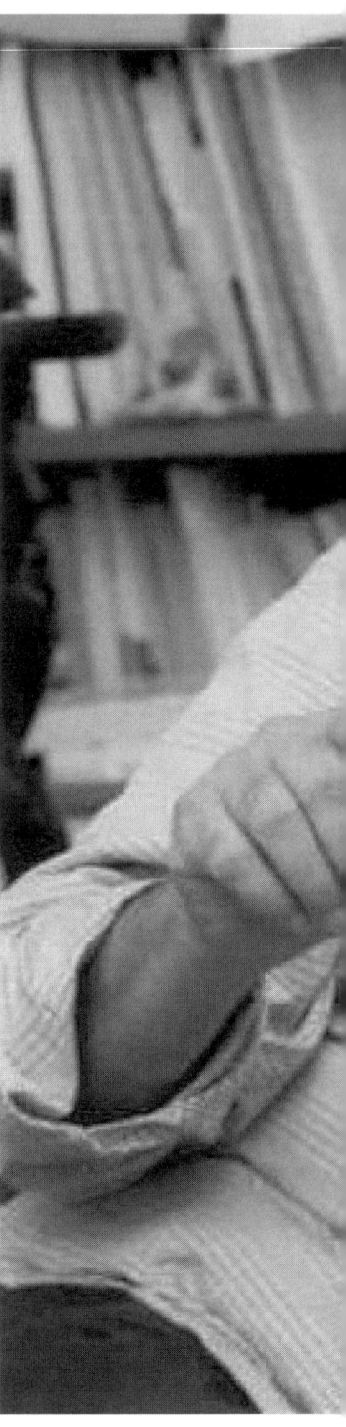

ALAA AL-DEEB

Lemon Blossom

CHAPTERS FROM THE NOVEL *ZAHR EL-LAYMOON*
TRANSLATED BY JONATHAN WRIGHT

1

He was woken up by the nine o'clock light, which began the day, harsh and disturbing on the upper floors of the buildings after streaming through the windows with their flimsy paper shutters.

Nine o'clock on a Thursday morning. It was Thursday and it would be Friday tomorrow. It was a sudden razor-sharp summer light that touched the edges of the sparse furniture and filled the void of the empty room where Abdel Khaliq al-Messiri lived, on the roof of an old house in tranquil Suez.

The ordeal of getting out of bed was now a routine, with familiar rituals and rhythms, an ebb and a flow. There was the desire to get up and the fear of getting up; the fear of lying in bed and the desire to lie in bed. Every day new details were added, depending on the night before and the day to come. Loneliness was now a fully woven cocoon, the shell of an old tortoise. The head of the tortoise came out, saw the light and heard the sounds, touched things and people, and then the soft white neck pulled back into the old tortoise shell. Loneliness: Abdel Khaliq al-Messiri's special loneliness. The loneliness of exile and imprisonment. Loneliness in the face of a mysterious present and an old distant world that once had been.

Today was Thursday and tomorrow was Friday. Today he would travel to Cairo. A monthly habit as irregular as the periods of a woman approaching menopause. When they asked him in Cairo why he was late in visiting, he would say: "My monthly periods have almost stopped," and they would chuckle. He prevailed against the ordeal of the day by laughing to himself and shaking the bedsheet

Alaa al-Deeb as a young man

with an enthusiasm that was less than half-hearted.

I'm not raking up the past. It's the past that rakes itself up. It's the only thing that lives with me here. It's the only thing that comes with me under the tortoise's shell without seeking my consent. Under the skin and into the veins. No one has yet invented a way to escape the past. It's always there, in your face and at the tips of your fingers. It's the one that rakes itself up and imposes its company on you without asking permission.

He was going to get out of bed with his right foot. When he did that the day would have a flavour, a flavour of busyness at least. His left foot, however, would cast a pall on the day. He smiled and adjusted his old pyjama bottoms.

He made a pot of tea and washed his face thoroughly in the thin trickle of water barely dribbling out of the tap.

He went back to wondering: which window should I open? The big one to the west that looks out over the roof, or the little high one to the east that looks out on the Gulf of Suez and Mount Ataqa? He could see that view only when he climbed up on a chair to open the window. He saw it for a few short moments, then stepped down from the chair and couldn't see anything. He could still see the view, but only in his imagination. All he could see of it was the light reflected off the dark mountain.

He opened the two windows together. Although he'd often seen the view, the solidity and immutability of the mountain took him by surprise. Timeless, dark and gloomy, it still held traces of the night. It would take sharp eyes to see through it and make out the folds of rock and time in this mountain.

The larger window overlooked a poor and desolate expanse of roof that smelled of heat and dust. On the edges stood tin drums and earthenware pots in which the plants had died, the stems dried out. The door to Umm Yusra's room, his neighbour, was closed. It had a large horseshoe on it and drawings in coloured chalk. Beyond the roof, as far as the eye could see, the city lurked quietly. Dirty roofs and closed windows that were deaf to the world.

He looked back into the room and said: "I'll let today pass. I'll glide along it as many days have glided along me." He could taste cheap soap in his mouth, and the taste was accentuated when he couldn't see clearly, when he looked in his head for an improbable concept or when he set his mind's eye to work in search of an old scene that he didn't want to see again.

He opened the door as well. He opened everything there was to open and sat on the small table in the middle of the room with his wet towel around his neck, running his fingers along the lines of print in the newspaper open on the table. "I thought a silent body was a sign of health," he said to himself. "Now I have no diseases, no bitterness, no urge to rebel or protest. My head isn't heavy and my guts aren't constipated. Might it be that this silence of the body is a sign of death?"

He rushed to the little mirror to comb his hair and check that his own face was definitely there. He had a close look, because the mirror was covered in black patches that didn't come off. His hair was soft and thin now and didn't need combing. Whose was this immobile face? This beautiful ugly face. Where had the feelings and thoughts gone? Shouldn't every face have an expression? What lay behind the pupils of those kindly amber eyes? They were the only things that moved. They examined the reflection of the sparse furniture in the mirror. Then they stared into the void and the silence. They didn't see the face of the man whose eyes they were. Those eyes are mine and my full name is Abdel Khaliq Hosni al-Messiri. He moved his face and withdrew from in front of the mirror, resuming that strange, determined smile.

Mona had said to him one morning: "Open your honey-coloured eyes. Let them take in people and things." And then she covered his eyes in kisses.

With the sharp taste of the hot tea that he made so well, the strange taste in his mouth disappeared and his arms and legs awoke. He heard Umm Yusra's footsteps coming up the stairs, so he covered his bare chest with a clean white shirt. He still loved the smell of clean clothes, while the smell of sweat offended him. Before Umm Yusra appeared, he could smell the fresh bread she brought every day from the edges of the market. She knocked on the door with the palm of her hand and her pleasant voice rang out, piecing together the fragments of the morning.

"Good morning, Abdel Khaliq, sir," she said.

He murmured many responses, as if speaking from somewhere distant. He could no longer break away from his private moments quickly, so at first the words came out as rhythmic sounds that vaguely conveyed his emotions. People were used to him doing this, and they understood what he meant to say. Umm Yusra went on to comment on the heat and the humidity, the damned staircase, the crowds, and the lack of fish and vegetables, while he drank his tea and repeated: "Please come in, come in, sit down." She put her plastic bag down on the floor and took out two white loaves, as she usually brought him when she went to market.

"That's very kind of you," he said, "but I'm off to Cairo today."

She put the bread back in her bag, and looked at him and the room with love and affection.

"Have a good trip. Don't forget to turn the water off," she said with a sigh as she turned to go. He suddenly regretted what he had said. Why hadn't he taken the bread? Why hadn't he held her back for a longer conversation? Why was he going to Cairo anyway?

The room had started to fill with tiresome morning flies, so he stood up to close the windows and finish off getting dressed. With the room dark now that the windows were closed, he set about re-arranging the few books scattered around – collections of old Arabic poetry, translated novels and books he had been given by visitors and some old friends. He stopped at the caricature of him that an old colleague had drawn, holding a wooden sword and with a coloured cloth bag on his shoulder. Then he read for the thousandth time the words written by a friend who got drunk at his place one night long ago. With a piece of charcoal he had written next to the window: People are lines that are written, but written in water.

2

Abdel Khaliq al-Messiri assured himself he was going to Cairo for fun, not because he'd been summoned for questioning, and that he wouldn't be taken off to be imprisoned or detained. But an unpleasant feeling lingered, a strange mixture of fear and dejection, and it was no longer any use trying to laugh it off and joke about it.

When he had come to Suez four years earlier to work in the cultural centre, he had had a vague dream that he would find himself in this isolation and that he would sort out the chaos into which his life had descended. He hadn't dreamed of any major change or great deeds, but he had said that cutting off his ties to Cairo would help him see things differently and that he would at least be able to adapt to the new reality and, most importantly, he would be able to put in order his relationship with the past.

The four years had passed like fragments of time, broken up and scattered. There wasn't any work worth mentioning to do in the cultural centre, and if there was, it was nominal, seasonal and trivial. He was usually excluded from meetings and other events because his communist past pursued him, or at least so he imagined, and he wanted it that way. The silly and noisy parties had nothing to do with his dream of working with people or for them. That hellish assumption that pursued him in reality and in his dreams. His bosses and his colleagues at work changed, while he settled in the library, without colleagues, with few books and with few people coming to read. It was a large room at the end of a long corridor, with open windows, and there he had tea three times a day, read all three newspapers, revised three notebooks and arranged three books. Those who wanted to read came, then left because they had changed their minds or because they couldn't find anything to read. Detectives came, then left because they found he had nothing to tell them. People seeking friendship and conversation came, but they found that his spirit had withered. They found him as mired in boredom as his bookshelves, and his old papers were covered in dust. He'd thought of writing his name on a wooden pyramid, as other civil servants did, and putting it on his desk. On the other side he would write: "Neglected talent and wasted time." He flipped the wooden pyramid in his mind's eye, first with the name facing him and then with the mantra for this stage in his life. He stood up to look out on the graveyard full of rubbish next to the cultural centre. Throughout the four years the presence of Cairo in his life had not diminished. It was a ghoul that consumed the days, not out of a craving for them, nor out of love for the city's days and nights and those who lived there. It was more like an incomplete sentence with some of the words missing. It wasn't in good order and it didn't convey any sense. A monster that blocked one's throat.

He could have liked Suez, but only if they kept him away from the main square, the provincial headquarters and the cultural centre, and if they kept away from him the new boutiques, the loudspeakers and the housing complexes that become dilapidated before anyone even lived in them.

He would have liked Suez if the big veranda overlooking the Gulf of Suez was still there, with the poet Amal Dunqul reciting his poetry in the darkness of the veranda, his face like Mount Ataqa and his frame like ships' ropes. If they brought people back as they had been, without coloured shirts, rolled-up sleeves, slicked-back hair, tight trousers and a gangly gait.

He liked the mackerel, the shellfish, the sweet tahina, the sesame bars, the men and the sea, before it was polluted by displacement, lies and thwarted hopes.

He liked all the streets before the filthy rats and the new thieves had gnawed at them.

He loved the ebb and flow of the tide by moonlight under Mount Ataqa on nights that were gone and would never return.

He loved the Arbaeen district, the fish market, the mosque of Sidi el-Gharib and the coffee shop chairs painted green.

When he went into the Ministry of Culture building with his friend Ahmed Saleh to meet Dr Mahmoud Fahmi, he was fighting off a sense of nausea that Ahmed had failed to dispel with the black humour that he aimed at everything around him. Ahmed Saleh was an old comrade and now he owned a jewellery workshop in the Azhar district. He had survived many conflicts and had moved on to new territory. The only thing that tied him to the past was lengthy and repetitive night-time conversations about politics and how people changed. He knew everyone – the dissemblers and the traitors, those who denied, those who clung to delusions and those who went astray. Ahmed was tolerant, capable and strangely serene.

Because Dr Mahmoud Fahmi had a particular liking for silver and because his relationship with Ahmed was very friendly, Ahmed brought him new pieces of silver, found rare old pieces for him, re-silvered old pieces for his wife and repaired ones that were broken. He saw him at home and in his workshop, and they were always on the phone with each other. "So, Abdel Khaliq," said Ahmed, "he won't turn down a request from me. In fact he really wants to help, and so, my friend, don't be difficult please. Besides, who knows if he might be moved from this job tomorrow . . . what matters is that he meets you."

Because Ahmed Saleh was smart and had an easygoing and reassuring presence, the meeting was easier than he had imagined. Ahmed kept himself busy drinking his coffee and then examining the pieces of silver – the bowls and medallions that filled the large office. Dr Fahmi stood up, put his hand on Abdel Khaliq's shoulder, pulled him aside to the large window and said: "Now, about the security and Interior Ministry procedures, I'll see they're completed with the minister directly. Such things have to come from the top so the junior people don't complicate them. So, sir, it's up to you to choose. Alexandria's crowded and Upper Egypt's a long way off. What do you say to Suez?"

The doctor had raised his voice in the last part of the conversation, and so Ahmed joined in. "That's very reasonable, thank you very much. And Abdel Khaliq has always loved Suez."

"Very well then. You'll get the job in a week."

Everything changed suddenly and simply. Ahmed picked up some silver medallions and cups that the ministry had won to re-silver them in the workshop.

Outside, he punched Abdel Khaliq in the chest and said: "Just so you know, my name is Ahmed Saleh the miracle-worker."

Abdel Khaliq smiled in gratitude and surprise.

3

You, my love, are the centre of the universe. With you everything is happy and pleasurable, even watching the workmen pave the road.

I want to live with you in a simple fishing boat with crudely made oars. We would park under bridges and go into small villages at night.

I want to wash your clothes. You don't know how good I am at washing. And are you good at fishing and rowing?

It was close to ten o'clock. He had to leave Suez before noon to reach Cairo by the afternoon and find them all gathered in the bar. Before that he had to find a good cheap piece of hashish as a present from Suez that they could enjoy.

He avoided the main streets so that he wouldn't meet any nosy civil servants. They might ask him questions that he would have to

"Although many excellent novels have tackled the same crisis as **Lemon Blossom,** this novel is a genuine addition to Arabic fiction in general, both in its artistic structure and in the way it reflects lived human experience honestly and profoundly."

Mahmoud Amin El-Alem

answer politely, which annoyed them, and annoyed him even more so.

He didn't want to know where the director of the cultural centre had been the day before, or what he had done. He didn't want to know who had arrived in the province from Cairo the day before, or what they had been asking.

He wanted to avoid the streets with pavement kerbs painted alternately black and white. He wanted to avoid the slogans written on the empty rubbish bins, and the traffic lights that no one obeyed.

He took a back way that circled the old city and brought him out on a dusty street flanked by a hill planted with a patch of ancient prickly pear plants, covered in cobwebs and dust. The street ran on until it left the town, and beyond it lay fields, their margins scorched by the dust of the highway and the exhaust of trucks.

He hurried along the dirt path, his feet kicking up dust behind him. The growing heat of the sun and the ghosts of passers-by created around him a time and place suspended in the particles of dust, skewered by a doltish forenoon sun.

"I'm Captain Fathi Farag, and I'm going to sear your skin. And then I'm going to give you new skin in exchange. You, you son of a whore, take all your clothes off, all of them."

The officer was short and fat. The brass on his uniform glittered in the sun and his eyes were black holes that glowed.

Abdel Khaliq repelled the memory of his years in detention by repeating an old song that a friend of his used to repeat. The tune had lost its savour and the memory had grown more brutal and more vivid.

Get away from me, you ghosts, you years of waste. Rise up and settle there, among the fields of prickly pear. Mix the blood of the old communist with the coverings of cobweb, or push the red flower of the prickly pear down my throat, or the thorny fruit itself. Only don't leave me captive, tearing myself to pieces by digging up and raking over the past.

The dust from the road gradually settled, and the dusty road handed him over to the asphalt. He went into the cool of the coffee shop, which was covered by a grapevine trellis. He asked for the hashish dealer and they told him he hadn't come yet, so he sat down to drink a bad cup of tea and wait impatiently.

4

In coffee shops and hashish dens Abdel Khaliq felt a mixture of unease and childish excitement. Here was a world outside the law, far from the rules that people obey; an antidote to the daily grind and the hustle and bustle of life.

The sessions were no longer as enjoyable as they had been. He wasn't addicted to smoking hashish or even a regular smoker. He was just killing time and watching. Inside him there was an old tradition of hostility towards hashish. They used to say: "Get drunk if you want, but beware of hashish because it's the quickest way to undermine the spirit of revolution and destroy any desire for change."

He didn't challenge or discuss the old tradition, but other things had intervened and words had lost their meaning. He never made anything, never did any work, so why was he remembering these old ideas?

At one time these coffee shops had been a stable and well-entrenched world. The towns poured into them all the stories and myths they had. Every coffee shop had its own flavour and character, associated with a part of reality that Abdel Khaliq had often spoken about but never experienced. The Cairo coffee shops – the Azhar, el-Hussein, Gamaliya and Maarouf – were the originals: solid establishments linked to history and old traditions, whereas the regional coffee shops that he knew were all built on the highway.

These places no longer had their old magic. New customers had invaded them before even the police raided them or had them knocked down. New customers had turned the hashish dens into boutiques. He had loved an old coffee shop in the Arbaeen district, and when he visited it recently he found a large window at the entrance offering liver sandwiches and the smell of the frying mixed with a fragrant smell of tobacco.

When he asked the waiter, the waiter said: "It's all to make a living, sir. Hashish makes you hungry and sweet things are now expensive." He left the coffee shop feeling as if he had lost a friend, the cool calm darkness inside having welcomed him on afternoons. From deep inside, the street was visible in the distance through the bright opening, like a silent world that had nothing to do with him.

Some of these places offered him a special sense of peace that he hadn't known since childhood, especially when he sat alone and drank coffee at his leisure, then followed it up with a glass of tea. When he came out he would find the city had signed a separate truce with him and all the city's other wars no longer concerned him.

Hashish was now expensive, too, and fraught with danger. It was of poor quality, without any flavour. It gave him a headache and made him feel sick. If it wasn't for his friend Fathi Noureddin, who asked him on every visit about the hashish in Suez, he wouldn't think of sitting here waiting for Saber, who sold small pieces of carefully wrapped hashish in this coffee shop – hashish that looked top-notch but was of poor quality. The only thing that made it hashish was the name, and a little of the smell. Anxiously he asked after the dealer again and, as he followed up his first cup of tea with another one, the boy said: "The boss is on his way right now, sir."

His mother had been fat and white. From early morning she bustled around their big house with its many open windows and doors, driving Saadiya the maid ahead of her to turn the house upside down and sweep it every morning. Saadiya was dark-skinned and a year or two older than him. She worked all day long without stopping or going out to market. Very occasionally she took a few moments off on the quiet to play in the dirt with him or let him grope her. If she was caught her mistress called her names and punched her firm brown body, whereupon Saadiya would weep loudly, then laugh and go back to running here and there until she collapsed at the end of the day on her dirty bedding beside the kitchen door. His mother would have a shower in the afternoon and change her clothes, including her headscarf. She had a particular smell that filled the house.

At the age of thirteen he pilfered fifty piastres from his mother's purse when she left it in the sitting room. It was during the summer holiday and the days were boring and long. His friends were going to the cinema and doing many things, while he didn't get any pocket money from his parents. The fifty-piastre note was carefully folded at the bottom of the purse and he didn't think his mother would discover it was missing any time soon.

He took it at about three o'clock in the afternoon when the house was asleep, and went out to have fun with his friends. He hid the coins he had left in his shoe and went home at around ten o'clock in the evening.

He found out that his mother had beaten Saadiya till she bled and that the girl had run away after swearing that she knew nothing about the money, that she would never come back and that they wouldn't find out where she was.

He said he knew where she had gone and would go and bring her back. He said there was a carpenter in the market whom she often spoke to and who said he was from a town near where Saadiya's family lived. "Go, and don't come back without her," they said.

He couldn't believe he was going out into the street again. In the darkness he threw the coins away and ran until he reached the carpenter's shop. They told him that Hamdi the carpenter had taken the girl to his house. He found her there with her hair tousled, curled up on the floor crying. He threw himself on her and started hugging and kissing her. "It was most unfair what you people did," Hamdi said. "You were responsible for the girl, and no one should treat good people like that. Suppose the money was lost or fell out, or the lady spent it on something and forgot."

The three of them returned in a sad procession. He was aware of Saadiya walking behind him and his heartbeats were deafening. He couldn't look at her. She was crying in a strange way, not like her crying that was followed by laughter. It was a long walk, and every now and then Hamdi the carpenter would say: "But why? You're good people and your father's a fine man."

They found the lights on in the house, with everyone waiting for them.

His mother welcomed Saadiya, hugging her and saying: "It's all over, my girl. Go and have a shower, and go to sleep in your bed. It's over, we've said it's over. Aren't I like a mother to you?"

His father had a few words with the carpenter, then sent him away. The carpenter wished him and the lady of the house well, saying: "We're all at your service, and may God bless you and your children. That girl is in your charge and she's the best maid in the whole area, I tell you, sir, and she loves the young master as her brother."

Abdel Khaliq walked around the sitting room, listening to Saadiya sobbing. His mother got up to put some food on a plate for Saadiya and then made sure she had gone to sleep in her bed.

At the end of the night his mother said to his father: "Money or no money. The girl's grown up and I no longer want her in the house. She'll have to go home."

When Saadiya was gone, he had an intense fever and was frightened that during the fever he might reveal his secret. He clung to the bedposts, clenched his teeth and cried, while his sister by his side changed the wet towels on his feverish forehead. The room and everything in it seemed to have turned into a single piece of silent marble.

When the dealer came into the coffee shop, the place suddenly sprang into action. He was wearing a clean white galabia, and acted with self-assurance.

He put a piece of hashish in Abdel Khaliq's hand and said: "This is something new, something nice for you and your friends."

Abdel Khaliq smiled at him incredulously and quickly left the coffee shop, the hashish still in his hand.

5

The bus and service taxi station was pure bedlam. Four or five cassette players were blaring from the bay where the buses waited or from the nearby fruit juice bars. Some were loud and weird-sounding recitations from the Qur'an, one was playing incomprehensible Upper Egyptian praise songs, and in another a woman was screaming in anguish about her man, who had gone away and hadn't written to her at all.

He stood next to crates of poor quality fruit, on sale at high prices, and the pedlar and his assistant almost pushed him into a crate of disgustingly ugly grapes. Women in hijabs were hurrying about in their long gowns, looking overweight and flabby. As their menfolk jostled to find empty seats in a service taxi, or a cheap ticket for a crowded bus, they hurried after them. The ground at the station was filthy and crates of soft drinks were piled high, like barricades for a war that might break out at any moment. The smell of food was pungent and offensive, but people were filling their mouths around the carts and throwing the leftovers under their feet. Young boys were washing plastic and tin plates in buckets of dirty water.

Who had released all these ghouls, and what did they want?

He almost had a fight with the pedlar who was pestering him. "I don't want any, man," he shouted in his face. "I don't want any."

The man turned away as if he hadn't heard, and went back to shouting his wares in a grating voice.

Amidst the chaos he set about looking for a taxi driver he recognised, to make sure he could sit next to him, but all the faces were new and in a hurry because today was Thursday and the next day would be Friday, so there was a chance to raise the fares or for new drivers to descend on the station.

He felt a hand tugging at his trousers and noticed a black beggar crawling along the ground, his legs contorted beneath him, pulling his trousers and saying something unintelligible to him. He felt a blast of heat shooting through his body and he jumped out of the way.

The fat white officer was standing over him and he was flat on his face in the hot sand. The officer was kicking him in the ribs with his shoe. "Eat the dirt so I can't hear your voice," the officer said. "Eat it or I'll stuff it down your throat." Next to the officer stood two soldiers with Sudanese whips hanging from their hands. In front of him was a long line of fellow prisoners, crawling along faces down.

"Abdel Khaliq, Abdel Khaliq, answer me, man. Aren't you going to Cairo?" The strident metallic voice was that of Mustafa el-Kurdi, a colleague who had been seconded to work in Saudi Arabia three years earlier. Mustafa took hold of his arm and pulled him away from the heart of the chaos. Oblivious to everything around him, Mustafa cut through the crowds confidently and skilfully. Abdel Khaliq followed behind.

Mustafa el-Kurdi had changed. His skin had turned white and the spots and pits that had covered his face and chin had disappeared. His face was now smooth as smooth can be and he looked as if he had been eating good food, along with juices and vitamins. He was wearing a loose, colourful shirt and trousers that glowed in the sun. In his hand he held a large brown leather bag that was like a portable wardrobe.

Abdel Khaliq had heard many stories about him. He had heard that he bought two flats for the two daughters he was preparing to marry off soon by pulling many strings in local government. He had heard about the presents he brought from Saudi Arabia and also that he was going to publish a collection of short stories at his own expense – stories he had written in Saudi Arabia.

The Peugeot taxi was waiting for them outside the station, with

Mustafa's wife and daughters taking up the seats in the middle. In the back were two faceless young men wearing full suits and dripping with sweat. The three women were wearing pink headscarves and long colourful dresses. They had made up their faces in the same style and pieces of gold glittered on their chests and hung from their ears. Mustafa introduced Abdel Khaliq to them enthusiastically, saying: "My colleague Abdel Khaliq al-Messiri, a great poet and writer who works in the cultural centre."

Abdel Khaliq greeted them all, mumbling words that no one could hear. He squeezed between the driver and Mustafa el-Kurdi, who sat with one hand on the seat back, turning so he was facing his family, all of whom beamed with a contentment that was oppressive.

Mustafa el-Kurdi didn't give anyone else a chance to speak. Only he spoke. He thought the country was in excellent shape. There were new buildings everywhere and people were doing well. What the country lacked was some freedom and opportunities for trade and business. There was a need to eliminate bureaucracy, the legacy of backwardness and poverty, and the effects of years of confusion and chaos. We don't yet know how we will benefit from our ties with America and the West, he said. Our ports, for example, are still far behind. You can't compare them with the ports in Saudi Arabia and the Gulf.

Then he turned to Abdel Khaliq. "And you, Abdel Khaliq," he asked with affected friendliness, "how's life with you? Anything new? You should get out of your shell, man. Travel, or get around a little. It would be a shame to let your life go to waste when you're a man of so many talents."

Abdel Khaliq smiled a meaningless smile and Mustafa couldn't sustain that theme, so he started telling him why they were going to Cairo. There were many things the girls wanted to buy in Cairo, you know how spoiled girls are, although they don't lack for anything. We've brought them everything from Saudi Arabia, not just one set, but two or three. Their mother goes along with them in thinking their father owns a bank. You know what, Abdel Khaliq, a day away from home feels like a thousand, but what can we do?

Abdel Khaliq felt he'd made a mistake by allowing himself to get caught in this trap. His brain was overworked and Mustafa's remarks and everything about him inspired him with no desire to comment.

Everything was false and artificial. The silent young men sitting in the back embodied for him the satanic trap of money into which everyone fell. The few pennies in his pocket were plenty to keep the wolf from the door. He didn't want any of the things they were talking about. They should learn not to speak about things that didn't concern them. What concern of theirs was the country, or people, or ideas, stories or poems? Why didn't they speak only about their money and their dollars? Why didn't Mustafa el-Kurdi take his calculator out of his bag and hunch over it subtracting, adding and multiplying? And leave Abdel Khaliq to himself, to look at the desert and enjoy the car's speed and the driver's confident driving technique. The driver was a silent, good-natured Nubian. He didn't speak; he was only a witness.

Mustafa apparently also felt he had made a mistake when he had stuffed this miserable and impoverished man into the taxi, so he turned to his wife and started to whisper to her in a private conversation that clearly addressed the meaning of life and other important matters. Abdel Khaliq shut his eyes and wondered: "Where has love gone? And sincere affection? 'Where have our joys gone?'" He yielded to the warm breeze that blew at them from the desert.

A year or more after he came out of detention into a paradise that seemed as vast as the skies and the earth, he came across her in the streets of Cairo. Or rather it was she who came across him. Mona al-Masri. Just Mona. How many times had he repeated that name in the night to wash away the sorrows of his soul? Mona and that's that. She came into his life as a delicate hand slips on a soft glove.

They would meet at the home of a foreign woman he knew. When he knocked on the door and she opened it for him, she repeated his name with passion and joy as if she had met him by chance in a strange world. She would lead him into their little room and close the door. The magical web they wove in their moments together was a secret they shared.

He had an old chair that looked out of the tall window. He settled into the chair, his body at ease. She didn't turn on the light. To the music of Mozart, together they watched the darkness come in. With his hands in her hair, he felt the music bring them together body and soul, and her lips seemed to shine with stars. How beautiful the calm is after the storm. They would make love passionately for an hour, then a strange serenity would descend. Was there a name for this thing that was? And how could there be life without it? A question he had never been able to answer.

It was winter and Alexandria was awash with rainwater. The café where they made themselves at home was empty except for lovers and some old Greeks. In the sunlight he looked at the soft fair down on her arm, which reached across the table towards him. He turned her hand over, ran his finger along the lines on her palm and stared into her eyes.

"You wouldn't have known but we've come to Alexandria for me to tell you something," she said. "We've completed the emigration procedures for my brother Wadie. I had a noisy evening with him yesterday. I won and he agreed to everything. You and I are going to get married today, or tomorrow, or whenever you want. He'll leave his flat to us. Wadie is now talking with Father and Mother, and now I'm yours."

He was about to speak, but she pulled her hand back and touched his eyes and lips.

He came around to el-Kurdi's metallic voice. "You fell asleep, lucky man. No sons and no daughters. We're going to stay downtown. The taxi can drop us off anywhere. We have some errands to do and we'll have lunch, and then go back tonight, we hope. Where do you want to get off?"

"Anywhere downtown. Anywhere."

"You must come and see us. I insist. Enough of this constant escaping. I want to hear what you think of the new short stories."

At the first traffic light, he thanked the driver and el-Kurdi and said goodbye to everyone.

"Goodbye, goodbye."

He got out quickly. With his folded newspaper, he beat imaginary dust off his whole body and slipped into the stream of the crowd.

Zahr el-Laymoon (Lemon Blossom) by Alaa al-Deeb
was first published in Cairo, 1987
This translation is from the edition published
by Dar el-Shorouk, Cairo, 2008

MAHMOUD EL-WARDANY

The Trans-generational Alaa al-Deeb

In 1969, I came across a tiny collection of stories entitled *Al-Qahira* (Cairo) by a writer called Alaa al-Deeb. I was 19 at the time, and all my readings were the conventional stuff, hence that collection came across as a veritable storm. Right from the first story – about a man who eventually decides to rid himself of all shackles and fly to the sky – it struck me as a different type of writing.

I met Alaa years later, in 1984, after my first collection of short stories, *al-Sayr fi al-Hadiqa Laylan* (Walking in the Garden at Night), had been published and I was surprised to learn that he had read it and written a review in his weekly page "Assir al-Kutub" (Juice of Books), in *Sabah El Kheir* magazine.

To me, a major trait of al-Deeb is that he was trans-generational. Born in 1939, he kept switching, while at university, from one political party to another, as was the norm amongst the youth of that era. For some time, he was part of al-Raya (the Banner), a clandestine communist organization, before he

Alaa al-Deeb's novella Al-Qahira, *published in 1964 by Rose El-Youssef's Golden Books series*

was dismissed for his "failure to deliver the party assignments", as he disclosed in an interview with *Akhbar al-Adab* published shortly before his departure. After graduating from the Faculty of Law, he joined *Sabah El Kheir* during its golden time in the early 1960s, and became part of one of the most important experiences of journalism in the Arab world, distinct from the mainstream press of that time with its liberalism and openness.

Mahmoud el-Wardany

Although *Al-Qahira* came out in 1964 (written in 1961), at a time when the literary scene was dominated by conventional writings (with the exception of Yusuf Idris), it presaged a different type of writing. It was striking how the vociferous political climate of the 1960s, with its mega lies and the high waves of Nasserism, was barely reflected in that collection, while feelings of doubt, suspicion, failure, fear, and muffled voices featured prominently. The collection was also distinct in its conscious avoidance of metaphor and rhetoric and its departure from the 'tale' style in favour of the time-neutral 'case' or series of events.

Two writers had paved the way for the torrential waves of writings of the 1960s, unleashed by the 1967 defeat. They were Edwar al-Kharrat, with his collection *Heetaan 'Alia* (High Walls), published in 1959, and Alaa al-Deeb with *Al-Qahira*.

In addition to his creative writing, al-Deeb made a trans-generational contribution to literature with his weekly column, "Assir al-Kutub" which continued without interruption for four decades, starting in *Sabah El Kheir*, and later in *Al-Qahira*, *Al-Masry al-Youm* and other papers when he had to leave *Sabah El Kheir*, voluntarily or otherwise. Each week, he would review a new book, mostly by an obscure writer whom he did not know personally. His selections included collections of short stories, novels, and books on politics, economics, and other subjects.

It is a task that is extremely difficult, to say the least, for someone to review a book every single week for four decades, but he did it, managing to avoid the traps of interest groups and winning the confidence of readers, who held him in high regard as an objective, conscientious writer. Rather than writing methodological critiques, al-Deeb chose to write in a simple yet profound style which appealed to the ordinary reader, and he considered that a task worthy of the trouble. He wrote about dozens of new and avant-garde writers from successive generations. Throughout that period, he dedicated his life to writing, getting in return only the most basic of his needs, perhaps less.

As a close friend of his for over twenty years, I was witness to the austere life he had voluntarily chosen for himself. He died in the same al-Maadi house where he was born. But he never felt sorry for the course he had set for himself.

Apart from stories, al-Deeb wrote the beautiful script of the famous film, *The Mummy*, directed by Shadi Abdel Salam. He also translated scores of books, such as *Endgame* by Samuel Beckett, *A Moveable Feast* by Ernst Hemingway, *The Road to Virtue* (about Daoism), and many other carefully selected texts.

Cover of Edwar al-Kharrat's novel Heetaan 'Alia *(High Walls), Cairo, 1959*

He had a short-lived experience of employment in the Gulf. That venture, which lasted for only two months, came to an end when one of his Egyptian workmates informed against him, telling their employers they had a communist in their employ. That experience provided him with a good opportunity to reflect on the impact of the oil era and to write his important autobiographical work, *Pause before the Decline, Papers of an Egyptian Intellectual*.

In addition to four collections of short stories, he

published six novellas, *al-Qahira* (Cairo), *Zahr el-Laymoon* (Lemon Blossom), *Atfaal bila Dumu'* (Children without Tears), *Qamar 'ala Al-Mustanq'a* (Moon over the Swamp), *Oyoun el-Banafsaj* (Violet Eyes) and *Ayam Wardiya* (Rosy Days). These novellas were published individually, spaced over several decades. Al-Deeb, however, eventually managed to publish them in one volume with Al-Okhra (The Other) Books in Cairo in 2012. It was the first time that he wrote an introduction for his works. Referring to the first three novellas that came out as "Alaa al-Deeb's Trilogy", he said: "The overall horizon of those narratives was occupied by two tragedies: the grand defeat of the Arabs in 1967 and the demise of socialism both within and without." It was also dominated by the "black gold experience: the petro-dollars that poured into Egypt at a critical time and played havoc with our life".

Cover of *Assir al-Kutub (Juice of Books)*, collection of articles by Alaa al-Deeb, published by Dar el-Shorouk, Cairo, 2010

Personally, I tend to believe that al-Deeb's major contribution to the Arabic literature was the novella. Surely, six successive works of the same style could not have come by mere coincidence.

It was striking that his departure on February 18, 2016, was not associated with the usual screaming and wailing. It was a fitting departure: serene and low profile.

Translated by Adil Babikir

YASSER ABDEL LATIF

A Lofty Eucalyptus Tree in Maadi

Alaa al-Deeb's literary and professional identity was formed by his long association with two major schools in modern Egyptian culture. These were, first of all, the journalistic school of Rose el-Youssef, and secondly, the 'sixties generation' in Egyptian literature, as embodied by the independent and avant-garde magazine *Gallery 68*. The Rose el-Youssef of which I speak here is not the company during its initial, liberal phase, which began with its founding by the pioneering dramatist Fatima 'Rose' Youssef, and the support of writers like Abbas al-Aqqad and Mohamed El Tabei. Nor do I mean the company's most recent phase, which began in the nineties under the management of Adil Hammouda, who oversaw its transformation into scandalmongering and yellow journalism. I refer, rather, to its middle phase in the fifties and sixties, when it was managed by Ihsan Abdel Quddous, the daring journalist and most famous author of best-seller novels during that era.

Abdel Quddous took over management of the company and its magazine from his pioneering mother, and assembled a crack team of talented writers and artists, most of whom were active leftists. During this era, the foundation brought in figures like the poet Fuad Haddad, the physician and author Salah Hafez, the graphic designer Hasan Fuad, and the illustrator Zuhdi al-Adawi. While Abdel Quddous is generally classified as a 'liberal', he revealed his socialist sympathies in his decision to assemble this team made up of individuals imprisoned under consecutive regimes. This second phase of Rose el-Youssef produced a new magazine in 1956 called *Sabah El Kheir*

(Good Morning), with the flashy slogan: 'For Youthful Hearts and Liberated Minds!' The magazine was committed to developing a fresh new kind of journalism for a generation that felt newly empowered after the departure of feudalism and colonialism. It was perhaps even more committed to showcasing new kinds of illustration, caricature and editorial cartoons. It owed its success to the efforts of some truly great talents, such as the poet and cartoonist Salah Jahin, the exceptional journalist Ahmad Bahaa al-Din, and the novelist Fathi Ghanem.

Yasser Abdel Latif

Sabah El Kheir had some daring ideas. It once sent the author Abdallah al-Tukhi on a journey along the Nile, all the way from Cairo to its source in Uganda, to write weekly reports that were accompanied by illustrations (not photographs!). It sent the novelist Sabri Moussa to the eastern desert to write his masterpiece *Fasad al-Amkina* (1973; *Seeds of Corruption*, trans. Mona Mikhail, Interlink, 2002). It would also dispatch a young author named Alaa al-Deeb to write an investigation, complete with photographs, about a bizarre homicide case in Upper Egypt.

In 1987, having just finished high school, and still emerging from a troubled adolescence, I tried my hand as a novice at story writing. For inspiration, I turned to literature to find that which might fill the desolate void of the eighties. My uncle, who was the financial director of Rose el-Youssef, took me to the company's headquarters to meet its writers and show them my own attempts at story writing. In a room on the fifth floor, where the offices of *Sabah El Kheir* were located, I met the very same three I mentioned above: al-Tukhi, Moussa, and al-Deeb! I had been following their work in the magazine, and had read some books of theirs that I managed to obtain. Among these was al-Deeb's *Lemon Blossom*, which I had read a few years previously in serialized form, accompanied by the illustrations of Ihab Shakir.

I read to them some of my first writings. Sabri Moussa encouraged me with some kind words, and al-Tukhi smiled without passing judgment. Alaa, for his part, asked me to come over to his home some time when I had something new to write about. I was surprised to discover that the writer whose book reviews I followed every week, and whose little novel I had become infatuated with, lived only a five-minute walk from my family's home in Maadi. Moreover, he was none other than the father of Sara Alaa, a school friend of mine since childhood, and I hadn't made the connection. I was about seventeen at the time, and he was in his late forties – about my age now.

One Friday morning, I gathered up some of the latest drafts of my stories and headed over to the house of Alaa al-Deeb. The house was on Street 73, and ours was on Street 68. In Maadi's numbered street system, there is no "Street 69," which meant we were only four blocks apart. Street 73 branches off from Street 9, the longest and most famous street in the suburb, and comes to an abrupt end at the wall of a German nunnery, which is totally hidden by the trees and the arrangement of the neighbouring houses. Coming out of the Maadi metro station, you'll take a left down Street 9. Street 73 will be up ahead on the right; turning in, you'll find the wall of the nunnery facing you, and the 'Rêve de nuit' villa on your right. The latter is rather different from the mansions of the Louza or Mosseri families – wealthy estates that once predominated in the southern part of Maadi. With a small garden, the house possesses a humbler elegance that reflects the aesthetic sensibilities of the Egyptian middle class in the 1940s. It was built by Alaa's father, Hubballah al-Deeb, who was director of landscaping for Cairo Governorate, back when Cairo Governorate had something called a 'directorship of landscaping'.

In all the thirty years that I knew Mr. Alaa, starting with the moment I met him at *Sabah El Kheir*, it was only twice that I saw him outside that house, or indeed outside Maadi. I could hardly believe it when a mutual friend told me how, one summer, he'd met Mr. Alaa on the balcony of the Hotel Crillon in Alexandria. Another time, I saw pictures of him and Youssef Fakhouri on a winter vacation in Aswan. He'd apparently taken a third trip, in the autumn, to Mersa Matruh. Otherwise, he would always be there, in his room, an eternal citizen of Maadi. Burying himself in reading each week in order to write his column, he was the most genuine recluse I ever met. And because he was the author of the most famous book review col-

Alaa al-Deeb

umn in Egyptian journalism, authors and publishers would send him dozens of books every week. The books filled his shelves and tables and piled up in towers on the old wood floor of his room, obliging him to give some away every few months and keep only what was precious or necessary.

In his office overlooking the garden, there would be a tall glass of tea with a couple of mint leaves in it, half-full, on the table in the soft light filtered through the trees. There would be music coming from behind the desk – most likely Bach, or perhaps Umm Kulthum. Maybe just a recording of the Qur'an recited by Sheikh Mustafa Ismail. He once pointed out to me how, in Bergman's film *The Silence*, the music makes a dramatic entrance: an elderly man dressed in black appears in the hotel corridor, and says to the mother and her little boy: "Johann Sebastian Bach!" As the music plays, through the window we see Nazi tanks patrolling the streets. In this very room, Alaa al-Deeb told me, his older brother Badr al-Deeb would meet with friends in the 1940s. Still a university student at the time, Badr would gather there with those who would form his first literary posse (did he say Youssef al-Sharuni and Fathi Ghanem?).

From his brother Badr, Alaa received inspiration, and his first lesson: writing is not merely a profession or a trade, it's how you prove you exist. To write, not to simply make up! One only writes with blood, as Alaa used to say. The same lesson was learned from Fathi Ghanem, too. Ghanem did not write *Zaynab and the Throne* merely to present a panorama of the journalistic field during the Nasser era, as an unobservant critic might say. He wrote the novel specifically to portray the character Youssef, the intellectual with sharp internal contradictions, who floated on the surface of events as a neutral observer, while at the same time complicit in the 'game of thrones'. Likewise, Badr al-Deeb didn't write *The Papers of Zumurruda Ayyoub* just to fashion a Coptic icon out of stained glass. His purpose, rather, was to put himself on trial, together with his entire generation, as part of a fierce existential coming-to-terms. Badr was thirteen years older than Alaa. His friend Fathi Ghanem was the one who set up the younger of two, the talented young man, to work in the Rose el-Youssef Foundation.

In the same room that Badr al-Deeb would meet with his literary group in the forties, Alaa would later meet with Ibrahim Mansour and Ghalib Halasa in the late fifties to exchange different kinds of books and different kinds of ideas. Badr and his companions had been interested in modern English poetry, surrealism, existentialism, and French and German literature and philosophy. This was due to the influence of their professors in the Faculty of Letters, such as Abd al-Rahman Badawi and Youssef Mourad, as well as their keen interest in the Art and Freedom Group, which was the Egyptian branch of the international surrealist movement. In contrast, the new generation in the room in Maadi became interested in American literature: Henry Miller, Hemingway, Steinbeck, Faulkner, Capote, and even Salinger, whom Halasa translated himself. Mansour and Halasa would go on to assume positions in the 'leadership' of the sixties literary movement, as it was manifested in the magazine *Gallery 68*. Although they were active Marxists, their views on literature were very open-minded and contemporary, in stark contrast to the dominant mode among leftist critics at the time, who practised a strict commitment to the tenets of socialist realism.

But Halasa was, in the end, a transient spirit, and Cairo was just one of his many stops. All Alaa had left was Ibrahim Mansour, his Maadi compatriot. Of their first meeting, Ibrahim would recall that he came across a kid just a few years younger than himself, standing at the Maadi train station reading *The Egyptian Gazette*. "My day's first catch!" he said to himself. Ibrahim, who had been politicized since the day he was born, succeeded in recruiting this 'kid' to the Marxist organization of which he was a member. But Alaa found himself unable to put up with the secrecy and stealth, and soon withdrew from the organization. In profession and politics, Alaa was not to follow Ibrahim and Ghalib's model of perpetual rebellion. In this sense he would remain closer to Badr. Yet he also managed to distance himself from the dense literary style and elitism of his brother by taking up the most refined form of journalistic writing, and by finding inspiration in the trends of the sixties' generation. One day much later, Alaa would point to a copy of a painting by Pieter Bruegel the Younger hanging on the wall above his favourite chair, and say: "I want to write a novel as clear as this painting. A poster-novel! Cities bursting forth from the Middle Ages, forming connections and creating new types of human beings. All of this in a single painting like this!"

When I began to visit him regularly in the late eighties and the early nineties, he had stopped going to work altogether, and would simply send in his weekly articles by fax. An employee from the company would come by at the end of each month to bring him his salary, since pay by bank transfer hadn't yet been implemented in Egyptian government agencies. It was effectively an early retirement, and a voluntary one. Retirement and exile are the fate of the protagonists in Alaa al-Deeb's last five novels. Abdel Khaliq al-Messiri, the protagonist of *Lemon Blossom*, exiled himself voluntarily to Suez. The novel portrays his weekend trip back to Cairo to see some of his friends and visit his elderly mother at their old house. In the event, the entirety of his painful past comes crashing down on him. The old house al-Deeb depicts in the novel is a near replica of his own house in Maadi, only he places it in Dokki on the other side of the river. Al-Deeb and his character inhabit the same house.

On his desk is a draft of his next article, along with small strips of paper on which he's written down notes for his next novel. At the time, his novel *Children without Tears* had just been published, and he was busy at work on its second part, *Moon over the Swamp*. I was impressed by *Children without Tears* even more than I'd been with *Lemon Blossom*, especially the final scene. Rushing to board his flight back to his life of exile in an oil-rich Gulf country, Dr. Munir Fakkar drops his suitcase and spills its contents all over the ground, as though his life were unravelling before his eyes. But *Lemon Blossom* is a cunning novel, with a deceptively calm surface. I wouldn't truly appreciate its effect until I read it again twenty years later. Only then would I perceive how Alaa's simple and poetic style had flowed into my first narrative work, *The Law of Inheritance*.

In the mid-nineties, after one of his bouts of ill-health, I went out to walk and shop with him one morning in Maadi. We walked down Street 10, then took a left down Damascus Street until we reached Sawaris Square. We took a right onto Wahib Dos Street, then went back across Street 9. On Damascus Street, he stopped in front of a huge villa once owned by an Iranian family of carpet merchants. He pointed to a lofty eucalyptus tree, several dozen metres tall, with a white trunk and a spherical green head up above. He pointed at it and said: "I've known this sweetie since it was little!" On Street 9, he would stop by all the shop owners he'd known for decades, buying cigarettes from Ayyad, brandy from Aziz, cheese from al-Yamani, and bread from al-Sawi. If he didn't need anything from one of the shops, he'd make some small symbolic purchase – a box of matches, for example – then come back the next day to get something more substantial. The very same Iranian eucalyptus tree would appear later in his novel *Rosy Days*. With this book, he would take the themes of isolation and retirement to their extremes, portraying a mental hospital as an oasis amidst a desolate world!

In Alaa's oeuvre, guilt and sin are related to a loss of innocence, to disillusionment and deceit. Badr, by contrast, examined these themes within a context of political and moral complicity. If Alaa's works seem to form one long diatribe against the Sadat era and its aftermath, the trauma of the 1967 defeat also loomed large. He would state this explicitly in his book *Pause before the Decline*. This is usually classified as an autobiographical work, but is perhaps better described as an exercise in self-criticism, a sharply critical review of his own personal history at a particular moment. At one point in the book, he says: "A dear young man, who hung on my every word, once asked me, 'What did you do in '67, and what did it do to you?' Without hesitating, I said, 'It killed me, and I've been dead ever since!'" It's no wonder that the book would become tremendously popular among young people in Egypt after the defeat of the January 2011 Revolution. It would share an audience with *The Stillborn*, a similarly painful work written by the communist activist Arwa Saleh.

Alaa would always describe his personal crisis as that of a middle-class intellectual. This was because he had made the decision to stay out of trouble, in contrast to his lifelong friend Ibrahim Mansour, who had committed himself to the cause and ended up paying the price with prison and exile. Ibrahim represented the daring side of Alaa, whereas Alaa represented the artistic spirit that had departed from Ibrahim. It was from Ibrahim, too, that he became interested in translation, and the two had rigorously trained in it from the beginning of their youth. His contributions to the field were few but of genuine quality, such as his marvellous translation of the Hungarian author Sarkadi Imre's novella *A Woman at Thirty*, and the short story *Return to Brooklyn*, which is one of the most beautiful things I've ever read by Henry Miller. He made a number of political translations, and also took on the *Tao Te Ching* by Lao Tzu.

I last met him in October 2015, four months before his death. I was back in Cairo for a month-long vacation. The 'Ustaz' was busy reading the works of John Coetzee, since he hadn't read him at the height of his popularity back when Coetzee had won the Booker and then the Nobel Prize for Literature. He wasn't one to follow the prevailing fad, however powerful the advertising – although Coetzee certainly deserved all the buzz. While he was evidently enjoying Coetzee's books, on the inside he was beset by depression brought on by his physical weakness and his sense that his time was nearly up. "When you read this guy," he said, "you feel that everything we've written is just a handful of sawdust!" I understood where his pain and desperation were coming from. Still, I didn't want to contradict his assessment, lest he think I was just trying to flatter him. Instead, I said, "Is Badr al-Deeb just a handful of sawdust? What about *The Papers of Zumurruda Ayyub?*" Catching my trick, he smiled from behind the darkness and said: "You're right!"

Translated by Ben Koerber

MANSOURA EZ-ELDIN

The Defeated Leftist Intellectual

In a press interview I conducted with Ibrahim Aslan in 2010, the Egyptian novelist talked affectionately and appreciatively about the role played by Alaa al-Deeb in introducing the writers of the sixties and their works. The way he spoke of him seemed to suggest that he regarded him not simply as a writer of the sixties, but rather as a mentor of that generation. Indeed, he placed him among the ranks of Yahya Haqqi and Abdel Fattah el-Gamal, two of the fathers of that generation, who lent their contemporaries great support by writing about them and helping publish their work.

"I regard el-Gamal as one of the forces of good, along with Yahya Haqqi and Alaa al-Deeb," Aslan said, adding that people of such calibre "are capable of bringing balance to any cultural life".

This view is by no means exclusive to Aslan: in a cultural community characterised by its flattery and narrow interests, Alaa al-Deeb is widely regarded as a saint. Litterateurs of various generations view his writings on them as both an endorsement and a recognition of their talent. Indeed, what earned the late novelist his well-deserved stature was his objectivity and keenness to encourage the new voices in which he saw potential.

Moreover, Alaa has close resemblance to his protagonists. The following remark he made will suffice to demonstrate: "It has killed me. I have not lived a full day since."

The reference here is, of course, to the June 1967 debacle, or the Six-Day War. Though it may at first appear to be a gross exaggeration, those who are familiar with al-Deeb's works will see this state-

THE DEFEATED LEFTIST INTELLECTUAL

Mansoura Ez-Eldin

ment as an entirely fitting description, not only of his life but also the lives of his characters. For the 1967 defeat was a turning point when the dreams of his protagonists were dashed and their lives were spoilt forever. In almost all his works, that humiliating defeat embodies a lasting wound; an incurable disease.

Personally, I always saw in Abdel Khaliq al-Messiri (from *Lemon Blossom*) and Amin al-Ulfi, amongst other protagonists of al-Deeb, a reflection of the author himself. He seemed like a musician who is more concerned with creating variations within one main melody than composing multiple melodies.

In most of his works, we are confronted with almost the same protagonist, albeit with a different name: a defeated leftist intellectual, estranged from his surroundings, unwilling to engage with a world governed by strife and personal interests, and highly critical of injustice and flagrant practices. Other recurrent themes are marriages doomed to failure and old love affairs still lingering in the memory. More importantly, there are recurrent references to a particular moment of total collapse, when everything breaks down. This is by no means exclusive to political and military defeat alone, but encompasses also smaller individual defeats.

What, I sometimes wonder, would have happened if the 1967 defeat had not occurred, or if at least it had not had such an impact on Alaa al-Deeb's life and works? Such a speculative question is difficult to answer, of course. However, his few stories published before 1967 reveal more diversity and vigour than do his subsequent works. Yet this remains a personal view and may not be highly significant when we consider the fact that the same existential anxiety, and the feelings of estrangement and alienation, are dominant too

THE DEFEATED LEFTIST INTELLECTUAL

Yahya Haqqi *Ibrahim Aslan*

in his early works, particularly *Al-Qahira* (Cairo). In this novella, written in 1961 and published in 1964, there is a critical moment which marks a turning point in the protagonist's life: the moment he kills his mistress:

"Here the human being has been defeated. Here he killed. Here with his bare hands he had attacked existence His defeat was proof he had reached the peak. Here his consciousness had snapped and he had lost control. The thought had merged into one with the deed. Here Fathi stopped torturing himself and his ability to stand his life snapped."

Read this paragraph and compare it with similar moments in other works by the same writer, and you will gain the sense that the human being in al-Deeb's works is "pre-defeated" – that defeat is his fate. It is part of his identity as a human. A defeat on the scale of the 1967 debacle is therefore not necessary for his protagonists to experience feelings of emptiness, alienation and loss. Perhaps the military defeat was merely a means of affirming Alaa al-Deeb's deep contention that human beings are doomed to failure.

Translated by Adil Babikir

ALAA AL-DEEB

Fathi and Aqeela

EXCERPT FROM *AL-QAHIRA*

TRANSLATED BY RAPHAEL COHEN

At three in the afternoon the next day, Fathi married Aqeela. The *maazoun** came to the flat. With him were two men fit to act as witnesses. The marriage was made. Fathi was sullen and serious. Aqeela tried to smile. The *maazoun* and his lads looked on in astonishment.

Out of everyday cups everyone drank a pale sherbet of watery taste. The forced conversation with the *maazoun* stopped. May God bless them. The flat reverted to silence.

Aqeela went into the bedroom. Fathi stayed in the living room. She lay down on the bed and felt the world around her was empty. Fathi was still moving around in the living room, nervously smoking cigarettes.

One by one, he shut all the windows in the house. Then he went into the room where Aqeela was lying down and shut the door behind him. She smiled as he approached her. His steps were slow and heavy.

He leaned over the bed. Aqeela stared at him. He put his hands around her neck and strangled her.

In a few moments Aqeela was a lifeless corpse.

He opened the window and saw a ring of policemen surrounding the building. He quickly closed the window and sat down in the living room. His two big hands rested on the table in front of him.

Life had just ended for him. It had ended and he had chosen the ending. It was he who had brought about the ending. He stared at his hands and thought that that was the greatest victory.

The windows were closed and the flat was humid, and he had turned into a god. Mankind has really become a god. What has happened matters now. Something real. It will illuminate the path for all those who come after me.

Here the human being has been defeated. Here he killed. Here with his bare hands he had attacked existence. His defeat was proof he had reached the peak. Here his consciousness had snapped and he had lost control. The thought had merged into one with the deed. Here Fathi stopped torturing himself and his ability to stand his life snapped.

Now I can talk to people. Now I have the right to talk, all of them standing there beneath the window awaiting weighty proclamations from me.

Me . . . the prophet . . . the murderer.

Many hands banged at the door.

A young police officer burst into the house smiling and ran quickly through the rooms. He put his hand on Fathi's shoulder and said: "You're coming with us."

The police seized Fathi. He walked down the street with them surrounded by a circle of policemen.

The stairs leading up to the flat were crowded with dozens of men and women. The lift meanwhile had broken down holding four journalists and their cameras. They were shouting at the doorman. The front door of the flat was open, and an old policeman stood guard not understanding what was going on around him. The women from the building had come out in their nightdresses to stand on the stairs and gaze around in stupefaction and fear.

"A monster."

"God preserve us."

"I knew it. He looks mad."

The journalists shouted inside the lift: "Boss, we want to take pictures."

"It's already seven. The pictures won't make it."

The old doorman brought a key for the lift door, and the journalists crawled out on their stomachs through the doorway above where the lift had broken down. The lights in the staircase kept going on and off with a loud buzz. A child on the fourth floor was trapped inside a flat, shouting that his mother wouldn't let him out.

Aqeela remained as she was, lying motionless in the darkened room. Her cold body exposed to the dazzling flashes of the journalists.

In the middle of the living room, the public prosecutor was standing dictating to the clerk mundane coherent words. In the same place fifteen minutes earlier had been standing Fathi with violent incoherent words running through his mind. Before he had killed, Fathi had seen a large face on the sun's disc. The setting sun was filled by this black face. Then Fathi had closed the windows.

"The things found in the flat were itemized and sealed as evidence in my sight . . . You fill in the rest of the wording."

The public prosecutor looked around him. He ordered the flat to be cleared. He left. His steps were fast, as if running from something.

The corpse look horrific. Mouth open and around the neck traces of fierce resistance. The residents of the neighbouring flats all tended to the view that the murderer was insane. He had always behaved in a dubious manner. For sure, there were other dreadful secrets that the investigation would discover.

* * *

The police station was calm. Soldier number one stood motionless by the door. In the main room there was a large space and a single bench. In a corner on the floor, a woman was curled up into a black ball. A strange smell filled the place akin to the smell of dry blood.

Fathi was sitting alone on the bench, his jacket next to him, his manacled hands between his legs. The large light bulb near the officer's room cast a single patch of light and left the rest of the place in semi-darkness.

Fathi's face was set calm.

The place suggested that the crime had faded, mixed with all of life, to no longer have an existence in any place but in the atoms of everything here. It was therefore impossible to think about it.

The silence of the police station was only broken by the loud coughing of the officer chain-smoking. Smoke curled around the light bulb next to his office.

Fathi was now unable to prophesy what would happen next.

Everything would proceed normally. There were no longer any surprises. They were responsible for everything now. All he had to do was wait. He felt a strange sense of wholeness. That for the first time he existed in a real place. That he was doing something real.

* * *

Three senior nurses entered the flat. Their uniforms were off-white. Their bodies were large. Their faces looked alike.

They stood chatting for a few moments with the policeman guarding the flat. It looked as though they were old friends. They lit cigarettes. One of them gave a loud laugh.

They burst into the flat and opened Aqeela's room. A few moments later they came out with the body. The stairs were empty and the morgue ambulance was waiting at the door.

They all disappeared inside it. The loud siren of the vehicle started up. By the lamppost, three boys stood watching the operation. They started running after the vehicle.

* * *

Fathi went into a large room, carpeted, the leather seats large. A senior officer was sitting at the far end of the room. The young smiling office walked behind Fathi.

In a seemingly calm and firm voice the senior officer said: "Where do you work?"

In a determined tone, Fathi replied: "At the Agricultural Museum."

It did not seem that the senior officer wanted to know anything specific. He just looked Fathi over. "How old are you?"

"Thirty-six."

"What qualifications do you have?"

"A degree in agriculture."

"You waster. Would someone do that to himself?"

Then the senior officer started talking to the junior officer who was sitting on one of the seats. They talked about Fathi as if he wasn't there. But he was standing in the room. More present and realistic than anything else.

* * *

That night when Fathi went into the detention room, the streets outside were empty. The few passers-by spoke slowly. The shops were open. The shopkeepers inside stood silently staring at nothing.

In the darkness Fathi sensed that she was dead.

The truth weighed on him. The snoring of the man stretched on the floor of the room was regular and loud. Fathi leaned his head against the wall, and fell asleep.

The next day's papers carried the news. Discussion continued for days. Even some intellectuals tried to discuss the crime in their own get-togethers and at the cafes.

People's explanations for the crime differed, and strange incidents intruded into the story. Some said that he had discovered the unborn baby wasn't his.

However, an old man with glasses and white hair sat down at the table in one of the smart cafés and told some young people sitting around him: "I think it's a very serious crime. One with very serious social and psychological implications for the crisis of some . . ."

One of the young men interrupted him: "What matters is whether we can imagine the mental state of the murderer as he committed the crime."

Their conversation continued until it petered out of its own accord and most of them started staring at their empty coffee cups. The crime receded and moved onto the inside pages. Some keen editors kept an eye on news of Fathi in prison. One newspaper published an interview with his sister and put her picture in the paper. The most significant thing she said was that she knew nothing about her brother's private life, and that he always kept away from the family. A psychologist said that Fathi was suffering from a split personality.

After a week, the crime had been completely forgotten and disappeared from the city.

At the old bar that Fathi and Aqeela had frequented, the waiter often remembered them. But he did not talk about them with anyone. He hated to see people discussing the crime with their preconceived ideas on the subject. He found nobody to investigate the matter with on the level he wanted. He just continued to remember them whenever he took an order to the table where they used to sit.

* A state-religious official authorized to register marriages.

Translated from novella *Al-Qahira* (Cairo), published in 1964 by Rose El-Youssef's Golden Books series

ALAA AL-DEEB
Children without Tears

A CHAPTER FROM THE NOVEL,
TRANSLATED BY RAPHAEL COHEN

A Minx from the Westernized Quarter

At the beginning of the second year of my secondment abroad, my mother died. Then, during the end of year vacation of the same year, I married Doctor Sanaa Farag. Obtaining compassionate leave was the first real test of the relationships I had formed, but I understood how things worked.

I had learned the rules of relationships in the second homeland and knew how to be a, b, c, or d as circumstances demanded. I understood a new form to the relationship between means and ends. I trained myself to keep my feelings inside and always present an image of pristine success. I was pleased as punch at the money I was earning: I counted it, amassed it, multiplied it by the exchange rate. It seemed a vast sum in Egyptian money, enough to take me to another level and open up places I'd never entered before. Above all I had to remain composed, not display my delight, but bury it under a façade of superiority, dissatisfaction, and general annoyance with the state of the world.

My mother's death and my marriage, which I thought I had planned carefully, marked the launch of my journey into the orbits of the vacuum that is my oxygen. I gradually lost my real connection

Cover of Alaa al-Deeb's trilogy

with things and meanings. It all happened drip by drip. Over the months and years my blood drained away to be soaked up by the sand that separated my first homeland from my second and make what I loved and what I hated equivalent. Things were subject to new criteria. I became an empty vessel dressed in a new suit and white shirt.

Stomach cramps and a strong urge to expel wind by burping or otherwise leave the taste of death in my mouth. I can smell it and have a vision of my soul leaving my nostrils to hide in the nearest place, like a cockroach dusted with insecticide. Eventually my expression changes; without a soul, my skin tautens like wax; people talk to me and their voices echo inside my hollowness.

Why rake up all this hurt now? Why are you scared and upset today? Alternately cold then hot at your extremities, sweating, irregular heartbeat and respiration, hazy vision as your eyes stare unfocused into the distance. There is no longer any external threat to frighten me. My money defends itself and me, so where has this terror come from, stalking me and lodged between the moments.

Around midday, I became aware of his tall frame blocking the light filtering into my room in the empty hotel. I had been expecting his arrival since the start of the holidays, my cousin the peasant Mahmoud al-Sayyed Fakkar. My father's brother's son, the same age as me, or a little younger. He had not continued studying. His father pushed him onto the land, while my father sent me on the path of education. Something special between us persisted despite the machinations of the village and the small sins of its people against me. Despite his galabia, his big hands, and his clean skullcap, whose position on his head he never changed, he remained in my eyes wise, connected with something I did not have and connecting me with something I could no longer do.

We would spend a day or two together every summer holiday I was in Cairo. In the past he was free and strong, able to break through my privacy with an understanding uniquely his. More recently, however, and especially after I divorced my wife and left my children, he hid behind sympathy and commiseration, thereby concealing fear for his own life and future.

I stayed in bed while he sat looking through my papers and books at the desk where I wrote. He steeled himself to broach some subject. I watched him, captive to the old trust in him and an intimacy I missed but did not like. He was a peasant, and I was no longer like that. The paths had tangled, the circles overlapped, the details of what had happened between me and my family, my village, and him. The scab on a deep wound that I did not know when it had been pulled off or by whom.

He was the only one I trusted with the agreed cheque I sent my father every month. He would cash it in as well as my father's tiny pension, meaning that life just about ticked over in the home that had been devastated by quarrels, resentment, and greedy and unfulfillable demands. I could no longer get further involved in the affairs of that respectable family. All of them envied my new status but none of them thought about my concerns. Brothers and sisters stuck their nails into my flesh, imagining me as an oil well that never ran dry. They and their children looked at me without mercy or kinship. I gave all I could: gifts, presents, loans. But no one was satisfied. No one said thank you. They swarmed around me with their complaints, their issues, their accusations until I grew sick and tired of their faces and wanted to hear nothing more about them. He could work out how much I had spent, how many failed projects I had undertaken with them: partnerships in livestock, in plots of land, in extra stories on top of houses, in taxis and private cars, in a new supermarket on the fast highway, and in other fantastical projects.

I participated in everything and held dozens of family meetings to reach understandings, set conditions, and come to agreements. My big brother took what he wanted, then took off with his family for Assiut. The younger one also vanished by mysteriously emigrating to Iraq. Only my father remained in Kafr Shouk, with the girls and the girls' husbands and the girls' children, who would call me, "Uncle . . . Uncle." All of them fought over the old house, which was on the verge of falling in on the head of the old man who was virtually blind.

Mahmoud, even when we were boys, did not join in the sessions with Ragab by the railway station, near the bridge and the tree under and around which the daylight fractured. His father kept him away and forbade him from approaching there. That remained the main thing between us. He had no dream, no far horizon, no imagination, just soil, farming, and kids.

I opened the shutters and the room was flooded with light. We went out on to the balcony and looked out over downtown Cairo. We watched lots of cars pass beneath us, men who we thought were women, women wearing headscarves, and women sexy beyond our dreams. We heard loud voices punctuating what he was saying. He swallowed again and again, then I heard him say: "I want a urinary tract doctor, someone you know. That's all, I don't want anything else."

Finally I knew the subject he had been avoiding, and I relaxed.

* * *

My appointment with the psychiatrist was at seven. I arrived at the clinic fifteen minutes early. The clinic was empty apart from the receptionist who was busy reading an old magazine. He turned on some soft music and welcomed me with a neutrality that heightened my unease and constant desire to leave. I had been seeing him for five years following the divorce. Once the fighting and quarrelling was over, things settled down into their final pattern, but I suffered from a recurring nightmare that afflicted me both asleep and awake. I thought that Sanaa had taken something that we hadn't agreed about — I didn't know precisely what it was, but it was something valuable I had hidden somewhere but forgotten where. The image played on my mind and made me very uneasy so I would start rummaging around the room I was in. I took things out of suitcases then put them back, very anxious and upset and not knowing how to stop. I would catch myself looking under the bed or climbing the wooden stepladder to look on top of the bookshelves or among old paperwork. I would perspire heavily, winter or summer, and felt my legs would give way. I would lie down on the bed and fall into a disturbed and interrupted sleep.

When I went into the doctor, he greeted me with studied friendliness as though I were bringing him good news. Whenever I saw him, I felt soft fingers caressing my bare skin and a coolness touching my heart. I feel happy, as though nothing dangerous could ever happen to me there. I would then once again want to leave, but would compose myself. I'm not completely mad, yet. In fact, my mind was the match of the man sitting opposite me and another dozen like him.

I knew the adulterated wares he was dealing in, those hollow words of clay he beat out with his fingers and tongue, making sounds with a narcotic effect, like smoking a joint in the morning. He slid his chair back, his face covered with a brittle and fake self-confidence, and talked to me about the travails of mid-life and delayed adolescence. He showed admiration for my ability to cope with estrangement and all the hardships that had come to me and my family. Then he talked about general standards and personal standards, about adaptation and psychological burdens.

He always prescribed a mild sedative morning and night, abstinence from drugs and alcohol, and regular exercise or a daily walk. When we talked about my marriage or divorce, or when I felt like talking about the children, I felt that he wanted to change the subject, as if he were saying that those were social problems outside his remit. That I had to solve those problems myself in the framework of the general principles we were talking about.

I tried to talk to him about the image of the children that haunted me. Tamer and Lamia grab my shirt and are screaming at me silently. Everything about them is normal except their eyes, which are made of stone and full of tears that do not fall. I grab their faces and shake. They make no sound and no tears flow.

He listened to me with a hateful smile on his face. I stopped talking and the horrific image overwhelmed me. I was still hearing the same old record from him that human existence was a holistic whole created through choices, and those choices were always right provided they were your own. The issue was one of endurance and the ability to adapt. My sense of being burdened grew and that he understood nothing, that what obsessed me was my own cursed fate, that the young man sitting opposite me could never understand what I was saying.

I told him again the story of the fire that I saw burning at my extremities and in the blanket and the heavy pillow I used to cover my head with when I slept. He reiterated to me the need to be active and exercise, and to rely on the mild sedative. Why didn't this man ever shout in my face? Why didn't he ever pick up the phone to report an insane criminal running from the law? Instead of which he smiled at me and put his hand on my shoulder in support and reassurance. Once again, I felt I was walking calmly between two rows of sheep staring at me. I stared at them looking for any difference in their faces and features. This brought back the children's eyes in infinite ranks. Then we all drowned in a sea of nothingness. I sensed his cold fingers brush my bare skin as though he were a small lizard.

Although I could hear an inner voice swearing I would never come back, I knew that I would come back before the end of the holiday for the appointment he made with me.

In that place I drank a bitter draught, and by the cupful. In that place I was relieved of nothing but the few pounds I threw to the neutral receptionist.

In that place I was relieved of nothing, but I did receive support and backing from the highest power: the power of reason, the mind, the nerves, the power of the spirit. My game fooled them all and I won the world championship for evil. Real evil is to evade punishment, to get away with the crime and hear words egging you on. In that place I became a real demon, a nice and clever demon. Then, afterwards, you succumb to whatever sadness you please, creating your own particular torment. Conscience is a good companion. You enjoy its presence when you're eating a jam sandwich in the morning. It speaks to me about norms and choices. Only the victorious are applauded, and I am the ultimate victor.

* * *

Over recent years, a balanced state of mind has become somewhat difficult to achieve in Cairo. Here in my second homeland, I live in a constant state of caution and vigilance and am ever on the alert. But as soon as the airplane's wheels have touched the runway, that starts to crack and then collapses completely.

Once I have reclaimed my papers from passport control and got my bags through customs, I find myself floating in a womb pregnant with every possibility: I might be weak or strong: the possible, the faint hope, the impossible.

The noise of my streets, and the light of my days. What does Egypt mean to you now, you miserable voyeuristic rat? In which of its streets do you get lost? In which alley or cul-de-sac in one of its villages do you hole up? What do those villages, sprawling over God's land, mean to you? Villages where the horizon is vaster than His mercy. The distant trees in the fields . . . merciful . . . merciful, with infinite mercy. In their shade, evil as a reflex does not dwell; my subtle demons made of wrapping paper and plastic do not live next to them.

That key image of mine, my only landscape, comes back to mind: Kafr Shouk railway station, one side frequented, one side desolate and abandoned. The abandoned side all sleepers and rails, like an ancient temple for extinct tribes. On the other side, the ticket office, and the tree, under and around which the daylight fractures, where Ragab sits, with the pictures and the doum palm fruit, and me and Safi the mechanic, the story of the Cave, the dream of gold and sparkling coloured jewels, the slaughtered rooster running with blood on his neck and under his feet, pungent incense, and a nomadic Bedouin from Morocco tugging a blind girl along and calling on all those who have a dream or hope or ambition.

This vision comes of its own accord and flows like the blood in my veins. But Sanaa Farag's house in Korba, at the heart of Heliopolis, I have to evoke myself. As the first step on the ladder of choices and norms, I make it appear. In that house, things have stopped happening of their own accord, but need drafting or planning or calculation. In that house I make my reckoning and carefully plot how to choose, how to walk forward over the clean, stripped rug and in the empty corners with their brass pots where the leaves of plants still hang down verdant and tender. Sanaa's father, Farag Bek, was a retired senior civil servant living under the leaves of shade-giving plants in calm resignation after Heliopolis had sucked the life and vitality out of him, all his humanity, his being an architect, his dreams, and instead of all that had given him a senior government job, and a wife, sons, and daughters. He moved through the intersections of their complicated lives in straight lines.

He greeted me as his daughter's fiancé, agreeing to the match before we even spoke. Everything had been agreed in other rooms before I met him, between me and Doctor Sanaa, and between me and her mother, and between her and herself. All he had to do, before he died, was stamp the marriage contract of the Doctor, who was nearing thirty, with the seal of paternity.

The velvet chairs around him stood empty after his body, and the body of his lady wife, wasted away from diabetes and constant anxiety over out-of-stock medicines and a fixed pension whose value was forever dwindling, and over Doctor Sanaa, the last child to get engaged and marry. Her life oscillated between bouts of depression and fits of crying, mad late nights outside the house, relationships that fizzed like adulterated sparkling water, and wrong numbers on the phone, or long conversations, or conversations cut short for no discernable reason.

I married her here, in the shade of those drooping leaves, and the information available: "She's yours" provided she agrees. A doctorate in business administration. What could I say? He was a good man, may he rest in peace. His false teeth meant he could not stop dribbling.

Of course my wife wasn't a virgin when I slept with her. She must have known one or two or three men, at least, before me. When the door closed behind us, I knew that secrets and new circumstances declare themselves when the door closes on a man and woman alone in a room. I knew that there were many things under the surface that flowed without design, like a man suddenly ejaculating when he feels there is a woman beneath him shouting out.

Sanaa Farag was a Westernized she-cat. And I tried to be a tom from the south of Egypt, with my brown skin and my penetrating eyes. I had a visible manhood and a voice that tickled her tender skin. I don't remember exactly what she said during her first orgasm with me after we got married, but I remember she touched my nose and chin and my manhood, and whispered my name once or twice, then snuggled over to the edge of the bed.

* * *

Today was an onerous Friday. The morning and afternoon hours lumbered depressively by. I shuffled between the balcony and the bed, went through some of my papers, and remembered other important papers that I had left behind at my house in Dalouk. I opened the Friday newspapers, and between the lines could hear a kind of groaning that was unlike the human voice. I tried to make connections between events and particulars, but saw things juxtaposed chaotically, as though they had suddenly fallen from a great chasm that had opened in the sky. I adopt the air of an intellectual worried by public concerns. I expect a calamity and foresee a terrifying plunge into the abyss. I look for signs of the apocalypse in the news of my country, or my second country, but things seem coherent, running along in their own particular chaos, guarded by the angel of poverty, the demon of pleasure, and the lord of money and power. Thank God, I no longer have roots, either here or there.

I've become the country of myself. I am my money, my land, my properties. Everything else is ink on paper, words chewed in the toothless mouth of an old man. My country has grown decrepit with age before even having lived its youth. I, on the other hand, am a cosmic phenomenon. My strength lies in my oneness and in that impossible distance that separates me from people. I see them as one- or two-dimensional friezes. They are a page in a book I turn over whenever I want.

They are my children, yes, but she took them. The cow took everything she bore. She severed my link with them from the outset. She taught Lamia to see me through her eyes, as did Tamer when he grew up. He learned how to talk to me with a disdain derived from her feelings towards me, her that Westernized minx, no longer any good for this or for that. How many days were spoiled, how many nights wasted and ruined when she made me feel that I was beneath her, that malevolent minx, who could never have enough sex. My children were never happy with what I gave them, because she always ridiculed what I brought or purchased. She always thought it was less that her elevated status. Tamer broke an expensive toy and I smacked him. Then in front of them she shouted at me that I was a pleb and didn't deserve the blessings God had given me. Perhaps that was the paper she took without my knowledge, the one that disturbed me. She instilled those stupid words in me: I'm a pleb, I don't deserve, and she raised my children accordingly. It wasn't in good taste for her to make me feel that I had no taste. I know what taste is; I recognize poor taste when I see it assailing all our senses – sight, hearing, taste, smell, and touch. I see poor taste rising like a tide of sewage. But what can I do? What can I do about it? Should I reform the country, or rebel, or kill myself? Or just moan and nag like her, like a woman? Ridiculous things to do, with no sign of adaptation and conformity, that lack the magical sticky stuff discharged by the potent male who grasps the destiny of the age.

She didn't understand and never will. She came into my life with her judgements and left with the same judgements after I had signed and sealed them and said goodbye to her with a curse.

After Friday prayers, I dialled the number of their house in Korba. A strange uncouth voice answered me, a servant or relative. When he knew that I was Doctor Munir, he said that he did not know the address in Marsa Matrouh, and did not know when they would be back.

* * *

Someone who asks about my salary there, how much I make and how much I save, does not know I work hard there, harder than ten men.

My salary no longer means anything to me. I have forged my way in the fields of writing, translation, layout, the media, and publishing. My home has become my shop, my acquaintances my clients, and those who like me a means for me.

I have created an insulating layer around me to protect me from those with wealth and power. It puts me in a special position as a veteran expert who knows a solution to every problem. I am a psychiatrist there in my second homeland. I advise adaptation, conformity and freedom of choice.

Even Salmawi, the former seller of cloth in the state-sector shop who was caught red handed taking a bribe and absconded, leaving five daughters and their mother behind him, I even found a solution for Salmawi. He had no papers, and kept working and being fired, working and being fired, then hiding from the police, until I got him a job as a caretaker at a new building being built before me in Dalouk. I made him into the companion of my empty nights, and he would tell me how much he had made that month and how he was going to get hold of forged papers. He was good at making tea, and wrote strange letters, like carbon copies, to the five girls and their mother. He couldn't be happier than when opening a can of corned beef and laying out a few white loaves.

Years ago, Salmawi became my only friend in exile. He knew the regulars at my house, the visitors, and my students. He knew when to wear the clothes of a servant and when to take them off and don the garb of a guard or barman or companion. His house and daughters in Mahalla al-Kubra were a grand illusion that he could almost make disappear since they did not know his address. Only he knew their address. Clean papers were another illusion that caused him to use up twice the amount he had saved over the years. I didn't interfere in such cases. I didn't give an opinion. Even so, Salmawi remained my friend and me his.

He accompanied me as far as the plane door. He did not give me a letter or ask me to look anyone up. Yet he was anguished, imploring my bags and departing body with his eyes and whole being. It was a strange image of contemporary mute eloquence that I sensed and took with me.

In the seat next to me on the plane, sat a young man who looked like Adawiya or Katkout. He was one of the princes of the new migration and imported money. As soon as he sat down, he took out a wad of green notes that for no reason he had hidden in his sock, and checked me over with a clever, suspicious eye.

Shortly after take-off, he stopped pretending and asked me to fill in his paperwork because his handwriting was illegible. Then he went off on a tangent and said that he was on the flight taking home three coffins of worker colleagues caught in a scaffolding collapse. His fellow villagers had chosen him for that depressing task, but it was a holiday. A holiday, whatever the case, not so?

In the throng of passport control and customs, I remembered him. I turned around and spotted his head in the crowd. I made a run for it, without knowing how he would deal with the coffins of his three friends.

Translated from *Thulathiyat Alaa al-Deeb*,
the Trilogy of Alaa al-Deeb, comprising 'Children without Tears',
'Moon over the Swamp' and 'Violet Eyes',
published by Dar el-Shorouk, Cairo, 2009.
Alaa al-Deeb's works have been republished many times.

ALAA AL-DEEB

Moon over the Swamp

AN EXCERPT FROM THE NOVEL
TRANSLATED BY PAUL STARKEY

Thank God he'd gone. Hani Qabtan had shut the door of the flat behind him and gone. I hurried over to the large bedroom and shut the door behind me as well. I was alone, talking to myself without a sound, like writing on white paper with white ink, my voice in my ear, going up to my mind and down to my heart. And there it stayed.

I am happy when surrounded by nothingness, like swimming in soft velvet or silk. Forgive me, Lord, forgive me all this recklessness with the blessings that almost swamp me, and forgive me – please – for my inability to bear more of this torture.

Hani Qabtan had gone now, after depositing me, Tamer, Lamia and Nanny Najiyya in the furnished flat, while he went to his old hotel . . . Sanaa Farag – Dr Sanaa Farag – and her children in a sumptuous furnished flat in Mersa Matruh. I repeated my name and repeated the name of the place, though really I wanted to forget the universe and the place; I just wanted to remember him. Hani Qabtan: my lover, my companion, my suitor, and me. Okay, I'm nearly fifty, and my white knight wanted me to marry him while keeping his first wife, mother to Haniyya and Tayseer. He wanted me as a second wife: a fair-skinned concubine, a second bedchamber, a spare bed, quite ordinary, nothing new. Until we arrived.

A splendid, snatched summer holiday, ten days with my birthday in the middle, a joyful opportunity to flay the sheep after sacrificing it, okay, one step and I'll be fifty, forty-six, anyway, and the sea is before me and the rubbish behind me. The windows of the large bedroom open onto the back of the building and look out over apartment block skylights and desolate waste ground, where smoke rises from the burning rubbish. From the small window, I can see, amid the smoke, the edges of some manufactured plasterboard, and heaps of cotton and muslin, waste from the hospital next door. The small fires gave off a pungent smell. I shut all my windows and drew the curtains tight over them, turning the day into darkness, then took off all my clothes and stood naked in front of the mirror.

* * *

I still love my body despite the years. I still love my lovely, free body. In this mirror, with its gentle light, my face is calm, my face is real and steady. Once again, I recognise my features: my nose is still wide, a little like a man's nose, and my brow is wide. I recognise afresh the features of my body in the hope that I may find my soul, draw closer to it then withdraw.

My true nature always seems obscure and impossible to me, a bewitching embodiment of time and place, days and nights of flesh, belly and chest, blue veins here… and there, bouquets of light, hollows of darkness. I look out over my heaven that is turning into hell, at ease with myself. I love this body despite everything.

Dada Najiyya's voice calls me, naked in front of the mirror. I jump quickly to the door and lock it. I don't want anyone to burst in on me, neither Najiyya nor the children. She likes to consult me in both big and little things, although she knows that I am empty, with no views or wisdom. She knows how wretched I am. Najiyya has a magic mirror, a mirror like no other, I don't just see my body in it; even with no light, I see in it the wreckage of my life. It reflects my buried relationship with my children, who are with me, but belong to her. With no father, no country, no land – and a mother too who is absent even while present – they are Dada Najiyya's children, despite the pains of pregnancy and childbirth, despite the fact that I pay all the living costs.

I don't want anyone now, I want to remain alone with my naked body, alone with my face – the face from which I have removed all the makeup and colouring with the white cream whose smell calms

Alaa al-Deeb

me.

I want it to be a room to add to the dozens of rooms in which I have moved naked and free. All this annoying furniture, this so-so cleanliness, I shall spend ten days here; normal, impossible, dirt clinging to the curtains, a foul dampness despite the smell of the sea close by. Nausea and the urge to be sick that always precedes my delving into memory; panic, a burning in my stomach, at the bottom of my stomach, a feeling of panic rising, with the flavour of acid.

* * *

Ten days here in Mersa Matruh: I hope I can live them alone and free, gazing at my body, at my soul, listening to my voice that has changed a thousand times, its rhythm changing, sometimes coming to me from afar, sometimes scratching my face and making me deaf.

My voice is my memory, a tone between wisdom and mirth; thank God I bear no grudge, nor bitterness. All that has happened has happened, and I am still Sanaa Farag, on my feet, naked and alone on a new shore. Despite all those years, I still feel joy and a vague fear of the approach of my birthday on 15th August. In my head are the waterfall of my childhood, the torment of my adolescence, my loneliness and my eternal love, which I lost before I could hold it.

Ten days here with the man who wants me, whom I do not want, who says he loves me but I cannot believe him. I have come to know the various faces of love and the faces of lies. We have no fresh, virgin moments; where should I escape the memories of the past, the stumbling blocks of the present and the fears for the future? The future! Who is this deluded beauty that speaks of the future?

Hani Qabtan wants me for his second wife, these are the crumbs that are left to me. A night in my bed and a night with her; between us true lies and a false truthfulness; my children and his other children, the whole world turned upside down, nothing between us but empty seats and new flats, reception rooms, lights blazing in empty rooms, new sorts of drink, food and clothes, the wreckage of emotions and a life with no dreams.

A divorced woman, alone before the whole world, forty-seven years old, my period, my sex, my madness. A panic appears, overpowers and strangles me; I could throw my whole existence in the rubbish bin, were it not for that voice that resounds in my mind, which my lips all but give voice to. I replay the tape at the same speed or leave it to run at varying speeds; this has become my favourite game. Ordinary, ordinary, and sometimes impossible.

From the fingers of my husband Munir Fakkar I realised that he had entered a region of madness. His fingers that stretched toward me, grasped me, seized my flesh, any part of my body – a dumb force that left me only when I screamed. Despite the darkness, I saw a gleam in his eyes. My great victory was obtaining a divorce.

* * *

I went back to check that the windows of the room were closed, and the panic returned to fill my stomach and chest. I observed the figure of my naked body in the mirror and thought it a different person. I went to bed then got up again for no reason.

Inside me are death, laziness, challenge and rejection, folly and stupidity, but when I meet people I present another face – a strong, lasting energy that sometimes frightens me, and I feel I am on the verge of madness. I have learnt to laugh loudly with my throat, with my vocal cords, I smile with my face muscles, I leave my face to move, I strike the earth with the heel of my shoe and my heart is heavy. I don't want anyone to know my failure, my weakness, or my burning loneliness; no one deserves to know. After the divorce, I resolved to make a way, to pretend a real success, material but deceitful. I no longer have anyone to whom I can lay bare my failure or my need, or even my simple existence.

I covered my naked body and tried to sleep. My eyes were open and hot, and the tears poured out as I slept. If I shut my eyes, I would see strange things: geometric shapes, circles and squares, fighting each other and attacking my body, circling around my head. I would go into threads like the threads on the coffee cup Najiyya read for me for years, before I broke the coffee cups and stopped drinking coffee on doctor's orders.

The lines on the coffee cup rest under my eyelids whenever I close them to sleep. They carry me along roads and paths then leave me naked in a spot lit up like the middle of a theatre, my panic a sudden fall or a sudden nakedness in the midst of the crowd. For years, these moments have surprised me so that I leap up in terror. Impossible to go back to sleep without a sleeping pill.

I am much better now, since Hani, my sleeping pill, came into my life. He gives me everything except for his true self, but perhaps he is like that, with no true self – empty like me, a bright shell, a lot of money, his face smooth and moist. His sexual energy arouses me, he is never satisfied, he wants me at strange times, and if it's impossible he turns into an angry, stubborn child. I have learnt to deal with these moments, to open a window for the steam to escape from his chest, so that he follows me like a calm, obedient little boy. Only in those moments would something like love for him tease my spirit, and when he left me to go to his wife, I would hate myself even more than I hated him, hate his tall, thin, delicate frame, his bent back and the smell of men's deodorant with which he would disguise our tryst. He would come back a day or days later, his smile again visible on his smooth, moist face, encircling me with his chatter, his plans, his parties and excursions, and whisper about nights of mad sex, and I would give my time to him without feeling.

* * *

Sleep is my private sea, my warm, shady oasis. I seldom sleep, and when I sleep, I wake up bright, happy and rosy, as if I had bathed in milk and honey. My soul's happy smile comes back to me, as if the summer breezes had touched my face and breast, turning me once again into a confident young girl, loved and loving without limit. The hours of sleep take me back to my lover, to Aziz Shafiq, my love, who dwells in my body as if I had been created for him in a world made just for the pair of us. Despite the days and years, my memory of him has never faded. I speak about and to Aziz Shafiq in an old, private voice that I can no longer manage, a voice I can no longer find. I speak without words, for he understood everything about me; with him I was in no need of words, all words were born of him, in moments of love he would drown me in words. I stretched out my neck to him to breathe and put my hand on his mouth and moustache to silence him.

I got to know him when I was in the final year of Business School. He had graduated from the Faculty of Arts two years before me. He swept me away like an unexpected storm of gentleness, love, freedom, and understanding. He was a Christian, and thought that I too was a Christian. He told me: there is nothing in you that is strange to me; even my name could be Christian. He would call me by my full name, Sanaa Farag, as if he was merely giving me my due. On Sunday (but only on Sunday), there was a special schedule in their house, while our house kept what remained of the Friday rituals. On Sunday morning, he would go with his mother to church and spent most of the day with her. Friday he spent with us at home, never tiring of talking to my sick father, joking and playing with him, and holding endless conversations with the first of my brothers to emigrate about politics and the state of the country. Although we only occasionally spent the night together, there was nothing in my life except for him, night or day. It was a time different from the present time, and a country different from the one I can see now. I loved him on the road, in the corners, in the light of day, in the empty tram carriages, and I would cling to him during our long journeys on the metro. Even when the conductor shouted at us angrily, objecting to our exchange of a quick kiss, the man came back and laughed with us as he pushed us out into the nice quiet street to continue what we had begun. Yes, this actually happened to me, a long time ago. Lying on my back I tried to summon up his impossible fragrance.

* * *

My husband Munir Fakkar's crazy fingers and watchful eyes ravished my body and my whole being, reaching even under my nails. What did this stupid, frightening old bat want from me? He tossed and turned on a hot frying pan, he pounced on me, he hated me, he wanted me, wanted to play with me, to eat me and to put me on top of the cupboard as well. The oil money had already begun to flow through his veins instead of blood, and everything between us became hell upon hell. Even the city where we lived was like a film set still waiting for filming to begin. If and when people appeared, their breath was thick and hostile, and all the goods had lost the sparkle they once had. My cocoon, which I spun alone, was crushed before my eyes while still soft, trampled by his thick, bare feet, or his laughs that mocked me, and always, always his mad, dumb fingers. I closed my eyes and surrendered my soul to darkness in the heart of darkness.

What had I done that my destiny, my country, my family should have surrendered me to this fate? Why had everyone deserted me and left me with this crazy money dog? Somewhere around me too were my children, Lamia and Tamer; I stretched out my hand but could not take hold of them. I saw them, and my heart asked: Who are they? Their features were scattered around me; I gathered them up but they always eluded me. I fall down, feeling nauseous, with a deadly feeling of guilt.

Away from him, I secretly decided to take a ten-day holiday in Cairo. I secured the agreement of my boss in the university, and that was that. When my husband found out and had it confirmed, he kicked the door of the flat and said: On your own, like that, you idiot? Without saying anything, without saying goodbye, like a loose woman with no husband and no children? Shame on you and on those who brought you up!

Several dozen times, everything went up and down: my heart, my body, my hair in his hands; cups, plates, electrical appliances and the children in the corners. I tore his face and all my clothes with my nails, and spent ten days in intensive care.

Najiyya and Tamer are in the hall now, quarrelling loudly. His voice annoys me, it reminds me of his father's voice. The marks of his fingers are permanent, like burns on my heart, liver and gut. Tamer rushes toward the door of my room but Najiyya stops him and says: Enough, enough, Mother's asleep.

There is a strange relationship between me and this woman. I live in her shadow, and use her existence as protection when necessary.

* * *

I took my decision during the night, and in the morning, I was strong and determined. Only six months had gone by since I'd obtained my divorce from Munir Fakkar, but it felt as if I'd been reborn, despite the new material struggles and difficulties that I faced. He'd taken almost everything, though at least now I could breathe at night again. I also went back to reading and to listening to music in the morning, which was something he always made fun of.

I decided to resign from the university, to sever all the ties that bound me to the terrifying past that I had spent with him and his friends, and with the circles that we moved in. My friends had all changed after the scandal, when the police had been involved, and the newspapers had published every detail for gloating eyes and outstretched hands to rake over my most private affairs. I could sense them whispering to each other around me in a hum that never stopped. What was it in her that made him leave her, and what did he leave behind for her? Even the eyes of the professors who were my colleagues changed as they met my face in the morning. They didn't know how to conceal the way they looked at me as an 'easy' divorcée, as if they'd been cavorting with me at night in bed.

I had Tamer and Lamia with me, a small sum in the bank, and a small flat that we had snatched from the lion's claws. From this cave, with the resolve of a wounded lioness, I had to begin on my own. My first step was to remove from my life the nightmare that went under the name of my university life. People like us who took out loans changed into strange creatures, predatory sharks without colleagues or friends, taught by years of being ostracised how to prey on the living flesh of their brothers and how to climb on the shoulders of those closest to them. Those that didn't were strangled and emaciated by poverty; they began to smack their lips as they doltishly gazed at the clothes and cars that others brought back with them, as if everything in their previous existence had exploded in a single moment and fallen to pieces with no rhyme or reason. After I'd put an end to my torment with Munir, it was impossible for me to put up with this place for a single moment, for my professorial colleagues – the men before the women – moved from one faculty to another, conveying the rumours and the gossip about Munir and Sanaa in a resounding whisper, accompanied by laughter that proved a great source of amusement to the students and cleaners.

The nice Faculty Dean didn't ask me many questions, but scrutinised me carefully as he took from me the piece of paper conveying my resignation. As I quickly headed in my little car towards the University bridge, cutting through the crowd of students, it was like fleeing a forest of stupidity.

* * *

Through the bar window I could see the sea, stretching endlessly away in the darkness. The sea is the greatest thing in my life, awe-inspiring, absolute, unique. I love it, I feel it sweeping over me, and I plunge into it in an impossible, all-consuming competition. Looking at it makes me want to look for somewhere new, for a new spot to start from, a spot nearby but ambiguous, situated there in the unknown. There I shall find what I seek, there I shall find what I have lost.

After several glasses, Hani had started to relax. He had lost the tension that accompanied his talk and rapacious smiles, and had become a normal, unpretentious person again, really yearning for a free woman to love him and accept his faults and weakness in the same way she accepted the considerable material potential that he offered – a woman who would accept him as he was and pander to his vanity. I often sensed that his wife beat him and that he was afraid of her, but he always disguised this in front of me. He couldn't acknowledge it or speak about it, and when he spoke about her to me, he used repeated words and stock images. I had met her several times at gatherings and on visits to some foreigners they had dealings with, and found her to be an ordinary woman, pretty but a little artificial, with sharp nails, hiding it all well behind a curtain of contrived politeness.

I knew that the problem with Hani himself was that he wasn't the man to give a woman a justification for her existence so that she would no longer ask or be afraid, or want for anything. He demanded freedom but couldn't make it or give it. I often said to myself that he was just an ordinary, one-dimensional man, with whom the moments and days just slipped away. Now there was nothing in my life to stop me from going with him; he was entitled, as was I, to learn how to enjoy things together. He asked me to spend the night, or part of it, in his hotel. He reassured me how he had prepared everything and settled things with the management so that no one would disturb us. The evening on his balcony would be fantastic, he said.

* * *

My first days with my husband Munir Fakkar were terrible. We weren't children. He knew about my long-running relationship with Aziz and how he had left me when we were about to marry. Despite that, he strangely insisted on turning the fact that he wasn't the first man in my life into a sub-text, to which he would continually return – usually without any direct statement, and often with the rudest and vilest of images. I tried with all the means at my disposal to win him over and make him feel that he was 'my man', but it seems that the problem wasn't connected with me or my body or history at all; on the contrary, it was connected with him, and with his understanding of me and my relationship with him. He wanted to know from me the minutest details, and when I refused, he started to make up stories in his imagination, to believe them, and to hold me to account for them.

He continually surprised me at the most difficult moments by saying: You don't want me, you don't love me, you think about it – and then my whole body would be with him. At his hands, right from the beginning, I knew the curse of bad sex, sex that turns into a dumb struggle and ends with physical exhaustion and a void in the soul.

After pregnancy had made itself felt in my body for the first time, and I'd started to become aware of that fullness and power that a moving embryo can generate, I felt that I would be able to bind for him the wounds that had eaten into his soul. But he would always scratch them and reawaken them again, until I was convinced that he relished them, and that he was like an animal that likes the taste of blood from his wounds. So I left him to do it, and secretly drew a thick veil over the entire problem, though it seems that this just made him even madder.

The extraordinary women we hear about these days, who kill their husbands, chop them up and put them in plastic bags under train seats, or bury their children under their lovers' beds – I don't know what brought these images to mind, as I sat with Hani Qabtan in that chic bar. When I started to talk with him at length about these events, he insisted that all these things went back to sex, to the weakness or poverty of the man, or to overpopulation, and he started to repeat what the psychologists were saying in the newspapers. Images of the women continued to mingle before me with moments of my life with Munir and other men I'd known after him, and even with my moments with Hani, the gentle, cultured man who sat in front of me. Something changed in the universe I inhabited, something violent and explosive that insinuated itself into all the compassion, love and human emotions I possessed, strangling them all and turning them into knives and daggers.

It seems that the drink, the impossible sea (which had sunk into the darkness far away), or perhaps just that elegant place with no one else there – it seems that all this, together with a burning sense of loneliness, had brought mute tears to my eyes, although I didn't usually cry in front of anyone else. On the way back – the long, long way back – I asked Hani to leave me tonight, for I was no longer good for anything.

Translated from *Thulathiyat Alaa al-Deeb*,
the Trilogy of Alaa al-Deeb, comprising 'Children without Tears',
'Moon over the Swamp' and 'Violet Eyes',
published by Dar el-Shorouk, Cairo, 2009
Alaa al-Deeb's works have been republished many times.

IBRAHIM FARGHALI

Observing the Distortion of Intellectual Identity

When I hear Alaa al-Deeb's name, I instantly remember him as the "reader" whose book reviews have shaped our understanding of the literary scene of our time. Through his widely read weekly column "Assir al-Kutub" (Juice of Books), he continued for almost two decades to provide the readers of *Sabah El Kheir* magazine with thorough reviews of some of the most important books offered by this era. He demonstrated superb skill not only in selecting the books for review, but also in presenting them to the reader in a succinct, attractive way.

I also loved al-Deeb the novelist. I liked his style; the short sentences loaded with literary charges and emotions. That style was particularly evident in his celebrated novel *Zahr el-Laymoon*, (Lemon Blossom), as well as in his beautiful trilogy *Atfaal bila Dumu'* (Children without Tears), *Qamar 'ala al-Mustanq'a* (Moon over the Swamp) and *Oyoun al-Banafsaj* (Violet Eyes).

To me, al-Deeb was different from his generation. While most of his contemporaries were particularly keen to add flavours of experimentalism and fantasy to Egypt's predominantly realistic narrative, al-Deeb remained largely loyal to realism. The only explanation I can think of for this was his involvement in political activity, as he pointed out in his memoir, *Waqfa qabla al-Munhadar* (Pause before the Decline). It is certainly conceivable that his belief in political activism as an effective tool for change may have influenced his writing. Reading al-Deeb's trilogy brought to mind a number of other works which addressed the theme of life in exile, particularly the migration of Egyptians to the Gulf, which began in the 1970s. These works – including Ibrahim Abdel Meguid's *Al-Balda al-Ukhra* (*The Other Place*, translated by Farouk Abdel Wahab, AUC Press, 2005) and two other novels by Mohamed Mansi Qandil and Mohammed Abdul Salam al-Omari – focused on Gulf society itself, whilst al-Omari's work went even deeper in exploring the untold stories of that society.

Al-Deeb's trilogy, on the other hand, dealt with the psychological impact on the Egyptian intellectuals of the 1960s, driven by necessity to seek employment in the Gulf. It featured individuals with an overriding sense of double alienation, feeling estranged from both their native society and their new society in exile. The author did not, however, venture into detail over the causes of these feelings; namely, the intricacies of life in exile, and how it came to bear down upon the Egyptian expatriate.

Ibrahim Farghali

We meet Munir Fakkar, a university professor who divorced his wife, deserted his children and transformed into what he called a 'money-collecting machine' – a cliché drawn from the image of the poor Egyptian villager who, after acquiring some wealth, is money-hungry for the rest of his life.

Unlike Ibrahim Abdel Meguid in *The Other Place*, al-Deeb avoided getting into the details of the relationship of the expatriate with his fellow expatriates, or with the exile society. He also ignored a key influence that has had a tremendous impact on Egypt's sociocultural setup since the 1970s: the Salafi and Wahhabi doctrines adopted by low-educated Egyptians, and even some elites, during their stay in Saudi Arabia. Upon returning to Egypt, they brought with them new religious fashions and notions, such as the hijab and the niqab, and introduced superficial forms of worship, attempting to undermine age-old social norms on religious grounds.

Al-Deeb focused instead on the psychological conflict endured by Dr. Munir Fakkar, an Egyptian expatriate who, having lost the sense of simplicity and rural values of his home, and yet being simultaneously unable to gain proper recognition from the academic institutions of the Gulf, metamorphosed into a distorted identity. In reality, he is a typical example of a large number of academics who have been distorted not only by life in exile, but also by the deterioration in the quality of education in Egyptian universities. Al-Deeb traces the impact of these changes on the next generation: the children who grew up in a house dominated by hatred between Dr. Fakkar and his wife, Sanaa Farag, whom he describes as greedy and materialistic. He considers his marriage to her as the biggest failure of his life, a failure he continues to pay a costly price for by living away from his children, who stay with their mother.

Al-Deeb's preoccupation with the psychological changes in the Egyptian character, particularly amongst the intellectuals, is evident everywhere in the novel: in the protagonist's perception of the changes and deformities that Egypt underwent, and in his nostalgia for the village as the impregnable source of purity, whose inhabitants have not been subjected to the same degree of distortion as the city dwellers.

Indeed, it was the significance of these changes or deformities to al-Deeb which prompted his detachment from Egypt's literary circle. In his memoir, he points out that he had never been imprisoned for his political activity, but he did elect to put himself under 'house arrest'. He played host to close friends, as well as to scores of young writers who valued his views on literature and culture in general, and who admired his ability to remain aloof from the gossip and trivialities of the literary community.

In his real life as well as in his fiction, al-Deeb seems equally fearful and resentful of the state of backwardness that Egypt experienced for many years. In his memoir, *Pause before the Decline*, he says: "Backwardness is not driven by poverty alone. It's an octopus-like creature, a child of poverty and ignorance that was born in the dark, lived in mindlessness and stupidity, and fed on incapacity and narrow-mindedness. Backwardness is a body that I am wrestling against in every moment of my existence. At home. At work. In the street. In faces. In emotions. At entrances to cities. Under bridges. In interpersonal relations. In love. In what I read. In what I like and what I dislike."

In spite of this, he never succumbed to despair. On the contrary, he believed that monitoring the backwardness and the negative developments that society undergoes should render one even more determined in the quest to hold on to lost values and to recover the lost homeland.

Translated by Adil Babikir

YOUSSEF RAKHA

Five Memories of Alaa al-Deeb

1

It must've been 1996. I was working as a stage prompt with El Warsha theatre company. This would've been my second year at Hull University, but I spent the summer in Cairo to be with my parents. While I stayed I kept up with El Warsha through its director, Hassan El Geretly. Three or four times a week I'd make my way from the poorer side of Dokki where my parents lived to the leafy British Council villa opposite the Nile in Agouza. Rehearsals were held in a gym-like room on the top floor of the main building, where an audience was sometimes invited to cram around actors and singers. For the larger shows a stage or tent was set up in the garden. That must be where I first noticed the squat, leonine figure of a writer with the thick grey beard. He was leaning on a walking stick, glaring at the floodlight. Geretly had spoken often of Alaa al-Deeb. But the cane-wielding, Hemingwayesque intellectual in his late fifties was a genre of gentleman I could never have imagined. He was at once grave and gregarious; a magnetic but forbidding presence. I forget whether introductions were made on this occasion. But before very long I was regularly tramping down to Maadi to call at his house whenever I was in Cairo, and he let me.

2

When I started writing for *Al Ahram Weekly* in 1998, the editors I worked under were keen on me, but the head of the department remained sceptical. Yet when she interviewed me, it turned out that Ustaz Alaa – as I could never bring myself to stop calling him, such is the ingrained ageism of the Egyptian middle class – was someone we had in common, which seemed to greatly reassure her. Much later, when she and I became friends, she told me how the last time she saw him she had asked whether this Youssef Rakha was a friend of his son Ahmad's, and how, with an earnest look, he had replied: "No, he is a friend of mine."

3

Ustaz Alaa had the spacious ground floor of an old family house at the end of a tributary of Street 9: 9B. It had a gorgeous terrace and a small garden. It was so sparse and tasteful that it felt like something out of a Youssef Chahine film: a fragment of an older and infinitely more humane Cairo. Ustaz Alaa's Arabic too was the closest I have ever come to a pure Cairene accent . . . One bright winter morning over vodka when no one else was there, thinking I was speaking in confidence, I gathered up the courage to divulge to him my deepest, darkest secret. A short while later I found myself surrounded by elderly men in their underwear, discussing my predicament in the merriest way imaginable. I have not forgotten the resounding tones in which Ustaz Alaa announced my secret to his friends, glass in hand, although I still have no memory of when or how they'd arrived.

4

It was thanks to Alaa al-Deeb's position there that two of my very short stories – flash fiction-type writing – appeared in the mainstream magazine *Sabah El Kheir*. I would sometimes visit his office on Qasr El Aini Street, accompanying him back to Maadi in a taxi. It was thanks to his sensibility that I learned to string together several short pieces into a longer narrative, though when I finally had a book of short stories he could not help me publish it. It was thanks to his criticism that I saw what was wrong with my first attempts at a novel. He gave no instruction. He would simply read what I showed him, then he would respond in informal and spontaneous ways. He taught me how to write. He gave me a perspective on the sixties, on manhood and the national struggle long before I read his Fitzgeraldian fiction. He put me among people. He gave me confidence. He showed me that my secret was neither deep nor dark, and that I didn't have to protect it with such desperate shame. He taught me how to live.

5

I didn't see Alaa al-Deeb for many years before he died. Drugs, deaths and breakdowns had cut short our connection in the wake of 9/11. I saw a truly tender side of him tending to my imploding psyche in those days. Later he was depressed for a long time – dry spells prompted by physical illness always left him depressed – and I was trying to live anew. Later still there was this vicious circle of postponement: not phoning would make the thought of phoning harder, so I would put phoning off . . . By 2016 he had become irrelevant to my life, but I still had an image of him making his Turkish coffee on the kind of kerosene primus stove called a *sebertaya*, wearing a white galabia with the light pouring in through the shutters all around him, smoking and talking. And even now, that image is part of how I know who I am in this world.

ALAA KHALED

Alaa al-Deeb's Cairo

In Alaa al-Deeb's novella *Al-Qahira* (Cairo), published in 1964, the city appears to be suffocating. But this does not correspond with the image of 1960s Cairo that had become iconic, particularly apparent in footage of Umm Kulthum's concerts, where audiences effuse a joyful yet elegant spirit which pervades the streets, and the distances between people are bursting with roses. There was another Cairo that no one spoke of; a Cairo at the zenith of a totalitarian regime before its defeat. A regime that, without quite having complete mastery over the public sphere in which people moved, had managed to forcefully appropriate their psychological and personal space. Individual agency was snatched from them by a greater force, be it the regime and its manifestations in their daily and private lives, or the city itself that had turned into a piece of propaganda.

It is no surprise that Alaa al-Deeb plays on the Arabic word for Cairo (al-Qahira – the conqueror), as both a noun and an adjective. There is indeed something overpowering lying in wait for people in al-Deeb's Cairo, where we observe noise, crowding and garbage in the streets. This Cairo, post the 1952 Revolution, began to imprint its character on its residents, who inherited its intense psychological quality. Here, al-Deeb appears as the representative of the urban individual who deals with his city as a living mass and not as an imagined polity or abstract piece of propaganda, as would happen with Cairo after the 1967 defeat, which turned the city into a 'centre', both as a reaction to and revenge for its subsequent marginalization.

Alaa Khaled

This 'centralization' process had in fact begun to take shape after the 1952 Revolution with the emergence of [Arab] nationalism, later to become the defining feature of both the city and those who spoke for and narrated it. In this short novel, al-Deeb takes a different stance; he does not politicize the city, but at the same time he senses, at the peak of its haughty overconfidence, both its defeat and its detachment from the living body he once knew it to be.

In *Al-Qahira*, the city does not have a defined 'centre' to frame the protagonist's sense of loss, for it was not until later that this discourse of 'centrality' in Egyptian literature was crafted. The main characters are not described in more detail than their being ordinary people. This is of course before the entry of the marginalized intellectual protagonist into the Egyptian novel, with his heavy baggage and successive defeats, who establishes for himself a 'marginal centre' in which he is besieged after the 1967 defeat. It was this defeat which was to impact on the trajectory of Egyptian literature and imbue it with a sense of self-inferiority; in other words, reducing the whole sphere of literary production to serving this defeated spirit. The characters in Alaa al-Deeb's *Al-Qahira* move around freely within the borders of sixties Cairo, from Dokki to El-Ataba to Bab al-Louq to the Corniche to Shubra – the defining city limits during this period. The '*ashwai'yat* (irregularly constructed slums) and other suburbs were not yet in the picture, nor were the sharp class distinctions that surfaced with the expansion of the city. The author's perception of this lack of a defined city centre, with extended geographical boundaries, in fact created much more space for different types of protagonists – not just the marginalized who came to define post-1967 literature. Instead, he is the ordinary individual who sees Cairo from the window of his third floor office at the Agricultural Museum in Dokki, and from the low threshold of his dreams. True, the protagonist is marginalized by his feeling of being overpowered, but he still possesses a whole, homogenous city in which to move around. The public sphere still had spaces and empty pockets for the movement of these characters; for their impulses and unbridled ambitions.

The protagonist in this novel is not a writer, intellectual or political activist, nor is he full of existential angst in the sense that appeared after the 1967 defeat, when disillusionment became an essential quality of characters. Not only did they occupy a marginal-central space alongside the city, within it, or as an extension of it, but they also protected themselves by a geographic or psychological barrier which was often hard to transcend, for example in Ibrahim Aslan's *The Heron*. On the contrary, the despair and sense of disillusionment in al-Deeb's protagonist comes much earlier and warns of the defeat to come. He still moves freely within the city, not yet having been expelled from its centre, but at least occupying its centre in his memory; yet he also lacks a marginal-centre where he can protect himself. Al-Deeb's protagonist scatters his despair across the city's geography, carrying it with him from place to place. Perhaps this is to avoid focusing his despair on one sacred location, instead allowing its distribution across the whole city to become an image of his own despair and sense of defeat, or vice versa. There is a sense of kinship and patrimony, as well as a mutual exchange between the protagonist and the city, which is perhaps an extension of the paternal concept, or one of its many manifestations.

The protagonist is aged 35, but speaks with the voice of someone whose life is about to end and to whom the future has become crystal clear. Here perhaps, the writer attributes this to the city, which has emptied its ordinary protagonist of any social, political or even personal ambition. Who has snatched this young man's life away so early? The defeat is still three years away. Perhaps it is urbanity, or modernity, or the ways of modern life and the resulting compromises entailed within them. Perhaps it is the responsibility that the individualism of modern man can no longer put up with, or perhaps it is the repressive totalitarian regime of the time. All of these aspects have robbed this young man of his life, and each constitutes an image of the demise of the paternalistic era. A new era has begun, which places the son alone at the centre of life, and that drives him to age early. Perhaps the novel revolves around a forced separation from the intimate paternal world, vaguely reminiscent of Naguib Mahfouz's characters before their existential questions disappear, or before their journey to search for the meaning of life halts, becoming too complex and obscure for them.

The unexpected moment during the protagonist's free wandering in his city is when he goes to the graveyard quarter to bury his brother. Here, he feels that he is outside the city's mentality, outside the centre of domination, so his base instincts awaken, leading him to hatch the plot that will ultimately cost him his life, along with his girlfriend. Perhaps it is the personal freedom of the individual here that is being emphasized: you remove yourself from the domination of the city-god, the omnipresent intellect, in order to become the

Cairo in the sixties

god yourself. In this way, as the protagonist explains, you make your own plans, determine your own destiny, and, in your own image, take vengeance upon this other god.

In a lively interview I conducted with Mr al-Deeb about his university years, he explained how he wandered about in fifties Cairo, the Cairo that he loved, making his way to university in what he described as an "atmosphere of serenity". From his account, one could almost feel that the entire universe itself was in tune with him during his daily commute. In spite of the political turbulence, Cairo of the 1950s did not pose a barrier to this feeling of harmony and being in tune with oneself. The city was still a living mass for him, having not yet morphed into a domineering Cairo, or into a Freudian model of the patriarch, of which one would either wish to kill and be done with, or to run away from and never come back. Cairo at that time had a more benevolent system of paternalism in Alaa al-Deeb's view, which was also how he saw fatherhood. As he spoke to me about his relationship with his own father, there seemed to be a sort of appreciation, as opposed to a clash. This sense of the benevolent-paternalistic city in the 1950s would later be lost by al-Deeb's protagonist during his wandering through the Cairo of the sixties, perhaps owing to the heavy burden of totalitarian paternalism that was imposed by Nasser's regime.

We would always meet in Alexandria in his hotel room which looked out over the sea. There he would speak to me about Mersa Matruh, the place that was far removed from his Cairo. Alexandria and Matruh were for him akin to his old Cairo, where he could regain that state of harmony and active engagement. There was no longer a 'centre' to inspire, except at a distance. Yet the "serene" spirit that Mr al-Deeb possessed did live on. It cast its shadow and affection over everyone, making him observe his own life and others' from a shaded spot, as if he were taking a long stroll that lasted for dozens of years.

Translated by Suneela Mubayi

BEN KOERBER REVIEWS
Zahr el-Laymoon
(Lemon Blossom)
by Alaa al-Deeb

published by Dar el-Shorouk,
Cairo, 1987
ISBN 978-977-09-2289-9

Fallen, without glory, without scent

When *Lemon Blossom* came out in 1987, Hosni Mubarak had comfortably secured a second term as Egypt's president, and Farouk Hosny had just been appointed as Minister of Culture – a position he was to hold longer than any competitor. Neither, of course, makes an appearance in Alaa Al-Deeb's novella, a work of cogent subtlety. But the allied forces they represented – authoritarian neoliberalism in the political field, and capriciousness and hypocrisy in the culture industry – weigh heavily on Abdel Khaliq al-Messiri, the novella's tragic protagonist. The nature and extent of al-Messiri's manifold traumas are revealed through a series of vignettes, flashbacks, and ruminations as he undertakes a weekend trip from his current residence in Suez to his native Cairo and back again.

Time has not been kind to Abdel Khaliq al-Messiri. Divorced, he rues mixed memories about his ex-wife, who has emigrated to a more prosperous life in Canada. Once a committed communist, he finds most of his former comrades have sold out to post-infitah commodity worship. A frustrated poet, he ekes out a meagre living as a pencil-pusher at a branch office of the Ministry of Culture in Suez – a once cosmopolitan port town now reduced to a colourless and conservative backwater. And though Cairo is the locus of much of his distress, he finds himself drawn back once again. Partly, it is a matter of routine: in his words, weekend trips like this one have become "a monthly habit as irregular as the periods of a woman approaching menopause". Perhaps also, going home for Abdel Khaliq al-Messiri is less the result of a free-willed decision, than of the psychological compulsion to repeat, to linger over old wounds, that is so characteristic of victims of trauma.

The signs of his internal torment are visible not only in the language of narration – the repetition of key words like gharib ("strange, stranger") – but in his return to people and places he knows will only cause him pain. Soon after arriving in Cairo, he sets out to meet up with a group of old friends at "The Bar of the Princes". Pleasantries quickly give way to insults, however, when al-Messiri expresses his disgust at one friend's penchant for gossip, only to find himself outnumbered in the ensuing shouting match. Defeated, he is forced to leave. Subsequent stops include the home of his friend Fathi Noureddin and his wife, Ferial, whose warm hospitality only reminds him of his own divorce; a pottery workshop in al-Hussein, where the earthy, manual labour of the craftsman stands in sharp contrast to the writer's perpetual anxiety of production; the apartment of another friend, Hamdi, who appears absorbed in his own affairs; and finally, his childhood home in Dokki, where al-Messiri's ailing mother is tended to by his fundamentalist brother Saeed.

Al-Messiri's return to Dokki brings us to the physical manifestation of the book's title and central metaphor: the lemon tree that once grew in the yard of a neighbour. He says of himself: "No one needs him, there is no need for him. Not here. And not there. He's fallen, and his best days have withered away, like lemon blossom, without glory, without a scent". The fruit itself, *limun*, suggests *limuna* ("for Mona"), a dedication to his ex-wife Mona al-Masri, whose name doubly invokes the nation [*masri* is Arabic for Egyptian]. (Lemons or limes are also a tried and true Egyptian folk panacea for all manner of minor ailments; a medieval Arabic tradition recommends them as antidotes to snake venom). Yet it is not the fruit's symbolic load that places it at the book's core, but rather its capacity to induce in the reader the irreducible felt experience of its taste. In a work of such solemn minimalism, these mischievously placed pricks and pinches have the power to send shivers down one's spine.

In *Lemon Blossom*, a good part of the reader's task involves connecting elements from al-Messiri's past to his present emotional strife.

Whence his peculiar "strangeness", his inability to connect with those around him? It is clear that al-Messiri spent a certain amount of time in prison for his communist ties, and the almost unspeakable torture he endured there can explain a good deal of his current agony. Then there are the dual traumas of the 1967 Naksa and Sadat's "Open Door" (Infitah) policy. Abdel Nasser is a looming presence in the novella, and his defeat still leaves al-Messiri's friends split between memorializing the ideals of socialism and liberation that he embodied, and acknowledging the corruption and authoritarianism of his regime. The Infitah era has wiped away the economic and moral certainties of al-Messiri's generation, and thrown them at the mercy of fashions they can't comprehend and faces they don't recognize.

Cover of Zahr el-Laymoon (Lemon Blossom)

In the 30 years since *Lemon Blossom* first appeared, Egyptian politics and culture have undergone successive paradigm shifts. And yet, amidst the counter-revolutionary gloom of the present, it is perhaps not surprising that the novella has succeeded in reaching a new audience. In "Scent of Revolution" (2014), a documentary by Viola Shafik, Alaa al-Deeb appears with his novella to offer solemn reflections on the fate of Abdel Khaliq al-Messiri, whose story had ended without resolution. There is, perhaps, something of a morbid consolation in revisiting the thwarted dreamers of al-Messiri's generation: the "scent of revolution," and the taste of lime, are cognate sensations. Yet that is not the only experience that Lemon Blossom communicates. For while al-Messiri's story is suffused with melancholy, its ethical edge cuts not only against the oppressive apparatuses of state and society, but against the listlessness and defeatism of the protagonist himself. It is in recognizing and confronting these dual manifestations of power that *Lemon Blossom* offers hope for future generations striving for change.

ALAA AL-DEEB

The River beneath the Rocks

TRANSLATED BY NARIMAN YOUSSEF

My girlfriend and I sat in our darkened room. Her shoulders were bare and her dress was black. "I had been praying," I said.

"You pray?"

"Yes, I prayed before you came, and I cried. I knew that the light would rise from the East, so I opened the window. But I found only darkness outside. There was a murdered dog beneath my window. My neighbour looked out of the window opposite and said: 'Close that window and keep praying! Do not open the window again!' I then heard howls and screams and a noise of trees breaking. I could smell incense. So, I prayed once more until I passed out."

"Oh my love! Did all that happen before I came to you?"

"Yes, minutes – only minutes – before."

She hugged me and cried.

My girlfriend and I walked in a park. Yellow leaves were falling all around us. They fell on her hair and shoulders. She crushed a large leaf under her foot. Her smile was like the sun. "I want you know happiness," she said. "Come with me behind that tree."

Behind the tree was a large water well, and she fell in. I could no longer see her, but her voice continued to tear at my heart. "Know happiness! Go, and know happiness!"

Since then, I've been hearing that same voice out of every well.

I rented a small room on the roof of an old building. No one visited me anymore. Every morning before I left to work, I put out a bunch of clover for the white rabbit that I kept as a pet. He was a white rabbit with red eyes. He was my only friend.

He would sit in his small wire cage with his eyes looking towards my bed, where I would lie watching him. I would watch him until I fell asleep, his red eyes the last thing I saw and continued to see in my dreams.

In my free time, I would hold him by his long ears and gaze into his eyes until he fell asleep. I would stroke him and he would quiver in his sleep.

The rabbit became my life.

Last Friday I ate a big breakfast at the small wooden table – ful beans and fried eggs. The rabbit looked at me and chewed on something. The morning sun fell on him. His white fur was translucent and his red eyes sparkled. I felt a strange contentment. I finally had a home.

After I finished eating, I smoked a cigarette in the sun, then took the rabbit out of his cage and placed him in my lap. He moved his head playfully, his red eyes full of laughter.

Suddenly the wind blew and pushed open the front door, then the rabbit was out of my lap and in flight.

I let out a scream. The sun was behind the clouds. My rabbit leapt down the stairs. I fell at the bottom of the steps and stayed there, unmoving, for a few moments. It started to rain. The rabbit was lost in the busy street.

I was banished from my small room. I left the door at the mercy of the wind, the clouds still blocking the sun. A dreary, deserted darkness.

Night after night, the weight of that burden – the shore and the street, the street lamps, the shells of lupin beans littering the ground, pieces of paper carried on the wind down a long, tan street.

The voices of people from far away tumble off the surface of the mask I'm wearing.

Beneath the hard-edged, brutal rocks, a river runs. There, before me, under the clouds, in the night – beautiful, faraway eyes speak in a thousand tongues.

From *Al-Musaafir al-Abadi* (The Eternal Traveller), published by Dar el-Shorouk, Cairo. 2011

ALAA AL-DEEB

Pause before the Decline

CHAPTERS FROM THE MEMOIR,
TRANSLATED BY SALLY GOMAA & JONATHAN WRIGHT

Papers of an Egyptian Intellectual (1952-1982)

These papers are real,
fresh blood from an open wound
Writing them was
an alternative to suicide

I realised early what it means to be middle class or petty bourgeois. I came from the lower middle class, from a family that had no capital and no craft, just a government job with a fixed income, regular raises, and promotions to be celebrated by the entire household when my father received one every four or five years.

Understanding what it is to belong to the middle class is not the same as merely belonging to it. It robs one of the pleasure of enjoying its pleasures, its laziness and its futility.

Understanding where I belonged made me see the limits, where values broke down and the only fragments left in my hand were anxiety, frustration, and powerlessness.

My world was turning into an ocean of alienation.

It was common to hear in those years that the middle class was in control of the country. But seeing peasants toiling from sunrise to sunset and shift workers coming out of the factories told me, with incessant and strident insistence, that work was the only value and the world's great blessing, and that the middle class, with all its rituals, traditions, and codes of behaviour, was trying to alienate me from labour and teach me how to play dishonest games and pursue the vice of 'success'.

Here I am, still trying not to learn.

I went through most of the experiences of a petty-bourgeois intellectual, except for prison. I was never in prison throughout those many years. But there were times when I thought: "I'd rather be in prison than . . ." Sometimes prison would have been better than living in a wasteland where no opinions were voiced and one could not disagree even with oneself.

I had to live in the prison of my own home, my street and my job. Every night, I made love to the corpse of my lifeless dreams and my thwarted hopes.

My cause was not political only. I joined the Muslim Brotherhood chapter in my neighbourhood. I was a 'comrade' in an old communist organisation. I was a member of the Liberation Council and I enrolled in Nasser's vanguard organisation. In all these organisations I was there as a number, just a name that added one member to the list of members. I never felt I was doing anything real or effective.

An official in one of the organizations I joined once told me: "You're nothing but a Sophist intellectual. You're petty bourgeois. You don't want to do anything." I knew that the Sophists were the ones who killed themselves seeking the truth through questions, even to the point of suicide. I had questions, but I had no truth and no suicide. Another official in another organization told me in a secret meeting outside a small café on a side street: "We have to stop meeting. The security services are in turmoil. The police are at odds with the intelligence people. No one knows what could happen."

From the beginning, I knew that politics in my country was like wet clay or quicksand. You might drown in the sands or ride them. A deep chasm separated the rhetoric from the reality.

Once a critic who was preparing an academic study of the novel told me: "We can't see the reality of our situation or put it in words because we cannot talk to start with: not about religion, not about sex, and not about politics." I laughed, but it sounded like crying because there was some truth in what they said.

I'm leafing through the notebook of this petty-bourgeois intellectual. As I do so, I feel rather ashamed and insignificant. It's full of dubious attributes that are sometimes ridiculous, and sometimes pathetic. As far as judges or theorists are concerned, they might sometimes be seen as accusations or grounds for condemnation. Someone who possesses these attributes is usually seen as an "obstacle" or as someone who has no role.

But they are my attributes and I possess them. It is an accusation I do not deny and an honour that I can, with difficulty, claim.

The Horses of Dawn

I lost my job as a journalist. An order was issued to dismiss me from the magazine where I was working. No reasons were given.

I had been dismissed once before after being accused of taking part in a conspiracy I hadn't even heard of.

The first time it happened, I was robbed of any feeling of security. It made the weekly article I wrote for the magazine seem unimportant and unnecessary. I felt like a servant of no importance that the master kept at home so that I didn't starve or cause trouble.

But if the master were to be angry one day, or in a bad mood, or if I made any disturbing noise, even in one of the back rooms of the house, he would just point a finger at me and I would vanish and turn into smoke.

The days of unemployment were long and tedious. Alone, I confronted the futility of life and realized that the craft of journalism or writing was seriously flawed in our country, at that juncture, because it was a craft that needed strength, a special type of strength, to support it and sustain it.

At the beginning of my work in journalism, I had hoped that my literary and artistic desires and my dreams for society could be channelled in diluted form to a wide audience through journalism. I tried to convince myself that there was no point in being a writer who writes to be read by his friends or whose books, printed at his own expense, sell one hundred copies.

I thought that the compromises I had to make to be a journalist were necessary in order to have my writing published in a newspaper or magazine with a large circulation.

I used to say to myself that there was nothing wrong with clarity and simplicity. I did not see the slippery slope or the trap that had been set.

The basic sense that preserves a writer's dignity is his sense of importance, of freedom, his sense that when he writes he is accountable only to his art, his ability and his talent.

But when he writes within a mould, without transgressing boundaries, constraints or walls placed around him, he certainly turns him into something other than a 'writer'.

The only reward a writer can have is the joy of seeing his words come to life on paper, but I have often seen my words turned into mutilated creatures, stillborn like incomplete foetuses.

Zaki Mubarak [Egyptian writer and scholar] used to say: "I wouldn't like anyone to outdo me in patriotism" and: "No one loves his country as much as I love mine."

I can't understand how loving or defending one's country could be turned into a sword used at a threat against people.

My limited experience of being driven out of journalism and prevented from writing not only deprived me of my sense of security and my faith in journalism and writing. It also revealed to me an idea that had built up in our lives in the real world and that we always tried to ignore: that the real sense of the word citizen was still missing, and we were still looking for it.

Many a night I spent feeling homeless.

Many a night I spent feeling that, despite having my wife and my children around, I was unnecessary, outcast and superfluous.

> *I meet you in the turmoil of bitter astonishment*
> *You pass through the black passes, befuddled and miserable*
> *What has aimed a knife at your heart*
> *when in your eyes there's a question that silences the tear*
> *and eternal sadness?*
>
> Farouk Shousha [Egyptian poet]

During that time, I became addicted to sitting in a garden that had once been a garden and had turned into a wasteland filled with debris and garbage. I asked myself the same question over and over: "When does the end begin? When did it start?"

I looked for the answer in people's faces, in their clothes, in the way they interacted, in the way they jostled and shoved each other for no good reason, and in their ascent and descent.

I used to tell myself that 'home' was a stable set of values. But I was like a blind man in a rage, fumbling in the dark.

* * *

There are two types of conspiracy. There is the type where the prosecution is in charge and the interrogators take it up. The criminal intent is obvious and definitive and the law and the constitution make it an indisputable crime.

But there is another type of conspiracy, a collective one. This is the conspiracy that we all take part in. The conspiracy that all men embrace in order to advance or succeed, to achieve aims they consider legitimate, such as success or victory in the battle of life.

This is the conspiracy we hatch every morning as we have breakfast and drink our tea with milk. It is the ordinary secret conspiracy with which we face our bosses at work and our wives in bed; the ordinary quick conspiracy with which we face our friends when they fall by the wayside and our colleagues when we trample over their bodies on our way to more and more success, or to more money from Hell, or to empty delusions.

I admit I am part of this conspiracy. It was imposed on me. I found myself driven to take part and I cannot define precisely the moment when I was implicated.

I began to feel that it was gradually becoming part of the fabric of life. Its weft was the threads of life, its moments, its fears. Its horrible achievements began to wrap themselves around me like a cocoon. It infiltrated my thoughts, exaggerated my fears, and fed my ego until it wrapped itself around me like a chrysalis, from the time when work for me no longer meant making a real contribution and life for me was no longer a joy and a blessing.

Once again I discovered that cursing injustice is useless,

that praising justice is useless,

that pulling out thorns out isn't enough,

and saying poetry is pure treachery.

* * *

Sometimes a sad morning takes me by surprise. Sometimes the sadness lingers until noon. Then it accumulates intensely in the gloomy moments that separate my day from the night. At that point not even flowers or my child's laughter can take me back to reality of my simple life. In those moments I walk along until I reach a side street in Dokki. It is a street that used to lead to open fields and that had large detached houses.

I had a friend who lived there, a man from an Arab country, a politician and artist. I used to listen to music and poetry at his house. I made friends there and met women and sat till dawn on the balcony that overlooked the fields. He talked to me about the Bedouin in his country, about the desert, about struggle and the modest abilities of mankind.

In this furnished apartment, where no wife or children lived, there was always something being made: a story being written, a poet wrestling with the lines of his poem; college students discussing their causes. The real news about the country was told there without fear or hesitation. Small human circles contained within a larger one, more human and more vibrant. Intimate relationships with few demands. A future that called us without reluctance. Disappointment did not arise and had no meaning.

I return to that side street now, drawn by sorrow, like a criminal returning to the scene of his crime.

The street is crowded with tall buildings, ugly in colour and badly built. The café where I used to sit is now dirty with old, broken chairs. At its entrance, there is a display case of stale sandwiches which reek of rancid oil.

My friend is gone. A young man I know has taken his apartment: a loudmouth, vacuous and boorish. I ring the bell. A sluttish maid comes to the door. The man appears in his underwear. He insists I stay. The woman makes me a bad cup of tea. She swings her hips vulgarly as she asks permission to go out shopping before the stores close. I am surrounded by dust, by lies and cheap perfume. He speaks pretentiously about politics. He says he feels sorry for me. He tries to make me believe he can find me jobs to add to my income. Every now and then he checks his face in an old mirror in front of him. We exchange addresses and phone numbers and make appointments we will not keep. I take my leave. Now, my sorrow turns into worry and disdain. When will the end begin? Has it started?

On my way out the old doorman stops me. How his face has changed, but he remembers me.

So you remember me! Do you remember how things used to be? As we stand here in the lobby of this squalid building, can you tell me how all this happened?

I hear him asking and answering, but what he says is disjointed. He narrates momentous events:

"The Greek woman who used to live on the top floor started walking in her sleep and she fell out of the window."

"Four of the ground-floor rooms have been turned into brothels

frequented by Peugeot drivers on the Libya route."
"The man who sold beans on the corner lost two sons. He demolished his shack and he and his wife went back to the south."
"There's no one left for me to serve or guard."
"We have to cry for everything
but may our crying be good.
We cry from the nose, and from the knees,
cry from the navel . . . and from the mouth."

I now come and go without being noticed by anyone at the house. I have bouts of pointless activity. But days pass when I wish I could close the windows and not see anyone.

On those days I wish I had a different trade, like being a plumber or a car mechanic. I want to put a tool box over my shoulder and go to fix a Primus stove, but they are all old things, taken apart, like the ideas that fill my head: nails, screws, and pieces of old torn rag.

A monkey that spends its day nervously jumping on the bars of its cage does not sweat. Beads of sweat do not form on its mischievous brow. The free horse that gallops in the desert or works in a field is covered with beads of sweat. It raises its neck and head high, seeking more freedom and air.

I was sick of my emptiness. An air bubble on the move, with the colours of the rainbow changing on its surface. "Walking in the rooms of my empty house is . . . mysterious." "My house is turning into a cave of much sleep . . . that might give me a headache." "Everything happens inside me, while my face is still the same."

No one notices how lonely, isolated, and outcast I am as I collapse in front of the television.

Gigantic . . . oafish, stripped of willpower.
There is no shortage of food in the house.
The world around me is turning into a stomach
a vast intestine.
It will not shout until it gets hungry.
Where is the rice, the salt, the soap, the matches, the lentils?
The television is gigantic.
And I'm gigantic.

"An old man who has lost control over his body." I left my house suddenly. I now prefer streets to houses, and cafés and bars to rooms.

My wife said: "Would anyone in his right mind go out now?"

The streets in Cairo were empty. Wretched horses are dragging vegetable carts. The bells around their necks are faint and monotonous. The men next to the carts drag their feet along the asphalt road at the entrance to the city.

A new dawn broke, from behind the railway station. A dawn that brings new dust and new noise.

My Freedom and A Little Money

The hot humid weather in the Gulf port where I arrived to work was a slap in the face. The air in the streets was heavy and dense. It had a smell in the nose and a taste at the back of the throat. Was it the humidity? The smell of petroleum? Or the smell of my own sweat, which stuck to my whole body? The disc of the sun, obscured by dust, gave me no reason to believe I was in a real place. I might have gone to the edge of the world or to the gates of hell.

Where was Egypt's afternoon breeze? Where was the Nile?

When I reported to the official at the news organisation where I was to start my new job, he said, "Welcome" in a Levantine drawl. He gestured for me to sit in a chair next to his desk and disappeared.

From this corner, I could see the whole large room and the room could see me. I sat there awaiting my fate. The room was full of empty desks with a few papers scattered here and there. The official took all my paperwork with him, including my passport, and left me alone for quite a while. I took stock, thought about why I had come here. I thought back over my life, quickly and fearfully, as if I were flicking through my notebook, like a merchant waiting to declare bankruptcy.

I had read about the nightmares of mental illness in books of psychoanalysis – nightmares in which other people's eyes turn into Hell, where the patient imagines that every whisper and every laugh is directed at him. They were no longer nightmares but a reality I experienced. The staff came in and out like spectres and busied themselves looking through the papers scattered on the desks. All of them threw secret glances at me.

"Are you the editor that's come from Egypt?"

"Yes, I'm the editor that's come from Egypt." The office messenger hurried off, and I followed until we reached the office of the editor-in-chief. He opened the door and showed me in.

I had never met the man before and he didn't know me. I had come as part of the great gang of itinerant workers, leaving Egypt in search of a livelihood. The doctor had written on my medical report that I was "fit to work in any climate". This phrase was the standard formula that doctors wrote: it meant that I didn't suffer from any infectious or serious diseases that might cause problems or unnecessary expense for the institution where I would work. But the phrase stuck in my head as I listened to the editor explaining the work that awaited me. He was cunningly polite, artificially cordial. Despite all the platitudes and polite clichés, he seemed to be telling me that he knew why I had come and what my price was for coming, and since I had come, then we should first of all sort out the details.

This was not an illusion. His demeanour suggested this. With my passport in his hand, he flipped through it, looking at me. He spoke little. He spoke on the phone and scratched his head.

Finally he let me go to rest, with an optimistic promise that we would meet again soon and, *inshallah*, collaborate fruitfully.

When I was alone, in the stubborn midday period, the sound of the air conditioner reverberated through my room. I thought to myself: here I am in my new room. Here I own nothing. Nothing here has a history.

Now I can write my memoirs.

Only reality. Only real events. Faces and how people act. The succession of events. From their sequence, I would find out:

Whether I was nothing but a smooth surface

Whether I meant anything and had any purpose

Whether it was enough for me to be just an observer

Whether ants or bees had memories.

Any civility or tolerance Egyptians may have had in their hearts was transformed in the Gulf countries where there was oil into harsh coarseness. Their burning and impatient desire to make money changed people into beings of another kind. There always had to be a clear and quick justification for living in exile in such misery.

Once I became more familiar with the ambiance and the new rhythm of the work, I realized that the game had different rules that I had not mastered. You had to be "present and pleasant" even if there was no justification. There was a very insignificant amount work. It didn't matter if you did it or how you did it. What mattered was to make a big commotion about it.

The news organisation was full of "fellow Egyptians". They were the experts in the field. They had the understanding and felt at home in the trade. There was one assertive young man in particular who was quick on his feet and always laughing. He constantly proclaimed that he was "happy". He was happy with the money he made and could hardly believe his good fortune.

When I met Shukri, the well-known journalist whose name I had heard in Cairo, he was tired and drained. Throwing himself into a large seat in an empty room where we were almost alone, he said: "What's brought you here?"

While I was thinking how to answer, I felt him examining me with a glassy eye full of depleted intelligence and exhausted insight. I felt he was saying, "What do you want? Have you come here to watch us, or have you come here to have your share?" I couldn't offer a quick answer and his series of questions started to take a clear direction: he simply wanted to find out how I got there, what connections I had and what my ambitions really were. After a few moments he relaxed when he found out that I had no claws and did not pose a threat to him.

After that we kept an amiable distance and comfortably avoided each other.

* * *

I wait for dawn
but it doesn't come.
Dawn is not a specific time
it's perseverance . . . persistence,
an impatient, reckless voice that tells me:
"Either this . . . or death."

* * *

It is very painful to see a grown man going where he does not belong for the sake of money.

Mr. Fareed had been a senior civil servant in the Ministry of Culture in Egypt and had come to work with us in a junior position. It was that usual old story – he needed money to marry off his daughters and support his children. He told his story as if recounting a soap opera, affecting a tragic and deferential tone of voice that led to nothing. He was always miserable and in a panic over money. The younger staff often treated him as a laughing stock. But Mr Fareed was not miserly and certainly did not have all the aches and ailments that he claimed to have, for he could climb five floors without getting short of breath. It must have been the damned humidity and being far from home.

I don't know how time brought Mr Fareed to his rapid demise, for one of the rules of the game here, according to those who know, was never to appear too eager to survive or to make money, and because he couldn't hide that, or at least pretend to be preoccupied with something else, he soon fell from grace. He was subjected to what is known there as "finishing", i.e. his contract was terminated. (It was impossible for us to see everything around us change so quickly and not go mad.)

My only friend who was a local citizen was called Ali. He represented something new to me. He was free and had an unnatural longing for knowledge. Even a simple conversation with him had real depth, as if what he said was being said for the first time. He was crazy about Abdel Nasser. He kept a photo of him in his wallet and collected his old speeches. He followed in Abdel Nasser's footsteps wherever they led, in search of a primal truth he carried inside him. He thought the Egyptian newspapers were wonderful, and followed news of Egypt impatiently and persistently, as if he would soon have access to the whole truth.

But he was "funny" too. He could see himself and understood how backward he was and how restricted his horizons were. He realised that the world was much bigger than his country that had such a vast amount of money and also much bigger than Egypt, "the Mother of the World".

When he was at peace with himself and not mad at his boss who hated him or at some colleague who was an opportunistic bastard, he would say that he wanted to write a great comedy like Ali Salem's *School for Troublemakers*. It would be about a rich Arab who goes to the United States, where they trick him and turn him into a woman. He soon returns to his country to enter the world of women. There he can see everything and know everything because he would have seen the two faces of society. "But, you know what," he would say, "only an Egyptian could write this comedy because of the jokes."

My friend Ali was active and energetic and had a brilliant mind. Philosophising earnestly, he would say: "We are holding on to a small car whose engine is running in reverse. We're holding it with a rope and pulling and the engine is turning, and we're resisting, but all we are doing is kicking up tons of dust."

* * *

All great poems have value as documents because they include the way the author speaks and an author is a human being – an important one.

* * *

"Are you from Buheira province?"
"I'm from Buheira too."
"Which district?"
"Itay district."
"So we're neighbours."
"That's right, neighbours."

And we became neighbours. We smoked shisha together and became more than friends. He didn't even speak the bizarre Egyptian dialect created for the Egyptians working here – a mixture of colloquial and corrupted classical Arabic. Despite being a jack of all trades, he was completely at a loss. There was something wrong with his papers. He might have been a fugitive or wanted for some crime. He kept his sharp eyes on details of his poor family's life in the village like a hawk. They came to his mind like a fleeting dream.

He had been living here for several years and knew people. He sorted out thieves and cheats no matter how pious they seemed. He knew the market and prices. He could tell how much money you had in your pocket by the feel of your hand. His life there was a mystery. He worked at dozens of trades, made a lot of money and was often out of work. He had even been deported from the country once, but he managed to get back in.

No matter what, the one thing he did at the beginning of every month was to send more than enough money to the family he lived for. At the time he was living in a small room under the stairs of an apartment building. At the age of close to fifty, his only substantial possessions were an old leather suitcase, a small stove, a tea kettle, and a waterpipe for smoking shisha tobacco. He had lost his appetite for food. A loaf of bread in the daytime and a tin of fancy food . . . and after that he would take whatever turned up.

* * *

I saw Egypt in a dream
How different it looked.
Here I am leaving you
only to return one day.

"What upsets me is I that I don't feel at ease with hardly anyone." Homesickness descends heavily upon me. I can't even keep a diary. My desire to own things or earn any money turns into a delusion. No, it turns into a mistake.

* * *

I am not brave . . . when it comes to writing
but I am cautious. . .

* * *

The censor who sits inside my head is stranger than the one who used to spend a few hours at a small desk reading a few articles or news stories and who rarely raised an objection. If he did, it would be superficial and insignificant or easily avoided by simply restructuring the sentence, omitting a pronoun here, replacing a conjunction, or using a different voice or tense.

The censor who now sits inside my head is hard to describe. He is a strange mixture of police officer, fanatical sheikh and obdurate priest. He is a mixture of whips and rough sticks, of the Camel Corps soldier with a Sudanese whip and the indolent soldier on patrol, of the detective disguised in an overcoat and galabia or in dark Ray-Bans with gold frames. He is a censor who can take me away from myself, from people and from the Earth. He makes the beginning of the sentence different from the ending. He censors me through the eyes of friends, who are no longer friends, and through colleagues who once shared my ideas and then disagreed with me without debate, and who then cast judgment on me, saying "You've changed".

My censor is the old conservative bourgeois who still has a place in my morality and who prevents me from exploring the real possibilities of ideas, values and ethics.

My censor is Egyptian, European, religious, cultural, sexual and political. My censor prevents me from expressing myself and communicating with others. He denies me my freedom and turns it into a packaged commodity that you need a ration card to obtain.

* * *

PAUSE BEFORE THE DECLINE

The flat was built of red brick on top of an older building. In front of the white door there was a large empty space which the Muslim Brotherhood used for training, exercise and communal prayers.

This flat, which was the local branch of the Muslim Brotherhood, had clean matting on all the floors. It had several new chairs, one big table, a small bookcase, posters with slogans written in red and green ink, little new copies of the Qur'an, and several framed Qur'anic verses in a clear, simple font, fixed to the walls with small nails. The branch was open all day until hours after the evening prayers. It was always lit with electric lighting, the warmth of faith and the enthusiasm of the young. Three or four Muslim Brothers would bring the place to life with conversation that was magical and beguiling. They radiated cleanliness and honesty. To my heart they conveyed the comfort of faith and the stability of knowing the right path to take. Life in those days was not as loud as it is now.

The rhythm of the day, especially during the summer break, seemed slow and drawn out. The habitual practice of abluting and praying brought about a certain contentment and a sense of maturity – a sense that I was in contact with these adult men and that I was, first of all, in touch with my Creator, who bestowed enough of his Grace to pardon all my complex sins of adolescence. Falling asleep after the long evening prayers and reading the Qur'an felt like yielding to a royal palanquin that carried me over lakes of silver and mercury.

My father was neither fanatical nor exceptionally pious, but he prayed to perfection. The way he stood before his Lord, his voice when he recited the Qur'an and the light that radiated from his broad brow after prayers led me into a world of pure light. For many years, my father was almost a Sufi and an ascetic. He would close the door to his room and in the large, quiet house we would hear the sound of him reciting the Qur'an in a pure, clear voice. Whenever the family faced a crisis or when some worry persisted and took root in the household, our recourse was to long recitations of the Qur'an at night, sitting on the clean white prayer carpet made from the skin of a sheep slaughtered for Eid al-Adha. We saw the magical effects on our lives.

On many nights, I prayed behind him in his room while the rest of the family was asleep. The soft light that reached us from the living room wrapped us in a strange kind of intimacy and created around us a very special link with God. Those night prayers were like our special secret, or a gift of Sufi love that we gave to family members so that our financial straits might come to an end, so that my brother might pass an exam after falling behind or so that my sister might recover from a long illness.

Praying at the Muslim Brotherhood's headquarters or in the clean open space outside was something else. It gave me a sense of power and belonging. The lessons after the evening prayers often left me with more questions than answers. Only two or three of the Brotherhood members knew how to talk calmly in a way that juggled carefully all aspects of life's problems and sort them out patiently. Others lashed out with sharp sword, slashing away but unable to convey warnings and threats. Instead they struck fear, guilt and a sense of insignificance in young minds.

We used to sit in a large circle in the inner room of the branch after the evening prayers. Everyone introduced himself, saying, "Your Brother in God so and so . . .", each in turn until the circle was complete. Once everyone knew each other, the speaker would start the lesson.

Some of the speakers would ask specific questions about the lives of the Brothers and their families, and how they behaved at home. Their answers were candid, honest and precise, but the questions often gave rise to various forms of embarrassment, to which the group responded with suppressed laughter or disguised ridicule. The large social and economic disparities between Brotherhood members led to various criticisms of members' conduct and behaviour, which were brought up and discussed. But no one could do anything about them and offer any solutions. Religious and sports activities prevented any frank engagement with the social and economic disparities between members. Words were often spoken about solidarity, equality and helping others, but meeting constantly and living together for most of the day highlighted those disparities and left a heavy deposit, like wet sand, in our minds.

I had a wealthy friend who lived nearby and was also a member of the branch of the Brotherhood. He was athletic, strong and well built, and his physical prowess gave him a privileged position in the chapter. He was the captain of the football team and one of the few in wrestling and boxing. His piety, his praying and his religious views were powerful and disciplined. He was almost military in appearance, but he had a kind heart and a young, excitable mind. At a discussion session after evening prayers, one of the Brothers spoke, without mentioning any specific name, about a certain Brother's sister, saying that she was going to a foreign school, that she was often seen coming home after sunset and that she wore clothes that were inappropriate for the sister of a Muslim Brother.

I looked around me, knowing that he meant this neighbour of mine and his beautiful sister, whose visits to our house brought much joy and delight. She was a friend of my sisters and my father and mother saw her as a model for the woman with a future since she combined a foreign education, including foreign languages – the weapon of the age, with a sense of humour and intelligence. My mother especially liked her and always prayed for her to prosper and succeed.

I saw that my neighbour's face had turned pale yellow and his lips and face were quivering, but he endured the rest of the lesson with difficulty, then hurried off without waiting to go home with me as usual.

Late that night as I was at home listening to an Umm Kulthum concert on the radio with my family, we were surprised to hear crying and screaming coming from our neighbour's house. My mother rushed to the neighbour's house in her house clothes, while the screaming grew louder and louder, as if someone was being slaughtered.

My mother came back in tears and said that my friend had started beating his sister severely. He had hit her in the mouth and fractured her head and was insisting that she stay at home and that he would kill her if she went back to school. He was the eldest brother and the head of the family had died some years earlier.

That was the first vicious act of aggression I saw committed in the name of religion. But time managed to solve the crisis and history did not come to a halt. The girl won and the Brother gave way, I don't know how. It was the force of life and no one can stop it.

The girl went to Europe alone and came back as a doctor. She now has a large clinic and a happy family. As for the brother, he disappeared. I found out years later that he migrated to the United States, where he has been living for many years.

Translated from *Waqfa qabla al-Munhadar* (Pause before the Decline), published by General Egyptian Book Organization (GEBO), Cairo 1995

A TRAVELLING TALE

LINA HAWYAN ALHASSAN

Journey to Yasser's Grave

CHAPTERS FROM THE NOVEL *WOLVES DO NOT FORGET*,
TRANSLATED BY SAMIRA KAWAR

A gravestone arose in my heart forever

1

"Wolf, why do you howl? The two of us are so alike."
An old Bedouin song

They say wolves have memories, that they do not forget, and that that is why they keep howling until the last words disappear. Has sorrow made some animals weep? That is one of the most persistent images that comes to mind as I hear my aunt mourning my brother aloud. "I will not forget you, even if the wolf forgets." An authentic Bedouin lament. I hear the echoes of the frenzied wolf's pulsing howls as it seeks an impossible forgetfulness. Not a single wolf can free itself of its memory. Khalaf, my grandmother's shepherd, who died long ago, used to know why wolves howled. He understood the howls of wolves from their rhythm, their length, and the intermissions between them.

Sometimes, he would say: "These intermittent collective howls are intended to frighten other creatures nearby."

"These short continuous howls are by wolves exchanging messages and agreeing a hunting plan."

"That short howl is a wolf courting a she-wolf."

"That long howl belongs to a wolf whose she-wolf has died."

Once, the howling went on much longer than usual. The howls were long, and lasted throughout the night.

That day, Khalaf said, as his eyes stared into the darkness of the desert: "That is the howling of a she-wolf that has lost her cub."

At the time, my intuition gave me no inkling about why those howls had attracted my attention, why they had pierced my hearing. I recall them as though they had never stopped. It was a savage, solo lament that longed to spread as far as possible.

The following evening, Khalaf returned with the herd behind him, preceded by his dog, who headed for a pile of food scraps consisting of cracked wheat cooked in stock. Khalaf went to his usual spot by the terrace, where my grandmother served him his food. He dejectedly told my grandmother about a wolf cub that had been hunted by a townie from Aleppo. The townie had circled the cub's body all night, gloating over his catch. The next morning, he had wrapped the cub's body in a plastic bag and surrounded it with ice, before taking it with him to Aleppo.

Khalaf's sympathy for the she-wolf was obvious, even though he used to stay up most winter nights to protect his lambs from her claws. The she-wolf was well known in the Qasr Ibn Wardan desert for her savagery, and her intelligence in tricking shepherds and grabbing their lambs. She had kept him awake for many a night.

Night fell again, and the howls of the Ibn Wardan she-wolf filled the desert air. We all breathed in her grief. Grief has a smell. That night, no young girls came to spend the evening by my grandmother's fireside, and no one chatted as the howls echoed the pains of hell, the merciless sorrow of hell.

2

"O wolf that strikes fear in the hearts of gazelles"

YASSER IS DEAD.

I scream and scream and scream.

Were it not for that scream, there would be silence. Pain lashes us and the most ancient exclamation made by humans bursts forth, from the time when they used their voices like animals. It is my absolute cry, the cry of a savage gorilla in a jungle never entered by man.

The highway from Damascus to Homs.

My sense of security? Wounded by merciless fear. My stuttering and despair have made me conspicuous.

In a single moment, life becomes like a ship that has lost its sail. It sways in the middle of the sea, neither drowning, nor reaching the safety of land. I who am fond of ancient pathways, have inherited my Bedouin forebears love for creating new roads. Here I am taking the same route that thousands of Syrians have taken towards grief.

Like a scene out of a silent film: everyone is sad, and any words that can be said tremble on dry lips, mine and theirs. We look like shells smashed by a sudden wave.

Before travelling, I went to buy mourning clothes, although my wardrobe was full of black clothes. But I had not prepared any black ones that were suitable for mourning.

When events had broken out in my country, I had resisted the urge to become one of a group of heroes. We know what happens to heroes. They die, they are killed. The cowards own the Earth. The hero's fire is smothered by the coward's mud. Heroes die because they are heroes of memory and do not forget. Be smart and get rid of your "heroism". My brother had not thought of heroism at all, but he died. Am I wearing the hijab? Am I taking cover? Disguising myself? Or am I protecting myself because they have left us no other choice except that miserable black?

The road between Damascus and the village cannot be travelled without wearing a hijab. It is the first condition that must be met for basic security, so that you can at least avoid the bullets of snipers, as the driver tells us. But which snipers? There are many of them, as we have discovered, and they belong to all sides. Death is like the wind, and when it blows, it comes from all directions.

The coach stops again as shooting breaks out, and the traffic behind it grinds to a halt. Everyone crouches down automatically. I am sitting in the first row behind the driver and his assistant, so I am in the line of fire even if I lower my head. I busy myself by turning around to look at the two seats behind me, where my sister Maram and brother Wael sit, having suddenly arrived to take me to Yasser's graveside, to reassure myself that they have lowered their heads. I am the older sister, after all, and continue to practise a kind of guardianship that all younger siblings find off-putting.

Twenty minutes elapse, the sound of shooting begins to subside and becomes intermittent and slightly more distant. The traffic begins to move. The question is: What lies ahead of us as we are still only on the outskirts of Adra?

My mobile phone rings and I hear the voice of our younger brother, Basel, who is also surrounded by shooting at the coach station in Haresta. I reduce my wishes in life to only one: that the shooting should stop until the last coach to Saudi Arabia has set off, so that we can ensure that at least one member of the family is outside of this hell. As the shooting on the road to Adra stops and we resume our journey, the coach leaving for Saudi Arabia also sets forth.

The driver's assistant tries hard to hide his tension by offering the passengers water and coffee, attempting to trick his wrecked nerves and theirs.

We arrive at one of the few cafés that is still open on the way to the disaster-hit city of Homs. Wael walks ahead of me and gives me his arm. I trip over my long robe like a child learning to walk. The "kindness" of the waiter at the café as he lists the various kinds of sandwiches on offer takes me by surprise. I cannot taste anything, except for the bitterness that is clumped in my throat. Wael assumes his role as a doctor, and insists that I eat something to avoid a sudden fall in my blood pressure. Grief and hunger are a health disaster, he says. I survey my surroundings, provoked by the silence that is reminiscent of a graveyard. All the passengers seem sad.

I am confused by my new hijab. I catch a fleeting glimpse of a small bird, slightly bigger than a sparrow, flying above. I want to tell Wael about my wish at this moment: If only I were just a bird. I try to move the large stone that blocks my throat, which has been worn out with crying, to get the sounds out of it. I am no good at dealing with the pin that is supposed to hold my hijab in place. Maram seems more at ease than me in her black abaya.

I keep my glasses on as I sip some tea on the outskirts of the city of Homs, of which more than half has been destroyed. Wael is smoking, and I follow him to the window, stretching out two trembling fingers to signify that I want a cigarette. I have never been a smoker, but one cigarette might not be a bad idea to release some of the sobbing that has frozen in my throat.

A loudspeaker announces that the break is over. Ten minutes have passed, and all the passengers head for the coach with a terrible calm. I trip again over the hem of my robe as I board. Wael and Maram's arms are close by, allowing me to reach my seat without falling over. The coach moves, and the driver's assistant starts to close the curtains, and strongly warns the passengers against looking through the windows or opening the curtains. He says this is to avoid snipers' bullets. But I catch some whispers around me that these are instructions issued by the security services to stop people photographing the destruction that local television avoids showing.

The coach draws closer to Homs. I am easily able to calculate the distance of a route that I have taken scores of times during seasonal trips to our faraway village in the countryside, east of Hama. The more accurate way of referring to it is "the Eastern Hama Desert", but the government fears the idea of the "desert, Bedouins and nomads", so it avoids names of that sort. During my years as a university student, when I used to tell my classmates that I belonged to the "tribes", they laughed in protest and disdain, because all of them were sure that there were no tribes in Syria. People were either urban dwellers, or villagers and peasants. So, for someone to be of Bedouin stock was strange, impossible and weird.

I steal a glance beneath the curtain. A blue sign reading "Homs" assaults my vision.

I see Homs in my mind's eye through a burning route, and the archway of a bridge that I cannot see assaults my imagination. This time, we will not enter Homs. A verse of poetry by poet Nassib Aridah was emblazoned on the archway. It read: "Take me back to Homs, even within a shroud." He had emigrated to Latin America, and his wish had not come true. But Yasser had passed by Homs "of the shroud". He had preferred it to Damascus, and had decided to live there with his small family.

Why did they kidnap Yasser from his place of work? To demand a ransom. Syria had suddenly turned into a hell when some had revolted against the repression of forty years and others had been willing to ride the wave and exploit "the revolution". Our country had turned into an unbearable inferno, particularly when the "revolutionaries" had decided that all state employees were their enemies. Syria had become entrapped by armed groups hiding behind the banner of "freedom" to cover up their blackmail and kidnap activities.

Yasser's sin was to be a state employee. They attacked his place of work in the city of Sadad at night. He was treacherously beaten on his head with the butt of a gun while he slept. They did the same to his colleagues. He was bloodied and unconscious when they tied up his hands and feet and put him in the back of a vehicle. They drove off across the Qalamoun mountains to get to a camp that raised the banner and slogan of "freedom".

The driver's assistant notices how swollen my eyes are. I have spent the previous few days crying. He hands me a plastic cup that he fills with tea from a thermos that he shares with the driver. He is sad and silent. He seems used to seeing passengers crying. Weeping has become the only outlet for Syrians. All Syrians are crying, without exception. Weeping is our fate.

I recall the sound of the she-wolf's howling thirty years ago.

How fragile our words and poems are compared to the howling of a wolf. They all have their words: the president, the party chairman, the imam at the mosque. Animals have a language that really speaks, whereas we humans speak to hide the truth. We speak without saying anything. Language is a big hoax.

I ruminate on all that as I listen to the driver stating his political opinions, which quickly turned into a rhetorical speech.

Some things cannot be written. The wound goes too deep, and the part of me that died with my brother's death disappears completely. My resentment burns against those who wounded this country and dragged it through the mud. Who are they? None of them will confess. They all raise the banner of innocence.

The howling of the past poisons us all in the end, that eternal poison that courses through us, the poison of sects. It will kill us and wipe us out of existence. Everyone kills and shouts that this is for the sake of the homeland.

The memory of Wansah, the young Yazidi girl who escaped from her sect about thirty years ago to marry a Bedouin man, comes alive. I met her after she had taken refuge with my uncle. She used to tell me about the god that she worshipped. His name was "Tawûsê Melek", and she explained to me that he was a "Peacock Angel". That day, I had asked my grandmother why we worshipped "Allah", while Wansah worshipped "Tawûsê Melek". My grandmother said without giving it any thought: "It is not important whom we worship. What counts is how we worship. Humans worship someone in heaven so that they become better. All we have to do to be believers is to become better." After living temporarily with my grandmother in the desert for a year, we had moved to a village near Homs because of my father's military career. The villagers were mostly Christian, and the teacher told my father that she was at a loss as to how to give me marks for religious studies. My father had simply said: "Just have her study the Christian religion." So I used to cross myself before breaking my Ramadan fast with my mother.

Humans have it in their nature to prefer being different. That is the only way to explain all these identities that have been created by the game of origins and religions. Artificial identities, some of which are fake, and all of which are ultimately fatal.

We come to the end of the detour. I have been unable to glance surreptitiously towards Homs, which is to the right of the coach as it heads eastwards towards the city of Selmiyah on the edge of the desert.

We stop at a roadblock as we arrive at the town of Mukhtariyah. It is an army checkpoint. I move the curtain slightly to the side, and the first thing I catch sight of is the gun of a tank. A ditch has been dug around it to protect it, and it appears to be below street level. The gun is very close to my window, and what I think is the district of Talbisiah can be seen in the distance. Columns of smoke connect the land to the sky, and the ground beneath us shudders to the sound of shelling. The coach also shakes as the shelling reverberates. One of the young men travelling with us is silently dragged off the coach. All the passengers look on sadly as he is taken away to an unknown destiny. Not one of us dares to move the curtains by even one centimetre to find out what is happening to him, but it is very unlikely that he will ever be seen again. Disappearance is a fate that befalls many in my homeland.

Once the officer on duty at the checkpoint has inspected all the passengers' identity cards, the coach moves on. At almost twelve noon, the landscape begins to change. The land gradually divests itself of trees, and its green cover gives way to the dusty colour of the desert, although some greenery persists in the shape of regularly spaced olive trees growing in small plots of square farmland. Nature takes on an appearance that is close to my heart, for the heart cannot love something unless it is complicit with memory. I catch sight of those wide-open spaces, and I feel that captivating sensation that anyone returning home recognises. I recall my recent Facebook conversation with a Syrian dissident who fled into exile thirty years ago. He told me that his sole wish was "to return to my village, so that I can die and be buried in its soil and be devoured by its worms".

Is it a sign of the intelligence of our Arab language that a faraway village is called a *day'ah*? It is very logical, for the noun is derived from the word *dayaa'*, which means "lost". My village fits that description. It is far away, on the edge of the desert, as well as on the edge of the fields and rolling hills to the northeast of Hama. Half the road leading to it is very badly paved, and the other half is unpaved. It is nothing more than a strip that twists like the mood of an old

Bedouin. Cars using it cannot increase their speed because the wheels would just turn and dust would pile up around them, behind them and in front of them, their passengers resisting suffocation only by dreaming about arriving and taking a bath.

We drew close to the city of Selmiyah, and my memory reacted like a bale of hay set alight by a running cat with a burning tail. The tears that my glasses had hidden welled up and I stifled my sobs. Fate can reawaken several paths, scrambling my sense of direction and confusing me. My papers fly around. Am I really a writer?

When you are sad, your memory becomes as stubborn as a mule, and it shows you the dark face of history.

Yasser is gone. He left us good memories and five children, including a girl, and their mother, who will grieve endlessly.

Cheerful, funny Yasser, fond of mimicking others. He transformed the simplest event into something to laugh about. He will never laugh again. Has he left me some laughter?

The coach passes through the entrance to Selmiyah and I wonder: "Will I ever laugh again?"

It is noon, and the streets are empty except for a few vehicles of the kind that only tribespeople buy: a small pickup truck, a Kia, a Chevrolet, a Toyota.

Time contracts on that sad afternoon, and we wait by our suitcases for my cousin Younes, who was supposed to meet us in a rented car to take us forty kilometres north.

The city lacks sufficient mobile phone coverage, and we have to stick to our spot as we wait. Wael distracts himself by smoking, and Maram looks around like an anxious gazelle surrounded by a mirage. I am the only one preoccupied by fear. Anxiety destabilises me, and a sticky grief confuses me. My father warned us against coming, because the roads are dangerous, and are paved by death more than ever before.

Because of the circumstances of Yasser's death, I had not been able to attend his burial, or to embrace his grave. Runaway memories seeking a refuge crowd into my head as the wind blows around it — the wind of dispersal. Although we are standing in the city, I glimpse the dust in the distance, eddies of dust, and the unending desert horizon. We are in the desert, and a man in his Bedouin garb passes us, transporting us instantly to the desert of beginnings.

* * *

A week ago, my mother woke in the morning with her heart set on fire by a vague anxiety. She tried to phone Yasser, but his mobile phone just rang, no one answered. So she concluded that either he was not well or something had happened to him. We were unable to set her mind at ease. We tried to call him again, but his mobile phone had been switched off – he could not be reached. The landline rang, and my father informed us Yasser had been kidnapped. I immediately began to spout a torrent of reassuring words, which I knew were lies. But I could find no other way of calming my mother down except for the lies I uttered in her hearing about the "noble nature of the Free Army", whereas a deep voice that I could not fathom kept wordlessly mouthing to me, "This is our rendezvous with death."

The day passed as we awaited a call from the kidnappers, hoping they would make their contact and demand a sum of money to finance their war for their "desired freedom". Anxiety filled our home like a rabid dog barking at the fog. We made endless calls to all our acquaintances – dissenters, loyalists, officers. Evening descended and an endless night prevailed, and the phone call we awaited did not come. Hope is like an uprooted tooth.

My father, who used to spend most of the year with my mother on the farm in our village after his retirement from the army, was 340 kilometres away. He called us almost every hour, but there was no news. It is very easy to die, and very difficult to live.

The black abaya, the hijab and the glasses increase my sense of suffocation, and my anxiety intensifies on that miserable afternoon as we stand on the side of the main road at the entrance to the city of Selmiyah. An anxious half hour passes, and Younes does not appear. Worrying questions emerge. The lack of communications in that area of the desert has facilitated the most horrible of crimes. For a moment, I regret we have come, but we took the decision collectively. Wael, Maram and I would be by the side of our father and mother, and our brother's wife, bereaved by the death of her husband and father of her five children. Yasser's family left Homs a year ago, after a shell had fallen on the lounge in their house, and they went to live on the farm. But death came in the wake of that shell and plucked away the family's father. Grief is the means of bringing us to this desert, where one searches for tears that resemble one's own. When you are scared, despair plays havoc with hope and takes over.

Finally, Younes appears. He has been waiting for us at another place nearby, where he thought the passengers from the coach would alight. After exchanging the usual words of condolence and a few tears, we put our suitcases in the boot of the hired car. My father has not dared to send his own car to pick us up. The white Mercedes is well known in these parts. It belongs to Brigadier General Hawyan. It has not left the farm for several months. My father, an ex-officer who retired from the army about eight years ago, is being asked to mutiny. Every now and then, he receives a nasty message from some low-ranking, immoral officer or other who has broken away, demanding that my father break away. My father responds: "Break away? In my retirement?" He is in his late sixties, and someone is asking him to join a new front that defines its enemy according to agendas that are backed by God only knows who.

The hired car sets off from Selmiyah, heading north to Deirat al-Shambal, a land that had often inspired me to write novels. Sunflowers line the sides of the road. A plant that follows the sun like a blind person that can only perceive the glow. The sunflowers rise along the edges of fields planted with yellow corn. A few neglected fig trees that have acclimatised to the desert's barren logic are scattered here and there.

The sunflower discs captivate my vision, reminding me of Van Gogh's famous painting. What freedom did this flower have to not follow the sun, and to not be called a "sunflower"?

Some vegetable patches appear around the houses. The mirage causes the horizon to merge with the range of low hills to our left and the remains of an upright castle called Shmeimis that perches like a heron separated from the rest of its flock.

Whenever we catch sight of a military checkpoint in the distance, we become anxious. We are passing through villages whose inhabitants belong to another sect, and our hijabs will make them suspicious, and might ignite the enmity that politics have crafted with an amazing deftness.

To ease my anxiety, Wael tells me about the various checkpoints he crossed with my cousin Khalid as they searched for Yasser's body. He tells me how a "Free Army" checkpoint stopped them on the outskirts of the town of Yabroud, where they had been told that kidnapped people received hospital treatment. Everyone at the hospital denied that a young man fitting Yasser's description had been treated, or had received first aid there. The aim of their denials was to negotiate over the body. But one doctor took pity on my brother, possibly out of a sense of complicity, since they were both members of the same profession. He secretly gestured to my brother to meet him at a corner in the hospital that was not monitored by cameras. That doctor saved us from the labyrinth of financial negotiations with the kidnappers, who had wanted to sell us the body. He described Yasser accurately, and assured my brother that he had arrived dead at dawn on one of the previous days. He pressed my brother's hand as he saw the tears welling up in the eyes of a man who had suddenly lost all hope of finding his brother alive. The question was, where was the body? Yasser had turned into a body that we wanted at any price.

Yasser, whenever your name is mentioned, a bullet passes by, a bullet that penetrates my insides, my memory, my consciousness, my insomnia. Perhaps that is why I am writing this now, in the hope that my resentment will decrease, if only by a few centimetres.

Before we found your body, there was a small rebellious hope inside of me that perhaps you were still alive, so I was the only one to cling to the belief that you were not dead!

But two days after your kidnap, the final news arrived: Yasser is dead.

I had been at work at the newspaper, pulling together everything I could about the nature of the "Free Army" and its methods of kidnap and how to pay ransom. Wael had called and had told me in a shaky voice: "Come home."

* * *

The she-wolf howls. Her howl is free and untrammelled.

In a single moment, all paths fail to get me there, to the land where night is passed in the company of wolves that do not sleep, that howl to experience mourning, howl to seek salvation. They release their howls to the high heavens. Has anyone told the wolves that the real road to salvation plumbs the depths? We are not washed of our grief without throwing ourselves into our own internal depths, our hell, to be born anew. Do not try to trick your grief, wolf, with all that howling. Descend to the depths of your hell, fight your battle alone to find salvation.

There, where all the paths are that the tribespeople drive down with covered faces in their large red Chevrolet vehicles. A Bedouin cannot buy a vehicle that is not red. Bedouins share a certitude that red vehicles can never get stuck in the mud. All the roads they use are unpaved and in the winter most turn into muddy traps. Only a red Chevrolet can avoid them.

Some of you might have your cities, your streets, your cafés. But I have other places: a Bedouin homeland and dirt tracks that throw up dust when I use them, concealing all other roads. You use asphalt roads that municipalities or governments have paved for you, but I use tracks that my uncle once created.

In the cities, when one of you has a birthday, you get chocolates and toys for presents. But one day, I received a very different kind of gift that I doubt anyone has ever had before. I got a dust track that I chose myself.

To get a track of your own in the land of your forefathers means you will carry a very special kind of burden. At the time, I was seventeen. There had been several rain showers that winter evening. My uncle rearranged his headdress, rolled down the car windows, and said: "I will give you a track as a present."

Why?

We must take the roads within us, our roads. We will be lost if we take the roads of others. Our roads do not exhaust us. As soon as we feel exhaustion, fear, and darkness, we conclude that we have taken the wrong way, one that is not ours. As soon as someone draws us onto their own way, we will be lost, time will be wasted and we will spend our lives in a world for which we were not created.

The tyre tracks of the Chevrolet could clearly be seen along the road, which had become wet with rain. Ever since then, my cousins had become accustomed to using that track as a reasonable shortcut when they made their way to the main roads towards the cities of Hama and Selmiyah. My uncle would certainly have had no inkling that my siblings and I would travel along that track that day in the summer of 2012 to mourn the death of our brother, Yasser.

We travel several kilometres northwards, nearing my brother's grave. My mind sinks into the jungle of memories from those terrible days when I was sure that Yasser was not dead.

My father had come to Damascus to be with us to share the ordeal of awaiting a phone call from Yasser's kidnappers. The phone call had not come. While in the district of Nabak, he had managed to get the phone number of one of Yasser's colleagues who had been kidnapped with him, and who had been released in return for a ransom, according to rumours. My father dialled the number, and the man's wife took the call. She did not realise the caller was Yasser's father, and thought the caller was a friend or acquaintance inquiring after her husband. She related the story of her husband's kidnapping, and how his brothers had sold a plot of land they owned in their village to collect the necessary amount of money. At the end, she innocently said: "My husband's poor colleague, Yasser, is dead."

My father was accompanying my cousin in a modest Skoda car to avoid attracting the attention of the gangs that were on the roads throughout Syria. My bereaved father hung up and wept, then called us and asked us to meet him in the village, where the wake would be held. He returned to the village to set up a black tent, according to the Bedouin way, to accept condolences for Yasser's death.

As soon as I came through the gate to the house, I heard crying, and I knew that some verified news about Yasser must have arrived. A single wail of grief can tear out your throat, and crying can become a pickaxe that digs up your insides. All the niceties that humans have invented are blown away when you receive news that your brother has been murdered. You beat your chest, bang your head against the wall, writhe around on the floor, but the outcome is the same: Yasser is dead.

"But where is the body? How can you hold a wake without a burial?" I had been the only one to ask that question. My grieving mother had left immediately with Wael and Maram, and I had propped up my broken self with the idea that since there was no body, perhaps Yasser was not dead. I let them leave Damascus, and remained alone in the house, holding on to the idea that Yasser might, for example, be wounded.

I was alone when I was finally able to speak with Yasser's colleague, whom the kidnappers had released. He told me frankly: "Sister, Yasser died on my shoulder. We were all beaten on our heads with rifle butts. We bled for a while, then regained consciousness. We had been blindfolded, and our hands and feet had been tied. Yasser was on my shoulder bleeding, but he did not regain consciousness like the rest of us. I heard one of the kidnappers speaking to someone else on the phone. He must have been an officer, because he was addressing him as 'sir'. I overheard him saying that one of the kidnapped persons was unconscious, and that he was still bleeding. It seems he was ordered to take him to the hospital. He ordered the driver to take him to Yabroud Hospital across the mountains. They dropped us off somewhere in the hills, and continued towards Yabroud, which seemed close to the camp where they left us. Three days later, they took us to the main road leading to Homs after they had contacted our families and received the amounts of money that they had demanded. I noticed that Yasser was not with us, and I asked them about him. They replied with careless indifference, 'God have mercy on his soul.'"

At the start of events, before the noble participants had been killed and the villains taken over, one of my colleagues at the newspaper sensed my great sympathy for the peaceful demonstrations. He told me: "Those who have been humiliated and repressed will achieve nothing more than revenge." The revolution turned into a dirty war, a war that all the political parties to it wanted, and a war that was nurturing itself on the blood of all Syrians.

* * *

Even daytime in the desert can rekindle the memory of a grieving she-wolf's howl that filled the night.

The rhythm of those long howls thirty years ago fills my hearing, as we cross those silent, dusty, empty spaces in the height of the heat. Silence is the desert's favourite wisdom. Silence humiliates all else. Life goes quiet, the sky goes quiet, and the Earth humiliates us with its silence and leaves us to chatter on endlessly. We imagine its heaven and its hell, and it allows us to cry with an unrestricted freedom.

We stop at the first checkpoint after leaving Selmiyah. The officer examines our identity cards with much suspicion. The driver's and my cousin's clothes – the traditional garb of any Bedouin – and the black robes that Maram and I have on are the main reason for his initial suspicion. The officer returns our identity cards after Wael produces my father's card, which indicates that he is a retired officer. The driver moves the car forward, murmuring: "God have mercy." He tells us painful stories about cars that aroused suspicion at government checkpoints, and their passengers who met terrible fates. There is nothing to prevent the soldiers' guns that are aimed at the road from firing. The checkpoint is manned by a few soldiers, who have recently begun their military service, and a low-ranking officer. They have been thrown into the desert, and have barely managed to dig a trench and surround it with a few sandbags that give them a temporary illusion of protection. Any car that appears on the horizon heralds a potential suicide attack by a non-Arabic speaking bomber who will blow himself up in their midst, destroying himself and them along with him. We have fallen into a futile web of hatred. We usually say: "history repeats itself", and it often uses the same kind of villains to wreck the beautiful dreams of the virtuous.

In keeping with the Bedouin tradition of laying out dirt tracks, we take the one that only members of our tribe are familiar with. This allows us to avoid the paved roads that everyone else uses, and that are peppered with checkpoints manned by parties loyal to different sides and espousing different ideologies. The only common denominator that links them is murder. Killing is the easiest thing to do, and it often seems more merciful compared to other crimes.

The hired car moves through the hills, like a mouse wandering through a palace. The windows are open, the hot air sears our faces and fear jangles our nerves. I had not expected the situation to be so dangerous, and the driver does not relent from recounting his tales about the terrible events that have occurred on such isolated roads. Any armed villains with a car could stake out a corner and improvise a temporary roadblock to rob and kill, even though their vehicle might be emblazoned with all the necessary slogans of freedom and democracy. The intermittently hot July air heightens my anxiety. My mother will blame us, with the look of scared birds in her eyes. She will say: "Why did you come? It's dangerous." I will be silent, and not say anything to intensify her pain. After death, the eyes of the dead shine like an exploding star, a star that has died, but whose shining light we see as it traverses through time. Yasser, how could I explain it to my mother? Who can say something appropriate to console a mother? To any mother who has lost her son. It is all over. The only thing we have left of him is his grave.

Translated from the novel *al-Dhiaab La Tansa* (Wolves Do Not Forget), published by Dar al-Adab, Beirut, 2016

BOOK REVIEWS

Paul Starkey reviews
No Road to Paradise
by Hassan Daoud
translated by Marilyn Booth
Hoopoe Publishing, Cairo, 2016.
ISBN 978-9774168178. Pbk,
304 pages. £11.99 / $13.95

Facing up to one's life . . .

Hassan Daoud is the author of ten novels and three short story collections, and has recently been described as 'one of Lebanon's most important living writers'. *No Road to Paradise*, originally published in Arabic in 2013 as *La Tariq ila al-Janna*, is a work that can only serve to reinforce that view, having already (in the Arabic original) been awarded the Naguib Mahfouz Medal for Literature in 2015. Set in rural Lebanon, and told in the first person, the novel explores the predicament of a Shi'ite rural imam who has failed to find fulfilment in either his religious or his family life. Confronted with a diagnosis of apparently terminal cancer, and forced to undergo a life-changing operation that leaves him impotent, he is led to question his religious values as he struggles to reassess his place in the world.

The narrator comes from a family of imams originally of some distinction, at least in the local context: '[his] grandfather Sayyid Murtada's fatwa on how a husband could return to his wife after divorcing her was still known and talked about, as was his ode to the Imam Ali' (p.131). The narrator's father, however, did not write anything, or 'utter anything that became part of a public legacy (p.132); and the narrator himself has inherited neither the piety nor the scholarship of his forebears; he took up his religious calling solely to please

his family, and his religious books remain almost entirely unread. The sterility of his sham religious life is mirrored in his family situation: having consented to an arranged marriage, he finds himself bound to a wife whom he does not love, and of the three children he has had with her, two are deaf-mute boys. In the course of the narrative, his long-senile father dies, adding a further element of emotional deprivation to an already bleak existence.

In this seemingly remorseless sterile environment, almost the only obviously positive element is provided by the narrator's brother's widow, with whom the narrator is in love, and it is the progress of their relationship that to a large extent gives the novel coherence, enabling the author to give his narrative at least the semblance of a logical progression. To speak of a 'relationship' is perhaps to suggest too much, however, for though the narrator's physical impotence does not put an end to his lust, it inevitably ends in frustration 'That I had lost what I had lost in the operation didn't lessen my desire for her', he remarks: 'No longer having it didn't stop those images of her body from pursuing me. The physical longings were just as strong as before.' Their intimate, physical encounter is described in sensuous detail, but a moment comes when she 'suddenly, quickly became alert to the fact that what we were doing together had ended' (p.210); declining a cup of coffee, the narrator leaves, pitched in every direction by a 'messy blend of rapture and dis-ease' as he drives home.

For the most part, this is a narrative that moves forward not so much on the basis of bold decisions or dramatic events as through enigmatic hints, through subtle shifts in the attitudes of the various players toward each other, and through the progress of the narrator's inner struggles, conducted against the background of his progressive physical deterioration. Suffused with an almost English tone of un-

BOOK REVIEWS

Hassan Daoud

derstatement, essential actions are often reduced to the bare minimum: when the narrator's father dies, for example, 'I did not even have to turn his face toward Mecca, the direction of prayer. He had already that for himself, many days ago. That was how he had prepared himself to die, suppressing any wish he might have to give his side and shoulder a rest by turning onto his other side.' (p160)

Despite the narrative being set in the specific Lebanese village of Shqifiyeh – and despite the obviously Shi'ite intellectual and geographical reference points – the novel probably tells us more about the human spirit, and about man's emotions, reflections and fear in the face of imminent death, than it does about anything in rural Lebanon, or indeed, the Middle East as a whole. Toward the end of the work, however, a more immediate reality appears to intrude somewhat, as the imam's mosque is all but taken over by what appear to be a group of Islamic fundamentalists. Although the process is described for the most part in elliptical terms, in line with the general tone and style of the work, the end result – as the narrator hands over his books to the group – seems ominously symbolic of contemporary events.

Although this novel has not met with universal approbation among reviewers, I personally found it one of the most powerful and impressive Arabic works that I have read in a long time, well deserving of the Naguib Mahfouz medal that it has already won. It has found in Marilyn Booth an English translator well worthy of the task, and her seamless translation deserves to be widely read.

BOOK REVIEWS

Laura Ferreri reviews
The American Quarter
by Jabbour Douaihy
translated by Paula Haidar
Interlink Publishing, October 2017
ISBN-13: 978-1566560306,
Pbk, 208 pages $15.00/ £11.15

Dealing with loss ..
and the past

Set in a poor neighbourhood in the Lebanese city of Tripoli, Jabbour Douaihy's *The American Quarter* is more than just a novel, it is a journey through the streets of Tripoli and into the minds of the protagonists; three people different in age, experience and aspirations that, however, have a lot in common.

Abdelkarim Al-Azzam is the heir of an important family in Tripoli. His grandfather was a prominent political figure, for whom the city of Tripoli erected a statue honouring his brave deeds. However, times have changed and Abdelkarim's father feels the need to protect his son, keeping him away from public attention. Not being allowed to mingle with the other children, Abdelkarim grows isolated finding refuge in poetry. When the Islamists start taking over the city with violent attacks, Abdelkarim is sent to Paris where he enjoys a freedom he has never had before. The French capital becomes the stage for his intense love story with a Serbian ballerina, Valeria, who becomes the centre of his life. After she suddenly abandons him, Abdelkarim, heartbroken, returns to Tripoli where he resumes his secluded life never losing hope that Valeria will come back into his life.

The second protagonist of the novel is Intisar, daughter of Imm Mahmoud, the maid of the Al-Azzam's family. Intisar's life follows a path that is the opposite of Abdelkarim's. She lives in the American Quarter free to do anything she wants until the day she meets Bilal Muhsin and falls for him. She marries him against her mother's will, but soon she realizes that he is a loafer and will not help taking care of his growing family. To provide for her family, Intisar takes over Imm Mahmoud's job at the Al-Azzam's family becoming ever more disappointed in her life. Her children are the only joy left to Intisar, especially her firstborn son, Ismael, the third protagonist of this novel.

Growing up at Imm Mahmoud's home, Ismael has lived a privileged life compared to his siblings, but, following his grandmother's passing, he is forced to move back with his parents. To help out Intisar, he starts working for a baker who slowly convinces him to join the Islamic Guidance Association, a radical Islamic group. After being recruited for a suicide mission in Iraq, Ismael leaves home without informing anyone of his plan.

Intisar is heartbroken because of her son's disappearance, but never believes the rumour about his death in a terrorist attack and lives her life convinced that Ismael will come back.

The protagonists of this novel share a feeling of loss and the hope that what is lost can come back, they highlight the vulnerability of the human condition when facing drastic changes and the instinct of clinging to the past hoping it will return.

The American Quarter is a work of literary beauty; Douaihy's style and his love for detail give a power to the novel that goes beyond a good story. Reading *The American Quarter* feels like observing an intricate painting and have the chance to get closer and study its details and feel like you are part of the it and you can relate to its characters.

Jabbour Douaihy

I particularly enjoyed Douaihy's descriptive style in the chapter narrating Abdelkarim's childhood. Abdelkarim's feeling of not belonging is beautifully conveyed through the narration of his trips on the school bus or on his father's Jaguar during which he observes the world around him. He wishes to be part of it, but he is kept separated from it by the vehicles' window. Reading this passage, you can feel the same melancholy and isolation the character is experiencing, it is as if you were trapped in the car with him.

Finally, it is worth mentioning the superb work of the translator of *The American Quarter* Paula Haydar. Her talent already recognized by the judges of the 2014 Saif Ghobash Banipal Prize for Arabic Literary Translation when she was highly commended for her translation of Douaihy's *June Rain*, she has spoken about the challenges Douaihy's style poses for a translator with his page-long sentences and extensive use of adjectives and metaphors. Not only has Haydar done an incredible job in giving the novel a rhythm and a style that can be appreciated by an English-speaking audience, she has also provided the reader with useful notes that help them understand Middle Eastern culture better and visualize the colourful scenes described by Jabbour Douaihy.

Follow us on twitter @BanipalMagazine
https://www.twitter.com/BanipalMagazine

BOOK REVIEWS

Susannah Tarbush reviews
Him, Me, Muhammad Ali
by Randa Jarrar
Sarabande Books, USA, 2016
ISBN: 9781941411315.
Pbk, 216pp, $15.95 / £12.38

Versatile mastery of the short form

The Palestinian-American short story writer, novelist, essayist and translator Randa Jarrar has emerged as an increasingly significant voice on the Arab-American and international literary landscapes since her coming-of-age debut novel *A Map of Home* was published by Other Press in 2008. The novel won multiple awards and has been published in seven languages. (Tamara Yousry reviewed it in *Banipal 35* – it can be read online)

Him, Me, Muhammad Ali, a sparkling collection of 13 short stories, is enhancing her reputation further. The collection won the Story Prize Spotlight Award for the best short story collection published in 2016. It also received a Before Columbus Foundation American Book Award, and was chosen by Electric Literature as one of the 25 Best Short Story Collections of 2016.

These multi-layered and assured short stories show Jarrar to be a master of the form. Many of them have Arab or Arab-American characters, and they speak widely to our times of dislocation, colliding cultures, fractured families and fluid sexual identities.

Jarrar has a gift for sharp dialogue and an ability to conjure up whole worlds and complex situations in uncluttered prose. She conveys the vulnerability and loss that may lie beneath the humour of her narrators, the majority of whom are women.

Jarrar was born in Chicago in 1978 to a Palestinian father and

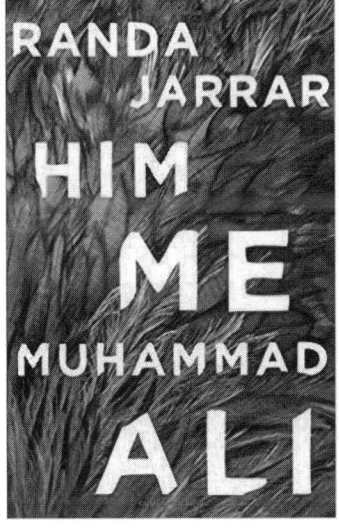

Egyptian-Greek mother. She grew up in Kuwait and Egypt, moving back to the US when she was 13 after the 1991 Gulf war. She studied creative writing at Sarah Lawrence College, and has an MA in Middle Eastern Studies from the University of Texas at Austin, and an MFA in Creative Writing from the University of Michigan. She is currently an associate professor of English at California State University in Fresno. In addition, she is president and executive director of the non-profit volunteer-run Radius of Arab American writers (RAWI).

Most of the stories in *Him, Me, Muhammad Ali* originally appeared, in somewhat different form, in magazines and journals such as *Guernica*, *The Utne Reader*, *Oxford American* and *Ploughshares*. Two stories – "Lost in Freakin' Yonkers" and "A Frame for the Sky" – were published in *Dinarzad's Children: An Anthology of Contemporary Arab American Fiction* (University of Arkansas Press, 2004) edited by Khaled Mattawa and Pauline Kaldas.

In 2010 the Hay Festival and Beirut Unesco's World Capital of the Book named Jarrar as one of the "Beirut 39" – the best 39 Arab authors under 40 years old. "The Story of My Building", first published by Hunger Mountain journal, appeared in *Beirut 39: New Writing from the Arab World*, edited by Samuel Shimon (Bloomsbury Publishing, 2010).

This deeply-felt story, laced through with irony, deservedly reappears in *Him, Me, Muhammad Ali*. It carries the dedication "after Isaac Babel's 'The Story of My Dovecote'". Set in Gaza during a time of savage Israeli bombardments in 2006 it is seen through the eyes of a 10-year-old boy.

"Lost in Freakin' Yonkers" takes place in New York in a heatwave in summer '96. The 18-year-old narrator, whose Palestinian-Egyptian family moved to the US four years earlier, is big with child having discovered she was pregnant at the end of her first year of college. She is living with the father of her child, an older violent womanising

Randa Jarrar

drunkard. She has been disowned by her family – although her mother keeps secretly in touch.

A Palestinian father is a recurring figure in the stories. In "A Frame for the Sky" a Palestinian father in America recounts his predicament in a series of worst days of his life. The protagonist of "Accidental Transients", 29-year-old virgin Dina, lives on a farm in the Jackson area Michigan. with her Palestinian father and young twin brothers. She has taken on the role of mother after her own had "flown the coop" to run away with a Japanese businessman. Dina is co-owner of a hair and beauty salon and gives lessons on hair styling at a college. She also has "a thing for birds" and is knowledgeable about different species. She compares a bird that has flown off course into Michigan to her Palestinian father: both are "accidental transients".

Several of the stories feature birds. The central figure in "Testimony of Malik, Prisoner #287690" is a kestrel originally from the Palestinian West Bank village of Aqraba. He has been imprisoned by Turkey in the belief that he is a spy, and tells his story while under interrogation.

"How Can I Be of Use to You?" is a wonderfully observed portrayal of a celebrated Egyptian feminist named Mansoura Metwally, reminiscent of Nawal El Saadawi. "Every young Arab woman or academic falls under Mansoura's spell at some point in her life," observes the story's protagonist who goes to work for Metwally while she is in Seattle and becomes her amanuensis.

At one point in the story Metwally meets a group of emerging

Arab women writers and asks the narrator to buy earrings for them. The earrings have feathers: "Now Mansoura resembled a mother bird surrounded by her dozen feathered chicks."

In the title story "Him, Me, Muhammad Ali" a 24-year-old American-Egyptian woman travels to Egypt with her father's ashes. Her father, a black American journalist, had told her he wanted to be buried with the old African kings, near the great pyramid of Khufu. The woman's father and mother, an Egyptian journalist living in Sydney, had first met in 1974 while covering the fight in Zaire between George Foreman and Muhammad Ali. The story's narrator has heard from her father about a photograph of her as a baby with her father and Muhammad Ali, but has never seen it. The comic yet sad truth behind the photo emerges only after her father's death.

Several of the stories have touches of magic realism. They include "The Lunatics' Eclipse" and "The Life, Loves, and Adventures of Zelwa" – a witty "Halfie", whose upper body is human and lower half Jordanian ibex goat. "Sadly, I do not have horns . . . but I am horny".

The haunting story "Grace" tells of a girl kidnapped at the age of seven in 1979 and brought up by a commune of women and children: "My childhood passed in gentle play and challenging work . . ." As an adult Grace becomes a teacher and discovers that her real sister has written a novel about her disappearance.

Two stories set in Egypt focus on female bonds of family and friendship. In "Building Girls" a 34-year-old Egyptian woman caretaking a seaside apartment block has an erotic encounter with a childhood female friend visiting from the USA for the summer. "Asmahan" is the story of two sisters who are driving with their daughters in downtown Cairo when they run over and badly injure a village girl.

The shortest story in the collection is the two-and-a-half page "A Sailor". It begins: "She fucks a sailor, a Turkish sailor, the summer she spends in Istanbul. When she comes home it takes her three days to come clean about it to her husband. He says this doesn't bother him, and she tells him that it bothers her that it doesn't bother him." This strong piece of flash fiction, with no dialogue, is further proof of Jarrar's versatility in the various forms of the short story.

BOOK REVIEWS

Margaret Obank reviews
Farewell, Damascus
by Ghada Samman
Translated by Nancy Roberts
Darf Publishers, UK, 2017
ISBN: 9781850772958.
Pbkk, 246pp, £9.00 / $14.95.

The boulder of Mount Qasioun takes wing

Ghada Samman's latest novel in English translation, *Farewell, Damascus*, was published in Arabic in 2014 and is set in mid-sixties Damascus and Beirut. At this time in the 21st century when Syria is in flames and existential turmoil, the author looks back to when she was a young woman in Damascus seeking freedom and independence. An important Syrian novelist and poet, Samman was born in 1942 into a prominent Damascene family – her father was a president of Damascus University – and worked as a translator, broadcaster and translator before starting to write fiction in the early 1960s. She was a force to reckon with, setting up her own publishing house so that she could publish her work uncensored. To date Ghada Samman has over 40 works of stories, essays, novels and dramas including, in translation, *The Square Moon: Supernatural Tales*, the well-known *Beirut '75*, *Beirut Nightmares* and *The Night of the First Billion*. The latter three are also translated by Nancy Roberts – what a successful partnership of great empathy this is!

The main character of *Farewell, Damascus* is 18-year-old Zain who has fallen out of love with her husband after almost a year of marriage as the continual demands of a traditional wedded life proved worse than the constraints of living at home as a single girl, not to mention an unwanted pregnancy, which was for her the last straw. She had to get rid of both for good so that she could concentrate on being a

writer. Instead of being a silkworm just producing its "precious, traditional treasure", she was going to "sprout wings and break out of her cocoon". Dr Manahili, who performed the abortion, turned out to be a friend of her father, and was very supportive of her writings that upset people who didn't "question inherited ideas and beliefs". He was born after his mother had tried to have him aborted, and he was obsessed with helping to ensure safe abortions for countless women.

The doctor was delighted to see Zain take "life by the horns rather than playing the miserable, helpless divorcée" as she forges a career for herself, writing, broadcasting, and studying. She has, like the author had, huge support also from her father, a well-known lawyer, who feels guilty that he was never supportive of the writings of her mother and so is always there to help his daughter.

The book is styled as straightforward narrative, following Zain's life from her abortion to her hurried departure for Beirut and her father's sudden heart attack when he finds a way to pay her a surprise visit there, interwoven with numerous flashbacks, musings, and the thoughts of the different characters as they react inwardly (and outwardly) to family situations, such as the news from Zain that she is divorcing her husband, that an arranged marriage is answered by an elopement, or a headscarf is not long enough to preserve one's modesty. Zain's grandmother has a clever and successful way of thwarting would-be gossipmongers – "just say, 'It was never meant to be!' After all, everybody believes in fate."

The central theme of the novel, which is carried through from the protagonist to most of the other characters – her cousins, aunts, former mother-in-law and the doctor, is the traditionally unequal, macho, chauvinist and abusive treatment of women by most men, the pressures put on girls to leave school, marry early and have kids, and basically give up on any chance of life apart from that of being a servant to the needs of their future husband. Zain's mother-in-law recounts to herself how she had been married off to her cousin, had

Ghada Samman

many children and forever regretted having had to stop her education. She didn't want that to happen to Zain.

The '60s was the time of social upheaval and rebellion against society's mores and customs when Zain and her female relatives are struggling for independence as women. The fact that the thoughts of most of them are only thoughts (and therefore italicized in the text) that they would hardly dare to say out loud, is a vivid part of the narrative – the voices of the silenced speaking out. At times the italicized font threatens to take over the story line as Zain recounts conversations with her cousins, and her dreams, and has many comments interjected into ongoing narrative, and this reader sometimes does a double-take.

The cronyism and corruption that are the adjuncts of the Syrian dictatorial regime are clearly described via a particularly unsavoury macho character whom Zain comes up against when she discovers she has to get an exit visa to leave Syria. She ends up being hunted down as a West German spy, but manages to cross the border to Lebanon when Dr Manahili calls in a favour.

Two other themes that run through the novel are Zain's relationship to Damascus and her mother's town of Latakia, and her love of writing and literature. The little owl, the spirit of her mother, that accompanies her, flying with her to freedom, is a hidden strength for Zain, who always, anyway, was determined to be a rock, "a boulder on Mount Qasioun", which overlooks the city of Damascus. However, when she looks out over her "beloved city", she imagines "My life is nothing but a tiny speck in Damascus's vast sky. Thinking this way makes my own troubles seem less scary."

When her father has a fatal heart attack in Beirut, and she follows the hearse containing his body as far as the border, she calls out the depth of her loss of country and her new predicament in a powerful inner thought: "Let it be known to Latakia, beloved of my mother, and Damascus, beloved of my father, that I'll never let anybody demean me again. I'd sooner live the rest of my life homeless and alone than suffer a fate like that." At that moment, also, she feels she is "no boulder. I'm just a speck of dust that's been blown by dark winds" . . . But she picks herself up when she describes how she thinks others see her: "Revolutionaries see me as some sort of petty, spoiled girl, who, even though she might be a rebel, is still loyal to her bourgeois class, and publishes books as a kind of decorative façade. The bourgeois see me as a dirty radical who needs to be straightened out with a blow to the head. The so-called Muslims want to have me flogged and hanged from their long beards. And as for my family in Ziqaq Al Yasmin, they think I'm a bad example to other girls in the clan." She concludes by saying: "I have wings, and I'm soaring."

Coming from the same generation as the author, and also powerfully influenced and affected by the worldwide social changes of the '60s, I welcome this novel as a heart-felt salutation to women who struggled to change society's traditional views of women's so-called "place" in the world, as well as a reminder to others to keep on doing that.

Millions of Syrians over the last few years will have also been saying "Farewell, Damascus" as they fled their country's borders, while the novel's protagonist reminds us that, though she wanted to "jump into the abyss" and end everything after her father died, all she really wanted (perhaps echoing the horrific journeys across the Mediterranean of the thousands of refugees) "was a hand to hold in these choppy seas – not to rescue me and draw me safely to shore, but just to keep me company as I battle the waves". Zain definitely has my hand, Ghada too.

BOOK REVIEWS

Paul Blezard reviews
The Book of Safety
by Yasser Abdel Hafez
translated by Robin Moger
Hoopoe Fiction, AUC Press, 2017
ISBN: 978-9774168215.
Pbk, 248pp, £9.99 / $10.02

Surgical analysis of moral descent

There are some books, all too few, but some, that grab you from the very first line, hold your attention tight, right through every single word to the end and then, long after you've finished reading them, keep delivering with their exquisite phrasings, stunning imagery and sheer, original, deftness of storytelling. Yasser Abdel Hafez's wonderful satire on modern-day Cairo, *The Book of Safety* is one such.

Not by any means a quick, easy 'lit-fix' read, Abdel Hafez's latest novel is rich, profound and has a depth of imagination and whip-smart narrative stratigraphy that will come as no surprise to readers of an earlier work, his debut novel *On the Occasion of Life* that was excerpted in *Banipal 25* (Spring 2006) in a special feature on "New Writing in Egypt". In the opening chapters the central protagonist, Khaled Mamoun, responds to a cryptically worded job advertisement, torn from a newspaper, that invites applicants to . . ."

BOOK REVIEWS

Yasser Abdel Hafez

"In your own hand, write the story of your life as you see it in 300 words. You may use any literary style or approach to convey your message . . ."

Successful in his application, he is employed to transcribe testimonies in the Palace of Confessions, a state run, shadowy organisation, where he meets Mustafa Ismail, a gifted thief-cum-University professor whose talent for breaking into the homes of the rich, famous, connected and powerful allows him ample opportunity to blackmail them.

From this modest opening we are treated to a surgical analysis of moral descent as Khaled is drawn into Mustafa's obsession for perfection in the business of theft and his book "The Book of Safety" is described as 'the ultimate guide to successful thievery'.

Thoroughly Orwellian in his treatment of dystopian, dysfunctional and downright dangerous politics, Abdel Hafez underpins the darker, more disturbing themes with a superbly clear-headed philosophical understanding and delivers the narrative with all the grip and tension of a bestselling crime novelist.

For those familiar with Cairo, many of the locations, tree-lined Shubra and Nasr City, not least among them, need no introduction. While sense of place is of course a vital ingredient in any well-told story, in *The Book of Safety* it offers a wonderful counterpoint of normality to the bleak and often terrifying absurdity. Imagine Catch-22 being set in an Arcadian flower meadow by a river, or all the horror of Stanley Kubrick's film "The Shining" taking place amid the gilt and grandeur of Buckingham Palace.

At this point, and perhaps rather aptly, a confession has to be made. Unless one has a comprehensive knowledge and understanding of Cairene and Egyptian politics it is possible that subtle, but important, nuances may be missed by the reader. This reviewer, whose grasp of such is through the prism of Western media, fears that this may be the case and thus although recognising the brilliance of the story-telling and the slickly imaginative twists and turns that Abdel Hafez creates for his characters, realises that he may indeed be missing the full importance of many of the delicately crafted observations that require such knowledge.

Notwithstanding this, however, *The Book of Safety* delivers punches aplenty in Robin Moger's top-notch translation, enthralling the reader with beautiful, cutting prose. It is entirely possible that Yasser Abdel Hafez's novel is an enduring work that in future will be viewed and lauded as a defining text of this extraordinary time in Egypt's proud history. This reviewer would not be surprised at all if this were the case and rather hope it is.

Darf Publishers & West End Lane Books
invite you to the book launch of
SUSLOV'S DAUGHTER
by Habib Abdulrab Sarori

7pm, Thursday 7 December 2017

All Welcome
to this FREE event

West End Lane Books
277 West End Lane
London NW6 1QS

For enquiries:
Tel: 0207 431 3770
Email: info@welbooks.co.uk

BOOK REVIEWS

Hassouna Mosbahi reviews
Tuyour al-Nab'a
Birds of al-Nab'a
by Abdallah Uld Mohamadi Bah

Published by Jadawel
Beirut, 2017
ISBN: 978-614-418-342-7

The "travel book" of a Mauritanian intellectual

Mauritanians have such a passion for poetry that their country is widely known as the land of a million poets. Ever since their forefathers had moved from deserts in the far-off east and settled in another desert sandwiched between the Atlantic Ocean and the Senegal River, Mauritanians have found in poetry a great solace from the harshness of their desert life as well as a channel through which to give vent to feelings of nostalgia for their ancestors' homeland.

One Mauritanian who probed a different path was Abdallah Uld Mohamadi Bah. Starting his career as a journalist with Arab newspapers, then as a correspondent for TV channels, he eventually forayed into business, travelling extensively around the world. Recently, he presented himself as a novelist. His novel *Tuyour al-Nab'a* (Birds of al-Nab'a) is a powerful narrative written in a superb style that draws on traditional oral anecdotes and reflects the influence of some contemporary Arab writers, particularly Tayeb Salih, who continues to inspire scores of writers in both the Maghreb and the wider Middle East.

The protagonist of *Tuyour al-Nab'a* has many things in common with the author. Drawing on the versatile experiences of his frequent travels, Uld Mohamadi manages to carve out characters that look quite familiar to us, characters that we have met, lived with, and accompanied in travels on board planes and buses, and on

BOOK REVIEWS

Abdallah Uld Mohamadi Bah, and the cover of Tuyour al-Nab'a

camel-backs across the desert.

The novel is set in many cities – stations or stopping points. The first stop is Madrid, where the protagonist lands after travelling from al-Nab'a (Spring or Well), his desert village that holds firmly to its Bedouin traditions in the face of incessant waves of modernisation. In Madrid, the villager will not indulge in city life as did Mustafa Sa'eed, the protagonist of *Season of Migration to the North*, but will rather watch from a distance while consciously preserving his Bedouin chastity. He is a spendthrift with a lot of money, yet he does not run after his desires. "Politeness dictates that I must restrain myself. I am forty now and it is just unbecoming for me to give free rein to my desires. The nightlife of Madrid is hard to resist but I have managed to curb my desires and to answer the call of my vigilant mind to keep quiet." The protagonist does not fail to exercise self-constraint even with Teresa, the Brazilian girl he loved, apparently because she served him as obediently as his village girls would have done. When the temptations threaten to take control, he rekindles the flame of Sufism in his "ever thirsty, bewildered soul" in order to regain his chastity.

The protagonist returns to his home country and to his desert village, not reluctantly as was the case with Mustafa Sa'eed, but rather because he genuinely believes that life is a series of stations, each with a turn of fate of its own, and that a wise man should accept this fact of life in the same way as his folks in the desert learnt to accept their fate. He believes that his life is "a travel book of endless chapters, each having a distinct colour, smell, and taste".

Back in the village, he tries to recall his childhood memories but they come across as blurred and confused. However, he does remember a grandfather who came from Chinguetti and built a mosque in the heart of the Sahara that formed the nucleus around which the village of al-Nab'a evolved. He also recalls Abdel Hadi al-Majzoub, the teacher who taught him the holy Qur'an and encouraged him to memorize classical Arabic poetry, and who ignited in his soul an unquenchable passion for Sufism.

After a brief stay, the protagonist leaves the village to work at the Mauritanian embassy in Kuwait. There he meets his compatriot Abdul Rahman, an addict of reading with leftist leanings who was a zealous advocate of Arab causes, particularly the Palestinian. With Abdul Rahman the protagonist will experience new adventures and will discover the inner world of Arab expatriates in Kuwait. "Without Abdul Rahman, my life is worthless. Thanks to him, I learned how to respect others' opinions even if I disagree with them." Along with Abdul Rahman, he travels to Doha where he meets some Sudanese and gets to know their fifth tone music and their Sufi poetry.

Back in his village, he notes that although some manifestations of modern life have started to penetrate village life, many aspects of Bedouin culture and lifestyle are still holding firm, such as gatherings for poetry recitations, religious hymns, and romantic tales.

Once again the old passion for travel takes hold of him and he sets off, this time to Guinea in search of the sons of al-Nab'a village who migrated so long ago that they had become fantastic characters in the memory of the village community.

Employing quite a large number of characters and a mixture of actual events flavoured with elaborate touches, Uld Mohamadi weaves a gripping narrative of a Mauritanian intellectual in frequent shuttles between his home village, Europe, and the Middle East. These trips, related in the style of folk tales, leave a spiritual imprint as well as a significant impact on the fates, ideas, and emotions of the characters – in the same way that ascetic Sufis might find opportunities for deciphering the secrets of worldly and heavenly existence through travel.

BOOK REVIEWS

Becki Maddock reviews
Maryam, Keeper of Stories
by Alawiya Sobh
Translated by Nirvana Tanoukhi
Seagull Books, July 2016
ISBN: 9780857423252.
400pp, Hbk, $27.50 / £20.50

A modern Scheherazade called Alawiya Sobh

"It started when she came to me towards the end of the war and said: 'The war is over. I want to write the experience of our generation. No…That's too ambitious. I want to write your story . . . the shadow of all our memories.'"

Although the Lebanese civil war does feature in this novel, affecting the protagonists' behaviour and emotions, many of the stories do not take place during the civil war. Maryam is not so much a civil war novel but rather a collection of tales about Lebanon, in particular Lebanese women. Alawiya Sobh has said that her book "is about the defeat suffered by the women in the Lebanese civil war." Sobh is interested in the consequences of the war, the changes it brought to Lebanese society, as opposed to specific events of the war itself.

Focusing on personal relationships and feelings, rather than politics, Sobh allows her female characters to tell their own stories of the fate of women in Lebanese society and war, describing the choices they face in terms of marriage, love, work and education. Her female characters suffer many hardships: honour killing, forced marriage, child marriage, domestic abuse, poverty, war, bereavement, miscarriage…Um Maryam remarks: "Men, they can't handle grief the way women can. Who knows why, but a woman can carry a heart full of misery."

Decisions regarding marriage are key to women's fates. Maryam suffers the stigma of remaining unmarried, describing herself as "the last grape hanging at the end of the bunch". She dreams of losing her

virginity with a man she loves but her first love Ali is killed in the war. She later has an affair with Mustafa who tells her that he won't marry her because she is too old. Finally, Maryam agrees to marry Ameen and move to Canada. "I dreamt of marrying a man whom I loved, one from outside the family whom I chose with my heart and mind. But here I am today, after all these years, marrying Ameen after having rejected him 25 years ago."

Maryam's generation feels the irony of women having fought for freedom but remaining trapped. Female revolutionaries imagined their male colleagues to be "progressive, partners wanting freedom" but find themselves still being judged and stereotyped by society. Kareem asks Ibtisam how she can be a virgin if she's a revolutionary, then ditches her after she sleeps with him. She then marries Jalal, who she does not love, who also judges her for her lack of virginity.

Sobh's protagonists' memories of both Lebanese life and specific war experiences demonstrate that, although the war is not the primary focus, Sobh's work is influenced by the experience of the war. Sobh transports the reader to wartime Beirut, the feelings, smells and sights, with a vivid description of Beirut under siege; the fear, anxiety and boredom. These wartime memories contrast with Maryam's childhood memories. She tells "the tales, woven and spun on the tongues of the people in my village", tales of her friends, neighbours and family members. The stories of her own generation and her mother's and grandmother's, demonstrate the repetition of women's dreams and experiences.

Sobh employs narrative techniques found in other Lebanese civil war novels, such as the absence of a beginning or an end. In common with other Lebanese civil war novels, memory is an important theme. The novel's fragmented chronology led the translator to include a note, clarifying that the inconsistencies of the novel are present in the original Arabic and, she explains, are intended to make the stories appear as many collective memories. As the Alawiyya of

Alawiya Sobh

the novel says, "aren't all women pregnant with the same story? The story of the foetus in one belly is the same one inside all women's bellies." These are the universal stories of women. "[Y]our story is not yours alone . . .", Ibtisam imagines that Alawiyya would tell her.

Nirvana Tanoukhi's translation successfully retains the amibiguities of the original Arabic and despite its fragmented chronology the novel is not a difficult read. The text is packed with beautiful, sparse yet impactful phrases, which contain layers of meaning. The confused narrative adds to the author's exploration of the nature of memory and appears to be intended to reflect the confusion of the protagonists. Maryam's parents each remember past events in their own way and are constantly fighting "over the truth of their stories" and Zuhair's neighbours have different versions of what happened to him. Even the writers themselves appear confused. Maryam says of Zuhair: "Clearly, he was mixing up theatre and life, just as she sometimes could not keep apart the lives lived from the stories written." Alawiyya herself confesses: "Too many faces, names, voices . . . I'm no longer sure whether Maryam is not the same person as Yasmine . . . I'm not certain whether the abortion was Maryam's or Ibtisam's, Yasmine's or mine . . . All of us aborted foetuses and dreams and memories."

Sobh, like many Middle Eastern writers, writing to understand experiences such as war or exile, writes with a sharp consciousness of the writing process, which permeates the novel. She has said: "The war silenced me. I felt as though I were one of those who go missing in war. I had to write this book to find my voice again. So I invented Maryam to tell the story for me." "I have created a modern Scherezade".

The majority of the novel is narrated by Maryam but in chapter 10 the narrator suddenly changes. "I know Alawiyya Subuh. I know her at least as much as Maryam does." From the new narrator's mention of Maryam's name we realise that the latter is no longer narrating. Ibtisam narrates this chapter, telling her version of her story, adding to what Maryam has already told us. The author herself is a character in her own novel, although her name is spelled slightly differently in the translation to the usual Latin-script spelling of her name . For most of the novel Alawiyya remains in the background, having apparently disappeared. She finally appears as the narrator in chapter 13, providing her thoughts on storytelling and the fates of her characters but as Maryam concludes: "Who was the one writing . . . the tales overlapped . . . Nothing was certain."

Alawiya Sobh is a Lebanese writer and journalist, born and living in Beirut. She has worked on and edited several women's magazines, including the popular *Al-Hasnaa'* and *Snob* magazines, and appears as a guest speaker on television programmes, addressing issues related to women, war and modernity in Lebanon.

Maryam, Keeper of Stories was first published in Arabic in 2002, excerpted in *Banipal 17* in 2003 in a translation by the present translator Nirvana Tanoukh together with a profile of the author, and in 2006 won the Sultan Qaboos Prize. Sobh's novel *Dunya* (2006) was excerpted in *Banipal 27* (2006) and her third novel, *Ismahul Gharam* (It's Called Love) (2009), excerpted in *Banipal 36* (2009), was longlisted for the 2010 International Prize for Arabic Fiction.

BOOK REVIEWS

Clare Roberts reviews
The Baghdad Eucharist
by Sinan Antoon
translated by Maia Tabet
Hoopoe Fiction, Cairo, 30 March 2017.
ISBN: 978-9774168208.
Pbk, 152pp. £9.99 / $12.03

To try not to remember

It was a day of notorious and brutal massacre of Christians in Iraq: 31 October 2010. That evening, at the Syriac Catholic Church of Our Lady of Deliverance in Baghdad, the tense political situation had left the congregation attending the Eucharist service on edge and fearful for their lives. As they rose to say the Lord's Prayer, jihadis entered the church and took them hostage. The attackers would ultimately butcher at least fifty people, leaving human flesh smeared over the walls of the church. Caught up in these harrowing and unimaginable real events, we find the fictional protagonists of Sinan Antoon's *The Baghdad Eucharist*.

Sinan Antoon's 2012 novel, released originally in Arabic with the title *Ya Maryam* (Ave Maria), and shortlisted for the 2013 International Prize for Arabic Fiction, draws us into the world of the often overlooked, dwindling Christian community in the Iraqi capital. The novel vividly depicts the challenges they face in this painful and deeply personal account of the relentless and unforgiving conflict unfolding in Iraq. This community's sense of forsakenness is all the more crippling when explored through the eyes of characters who have built their daily lives around their faith.

Although the narrative unfolds over the course of a tense 24-hour period, the challenges of the present compete with past memories for the attention of the novel's two protagonists – the elderly Youssef and his young relative and lodger Maha. The novel opens with

Youssef, whose flashbacks are dotted throughout the narrative. An evocative chapter focuses entirely on his old family photos, bringing home the very real challenge of not living in the past. In what unfolds into an uncomfortable argument, Maha accuses her uncle of falling prey to this, which he struggles to accept. As he goes about his day, however, it becomes increasingly obvious to him that Maha may just be right – the past is his "own paradise in the heart of hell".

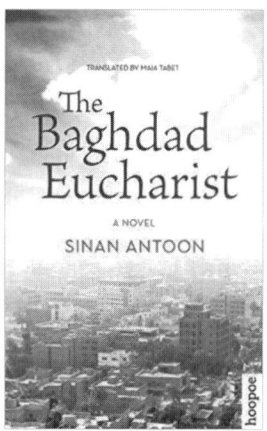

Sinan Antoon

Halfway through the novel the narrative shifts from Youssef to Maha, whose memories of growing up in a hostile and increasingly sectarian Iraq do not ring true with most of Youssef's own childhood memories. Dwelling on the past is an agreeable alternative for him; it serves as "the garden which I so loved and which I tended as if it were my own daughter, just in order to escape the noise and ugliness of the world". For Youssef, the horror of the present is also compounded by the fact that many of those who have played a key role in his life have long since passed away or fled the country. For Maha however, the past offers no such refuge. Despite her youth, she has experienced more than her fair share of loss and brutality since the day she was born: her "green eyes fluttered open to the ravages of war and sanctions; depravation, violence, and displacement were the first things she tasted in life". While different generations have conflicting views of the past, around them the city's maimed palm trees serve as indisputable evidence of the toll years of conflict have taken on Baghdad.

The Baghdad Eucharist, gracefully translated by Maia Tabet, is first and foremost a resounding call for tolerance, for peace in what is the bloody reality of modern Iraq. Ultimately, however, this novel underscores the continued questioning of an author trying to come to terms with the unbelievable reality of daily life in the land of his birth.

The Scent of Jasmine: Coming of Age in Jerusalem and Damascus
by Anan Ameri

Olive Branch Press, Interlink Books, USA, 2017
ISBN: 9781566560016. Pbk, 208pp, $20.00 / £15.99

"I grew up in a Muslim culture but I never knew if I was a Sunni or a Shia until I became an adult"

The first thing that struck me about Anan Ameri is how modest she is. The second was how enthralling and thoughtful was her writing, how she unfolded idea after idea, fact after fact, emotion after emotion, bringing them all together in the collection of unforgettable vignettes that is *The Scent of Jasmine*. Born to a Palestinian father and a Syrian mother, Anan was four years old in 1948, a student in Beirut and Amman in the memorable '60s – a rebel campaigning "against male-dominated societies, colonialism, and oppressive regimes", wearing a Che Guevara T-shirt, supporting liberation movements.

The vignettes, supplemented by numerous personal photographs, describe with humour and love the up and downs of her family, their constant moves from West Jerusalem, to Damascus, to East Jerusalem, to Amman. It is a wonderful mix of childhood treats and mishaps, family occasions, surprises and routines, with the bigger political picture moving between the background and the foreground depending on its impact at the time. The treasured transistor radio that was young Anan's "magic box" through which she and neighbourhood kids learned about "Uncle Mao, Patrice Lumumba, Castro and Che [. . .] Martin Luther King, and Malcolm X" remained with Anan through most of her adult life, during which she was to found the Palestine Aid Society of America and the Arab American National Museum. An invaluable glimpse into our past for future generations.

MO

Code Name: Butterfly
by Ahlam Bsharat
translated by Nancy Roberts
Neem Tree Press Ltd, UK, 2016.
ISBN: 978-1911107026. Pbk, 110pp, £8.99 / $12.19

"I felt alone in the world with nothing to relate to but my dreams and my hidden questions"

The young people's novel *Code Name: Butterfly*, by Palestinian author Ahlam Bsharat, offers a snapshot of life in Palestine through the eyes of a teenage girl, who is struggling to understand the political situation and the adult world, whilst trying to deal with more usual teenage concerns: falling out with her best friend or her sisters, waiting at the window for handsome Nizar to pass her house and trying to pluck her eyebrows without her parents noticing.

Butterfly has many questions: Why does her father work for the occupiers, farming land that used to belong to him? Do tears make a martyr impure? What is 'honour' that people talk about so strangely and why is it such a catastrophe to lose it? And how do the sperm and the egg get together if they start out in separate bodies? She tries to puzzle these questions out herself, afraid to ask her parents and afraid her friends will laugh at her if she asks them. So she hides her questions away in a secret treasure chest, along with her dreams for the future.

Bsharat's coming-of-age story was on the 2012 IBBY Honour List and is shortlisted for the Palestine Book Awards 2017. Young readers will identify with Butterfly's teenage concerns and also learn a little about what life is like for Palestinians.

BM

TRIBUTE

Denys Johnson-Davies
21 June 1922 – 22 May 2017

Plunging into the sea of life

In an interview back published in *Banipal 9*, Denys Johnson-Davies told me that translation of Arabic literature was for him "a consuming hobby at various times of [his] life". That hobby was to stay with him nearly 70 years, from his first translation of short stories by Mahmud Teymour (1947) until his last collection entitled *Homecoming: Sixty Years of Egyptian Short Stories*. Since we started Banipal he was always very supportive, and we much enjoyed meeting him whenever he was in London, and on occasions in Cairo or in Abu Dhabi.

He considered that "translation is, first and foremost, an art and not a science", and felt that "readability in a translation must be the main consideration, particularly in the case of fiction and poetry". He told me that he had translated "practically every word written by Tayeb Salih" and that he was his favourite author to translate as well as a great friend. He considered that "Tayeb Salih has had the advantage of being a sophisticated writer who deals expertly with simple material . . . and he has obviously thought deeply about the art of narrative – as is obvious from the way in which *Season of Mi-*

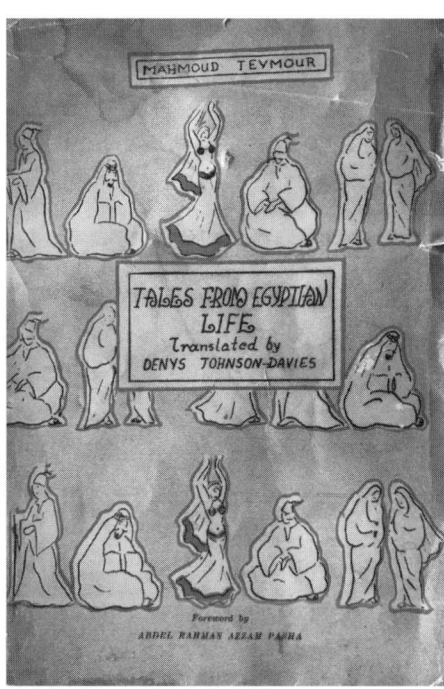

Denys Johonson-Davies with Homecoming, his last collection of translations. Above: his first collection of Mahmoud Teymour's stories Tales from Egyptian Life, whose publication he financed himself

gration to the North is structured". They were both living in London when Tayeb Salih started writing the now classic novel, and every week, as Denys recounted in a tribute after Tayeb passed away, he would receive from him "another sheaf of papers, another chapter written out in longhand. From the start, [Tayeb] was worried about certain parts of the book, particularly the long scene in which four elderly villagers, among then the much-married and outspoken woman Bint Majzoub, reminisce about the joys of sex."

Roger Allen wrote that "the sheer brilliance of his translation of *Season of Migration to the North* by Tayeb Salih . . . turned his English version into the one through which this novel has garnered such a world-wide reputation. This work remains for me the finest Arabic contribution to the worldwide tradition of the novel genre thus far."

Denys Johnson-Davies has left an invaluable and permanent legacy

TRIBUTE

Denys Johnson-Davies working in Marrakesh in the days of typewriters

to world literature and to literary translators in his consummate appreciation of the vibrant, living Arabic language, of enjoying the works he is translating. As Paul Starkey remarks in Banipal's own "Festschrift" to him by professors, translators, publishers and critics, *Banipal 43 – Celebrating Denys Johnson-Davies*: "It is no exaggeration to say that it was almost entirely through his pioneering efforts, not least through his establishment of the much missed Heinemann Arab Authors series, that modern Arabic writing in English translation was originally put on the map."

Banipal 43's celebration of the dean of translators, the doyen, the pioneer, the meticulous standard-bearer, the leading Arabic-English translator, a priceless treasure, a wise and witty friend, also included contributions by Roger Allen, Khaled Mattawa, Mark Linz, Peter Clark, Humphrey Davies, William M Hutchins, Musa al-Halool, Brahim Oulayhane, Samuel Shimon and myself. Each had a different relationship and connection with Denys, but all recognised the effect of how he valued the authors, who became his friends, as much the literature they were engaged in writing all around him, and the way he made its translation just something straightforward, in the normal course of life, part of life. Khaled Mattawa summed it up perfectly with these words: "The books he produced in English are ones he liked, written by people he grew to like. No presumptions, no other-ing, no historical burdens involved."

We, the bearers of his legacy, have to ensure that it continues to be passed on in his way, allowing modern Arabic literature to speak to the different readerships around the world.

MARGARET OBANK
PHOTOS BY PAULA CROCIANI

Denys Johnson-Davies and Tayeb Salih

Denys Johnson-Davies with Jabra Ibrahim Jabra in Baghdad

EVENTS

Sheikh Zayed Book Award opens up cultural dialogue in London

The Sheikh Zayed Book Award held a seminar on "Exploring the Arab Culture in Other Languages" at the Lanesborough Hotel in London on 20 September, which brought together an assembly of authors, publishers and translators.

The seminar commenced with a welcoming speech by Abdullah Majed Al Ali, Acting Executive Director, National Library Sector at the Abu Dhabi's Culture & Tourism Authority (TCA). Mr. Al Ali spoke briefly on the role of the TCA in fostering numerous cultural initiatives that include the Sheikh Zayed Book Award (SZBA), the International Prize for Arabic Fiction (IPAF), the Abu Dhabi International Book Fair, as well as Louvre Abu Dhabi, the Guggenheim Museum Abu Dhabi and the Zayed National Museum – with the aim of encouraging cultural dialogue, and bringing creativity into the spotlight."

One of the three panellists, Margaret Obank, publisher of Banipal magazine, spoke about the importance of dialogue, noting that "The Sheikh Zayed Book Award and Banipal have much in common since a central feature of the SZBA is cultural dialogue – dialogue that will enrich experience and knowledge of the other".

Dheyaa Al-Kaabi, a member of the Sheikh Zayed Book Award Scientific Committee, elaborated on the role of the Sheikh Zayed Book Award's category "Arabic Culture in Other Languages" in bringing depth to the cultural exchange between Arabic and other languages

Abdullah Majed Al Ali

Dheyaa Al-Kaabi, Haytham El-Zobeidy, Margaret Obank and Marina Warner

through the winning titles of that category. "Yet the role of the Award in this dimension has not been limited to this category; the Cultural Personality of the Year Award has also named prominent figures in orientalism," she added.

Professor Dame Marina Warner, inaugural winner of the SZBA Arab Culture in Other Languages Award, presented her experience with the book that won her the prize. *Stranger Magic: Charmed States & the Arabian Nights* tells the story of the Arabian Nights in western civilisation from a thoroughly new and, until recently, little understood angle. In it she introduces numerous references, not only from Arabic and Islamic literature, but across other cultures with similar traditions of mythography in storytelling.

This award category has celebrated the achievements of other exceptional academics and intellectuals, including Italian historian Mario Liverani, French-Egyptian researcher Prof. Rushdie Rashed, Prof. David Wirmer from Germany, and scholar Sugita Hideaki from Japan.

EVENTS

internationales literaturfestival berlin

Berlin International Literature Festival celebrates 20 years of Banipal

IN COLLABORATION with Banipal, the 17th Berlin International Literature Festival celebrated 20 years of Banipal publishing by hosting a special event with five authors published in Banipal issues – Algerian writer Amin Zaoui, Syrian poet Nouri al-Jarrah, Emirati writer Mariam al-Saedi, Egyptian poet Emad Fouad and Slovenian poet Veronika Dintinjana. Writer and translator Stefan Weidner moderated in Arabic and German, along with Jordanian interpreter Mustafa al-Slaiman.

The event was opened and introduced by Festival director Ulrich Schreiber, who spoke about the Festival's relation with Banipal and that he was keen to invite Arab authors every year. Each author read their original texts, while actor Matthias Scherwenkas read their German translations. Afterwards, Banipal invited all the Festival authors and guests to a wonderful Middle Eastern party in the well-known "authors' tent".

This event was one of several arranged by Banipal during 2017 to celebrate its 20th year of publishing.

EVENTS

l to r: Amin Zaoui, Mariam al-Saedi, Nouri al-Jarrah, Emad Fouad, Stefan Weidner, Mustafa al-Slaiman and Veronca Dintinjana. Inset: Festival director Ulrich Schreiber

l to r: ICORN writers Mohamad Alaaedin Abdul Moula (Syria), BANIPAL editor Samuel Shimon (Iraq) and Ashur Etwebi (Libya) discuss creativity in the Arab world at the Frankfurt Book Fair's Weltempfang, with chair Peter Ripken, former ICORN chairman

Literary responses to crises in the Arab world

The panel, with more than 60 in attendance on Friday, October 13, was organized by the International Cities of Refuge Network ICORN and BANIPAL magazine of modern Arab literature, which this year completes 20 years of promoting Arab literature in translation.

All three authors are living in temporary exile and all three were adamant that this did not really have a bearing on what they write and how they write. For Ashur Etwebi and Mohamad A A Moula, living and working in ICORN cities – Trondheim and Hannover respectively – gave them new opportunities to continue their literary work begun at home, while all three writers considered that crises contributed to a greater awareness of what stories had to be told, what poems should be written. There was general agreement that all good and decent Arab writers are aware of the great tradition of Arab creative writing and continue to struggle against the odds and to write as best as they can, even if there are difficulties in getting published, and even if there is no contact with their readers (wherever they are).

PETER RIPKEN

EVENTS

Assilah Forum Celebrates 20 years of BANIPAL

THE ASSILAH FORUM FOUNDATION of Morocco celebrated Banipal's 20 years of publishing with an entire day of discussions on the experiences of the magazine and publishing Arabic literature in English translation. The Forum invited a number of academics, and writers and translators of Arabic literature into different languages, and produced a special bilingual book in Arabic and English about the magazine's history with testimonies from translators and others.

EVENTS

Mohamed Benaissa

Kaoru Yamamoto

Fadhil Al-Azzawi

Robert Irwin

Charafdine Majdouline

Ahmed El-Madini

Walid Hamarneh

Latifa Baqa

Khaled Najar

Jonathan Wright

EVENTS

cover of Assilah book on Banipal

Margaret Obank

The symposium took place in the Hasan II Cultural Centre on 20 July 2017 and was opened by Mohamed Benaissa, the President of the Assilah Forum. He praised the magazine and its role in promoting and serving Arabic literature in the world while maintaining its independence, and saluted its achievements over 20 years.

Each speaker related their own experience of knowing the magazine and its editors over a number of years. They included Moroccan critic Charafdine Majdouline, Iraqi poet Fadhil al-Azzawi, Omani poet Saif al-Rahbi, Moroccan writers Latifa Baqaa and Ahmed El-Madini, British author and historian Robert Irwin, German translator Hartmut Fähndrich, Jordanian professor Walid Hamarneh, Moroccan writer Ismail Ghazali, British translator Jonathan Wright, Tunisian poet and writer Khaled Najar, Japanese professor and translator Kaoru Yamamato, Tunisian writer Hassouna Mosbahi, German writer and translator Stefan Weidner, as well as Banipal's publisher Margaret Obank, and editor Samuel Shimon.

The Assilah Cultural Festival is one of the best known festivals in the Arab world and next year celebrates its 40th anniversary. Banipal will be supporting that festival.

PLEASE TURN THE PAGE for some quotes from Assilah's bilingual book about Banipal and a taste of some of the contributions on 20 July.

EVENTS

Hassouna Mosbahi

Hartmut Fähndrich

Ismail Ghazali and Stefan Weidner

DENYS JOHNSON-DAVIES: For many years modern Arabic literature went on its lonely way without any magazine to help it. Then, without any official support, Banipal made its sudden appearance, and has done a magnificent job of making known to the English-speaking world the new modern literature that had taken its place among international literatures, providing the reader with short stories and novels deserving of attention … [keeping] the English reader informed about the modern movement in Arabic literature.

PAUL STARKEY: Banipal magazine is now in its twentieth year. The regular appearance of the magazine three times a year over such a long period may be reckoned something of a miracle. There was no ready-made market or readership for such a venture when it was first started, and many people were sceptical about its chances of survival. In a sense, their scepticism was well-founded, for the enterprise has never been a 'money-spinner', and its survival has often seemed precarious in financial terms.

RAPHAEL COHEN: Banipal at 20 – quite an achievement, and given the apparent paucity of English translation of modern Arabic literature at the end of the last century, an achievement that has played a role in widening access to world literature in English.

EVENTS

Mohamed Benaissa and Samuel Shimon, who is showing the Assilah book to the audience

ROBERT IRWIN: It is hard (for me at least) to think back to how it was for Arab culture in Britain prior to the first publication of Banipal in 1998. It really was a bit of a wasteland as far as British awareness of Arabic literature was concerned . . . The letter written by Margaret which accompanied first issue was the magazine's manifesto: 'It aims to be serious and passionate but quietly outspoken and thoroughly committed to presenting literature from around the Arab world in English translation, reaching out to the world of English readers.' . . . When the second issue of Banipal came out it was greeted with mild incredulity. It had not been expected to last. There was same reaction to third and fourth issues. The most recent issue I have received is number fifty-eight. The doubters have been proved wrong and Banipal has become part of the literary landscape.

CATHERINE COBHAM: Banipal has consistently published work by leading older writers who are unknown or little known in English translation, as well as that written by younger writers in search of publishers. The issues of the magazine that focus on the poetry or fiction of specific Arab countries, some of which are relatively under-exposed internationally, are particularly exciting and important for imaginative cultural bridge-building.

STEFAN WEIDNER: If anybody wants to know what is written in Arabic today but does not know Arabic, he or she just needs to read Banipal. But even for those who, like me, are able to read Arabic, Banipal is a treasure island.

EVENTS

HARTMUT FAHNDRICH: Admiration may be a sublime sentiment while envy certainly is a low one. And still, the two sentiments merge in my personal feelings about Banipal – there is admiration for the sustained effort in putting out such a journal three times a year, and there is envy that such a beacon of Arabic literature only exists in English. Arabic literature deserves to be spread in other languages as well!

ROGER ALLEN: In the years since its inception, the journal Banipal has become a crucially important symbol of the significance of modern Arabic literary culture in the anglophone context.

JOACHIM SARTORIUS: Banipal is a laboratory, illuminated by the flashing lights of its initiators, Banipal is a necessary bridge between Arab and Western cultures, Banipal is a valuable gift because it brings the wealth and diversity of Arabic literature to the anglophone world.

ABBAS BAYDOUN: We all recall that Samuel was the first to get in touch with us. We were still a lost generation when Banipal took the risk of presenting our work in the language of others. It did so with tremendous generosity and on countless occasions. It did so without a moment's hesitation in the face of anyone or apology for any text it presented too. It valued Arabic literature more than Arabic literature did itself. From the very first, Banipal saw the value and validity of its interaction with other literatures and cultures.

Humphrey Davies: Banipal gives me an insight into what is going on in literature across the Arabic-writing world, bringing me notice of new writers, new genres, and new possibilities. My collection of past issues is my Bibliotheca Alexandrina.

Abdo Wazen: How badly in need have we been for a magazine like Banipal, which has shattered the alienation of Arabic literature from the Anglo-Saxon world! It has succeeded in presenting Arabic literature as it should be presented: far from interests and background influences. I believe there is no other magazine that has been able to be beneficial to modern and contemporary Arabic literature like Banipal.

Fadhil Al-Azzawi: What makes Banipal a literary and cultural phenomenon is not only that it is daring, with a wide-open vision, and that it renews itself with every issue. Above all, it reflects the real achievements of the contemporary literature of Arab authors. Texts by established writers and poets are published side by side with those of the young and talented emerging generation of authors. Banipal is now in fact "a laboratory that illuminates the styles of modern Arabic writings" and in some way a mirror which enables us, as Arab authors, to see ourselves better.

Jonathan Wright: I first came across the magazine in the bookshop of the American University in Cairo in around 2008 and was immediately envious of the contributors whose translated excerpts the magazine had published. . . . Banipal is an invaluable resource for a working literary translator, as an easily accessible gateway to a wide range of writers in Arabic from all across the Arab world and in the diaspora. It's easy to miss writers and books in Arabic because Arabic-language journalism about literature is relatively undeveloped and often focused on one particular country rather than the region as a whole. Banipal brings them together and presents them to an English-speaking audience, giving them all due weight without favouritism or discrimination for non-literary reasons.

CONTRIBUTORS

Yasser Abdel Latif is a writer and poet from Cairo, Egypt, who has lived and worked in Edmonton, Canada since 2010. He has four works of fiction, two poetry collections, and has translated many literary works from French and English into Arabic. Some of his own works have been translated into English, French, German, Italian, and Spanish. His debut novel *Law of Inheritance* (2002), won the Sawiris Prize in 2005 in the young writers category. His collection of short stories, *Jonah in the Belly of the Whale*, won the same prize in 2013 in the category of prominent writers.

Adil Babikir is a Sudanese translator into and out of English & Arabic, living now in Abu Dhabi. He has translated *Mansi: a Rare Man in his Own Way* by Tayeb Salih and two novels by Abdelaziz Baraka Sakin. Other translations include two anthologies – of poetry and short stories.

Abdallah Uld Mohamadi Bah is a writer, novelist and journalist from Nabaghiya, southern Mauritania. His journalistic career began the mid-1980s with al-Sha'ab newspaper, then he was West Africa correspondent for al-Sharq al-Awsat, and later for the MBC TV channel, and for Aljazeera in Africa. His works include *Timbuktu wa Akhawatuha* (Timbuktu and its Sisters) and *Yawmiyat Sahafi fe Ifreeqiya* (Diary of a Journalist in Africa). He is currently CEO of Sahara Media Group in north and west Africa.

Paul Blezard is a writer and broadcaster. He presented "Between the Lines", the author interview programme that helped Oneword Radio win two Sony Gold Awards. He has chaired numerous literary events and was a judge of the 2014 Saif Ghobash Banipal Prize.

Raphael Cohen is a translator based in Cairo and a contributing editor of *Banipal*. His recent Arabic fiction translations include Mona Prince's *So You May See* (2011) & *Status: Emo* by Eslam Mosbah.

Mansoura Ez-Eldin is an Egyptian novelist and journalist. Her first collection of short stories came out in 2001. This was followed by four novels, *Maryam's Maze* (2004, with English edition in 2007), *Beyond Paradise* (2009) shortlisted for the 2010 IPAF and with Italian and German editions, the award-winning *Emerald Mountain* (2014) with French edition in 2017, and *Shadow Play* (2017). In 2009 she was selected for the Beirut39 project as one of the 39 best Arab authors below the age of 40. Her second collection of short stories *The Path to Madness* (2013) was awarded "Best Egyptian collection of short stories" by the 2014 Cairo International Book Fair. Ez-Eldin is co-editor of *Akhbar al-Adab* literary newspaper.

Ibrahim Farghali is an Egyptian writer, born in Mansoura in 1967. He has a BA in Business Studies from Mansoura University and works as a journalist on the staff of *Al-Arabi* magazine in Kuwait. He has previously worked in the UAE and Oman, and for *Al-Ahram* newspaper in Cairo. He has published three short story collections and six novels, including *Smiles of Saints* (2004) with English translation (AUC Press, 2007), *Sons of Gebalawi* (2009), winner of the 2012 Sawiris Cultural Award, and *The Temple of Silken Fingers,* longlisted for the 2016 IPAF and winner of the 2017 Sawiris Award.

Miled Faiza is a Tunisian poet and translator. He is the author of the collection *The Remains of a House We Once Entered* (2004). His poetry has been translated into English, French and Serbian and has appeared in many periodicals and anthologies. He teaches Arabic at Brown University and lives in Rhode Island, USA.

Laura Ferreri has a BA in interpreting and translation (Trieste University, Italy) and an MA in Arabic Translation (Edinburgh Univ. CASAW). She is a regular *Banipal* reviewer.

Sally Gomaa was born and raised in Alexandria, Egypt. She has a BA in English Literature and a PhD in Rhetoric and Composition. She is currently an Associate Professor of English at Salve Regina University, USA. Her publications include an English translation of Amina Zaydan's *Red Wine* (AUC Press, 2010).

Julia Ihnatowicz was born in London, where she is currently working as a freelance translator of Arabic. She studied literature at Warwick University, prior to living and working in the Middle East over several years. She has subsequently completed an MA in translation at SOAS and worked on projects ranging from the commercial to the creative.

Samira Kawar is an energy journalist and

CONTRIBUTORS

literary translator. She has contributed translations to *Banipal* since its foundation in 1998, and is a trustee of the Banipal Trust for Arab Literature. Two of her literary translations from Arabic to English have been published – the novel *The Eye of the Mirror* by Palestinian writer Liana Badr, and the autobiography of the late Saudi writer Abdul Rahman Munif *Story of a City: A Childhood in Amman*.

Alaa Khaled is an Egyptian poet, novelist and literary editor from Alexandria and founder of the literary and cultural magazine Amkenah (Places). He has published six collections of poetry, three books of essays and reportage, among the latter, *Everything Happens Quietly With No Surprises* (Alexandria, 2004) and his latest work, *Alexandrian Faces*. He was a featured author of *Banipal 58*.

Ben Koerber is an assistant professor of Arabic in the Department of African, Middle Eastern, and South Asian Languages and Literatures at Rutgers University. He is the translator of Ahmed Naji and Ayman Al Zorkany's novel, *Using Life* (Istikhdam al-Haya), forthcoming from the University of Texas Press in 2017.

Becki Maddock is a translator and researcher living in London. She translates from Arabic, Persian and Spanish into English. She has a first class BA in Arabic and Spanish (Exeter University) and an MA in Near and Middle Eastern Studies from SOAS, University of London. She is now taking Kurdish language classes, also at SOAS.

Lamia Makaddam is a Tunisian poet and translator Dutch to Arabic, and the author of two collections of poetry, published in Beirut, 2007 and in Cairo, 2015. Selections have been translated into English, French, Dutch, and Kurdish. In 2000 she was awarded the Netherlands El Hizjra prize for literature. She studied Arabic language and literature at the Université de Sousse in Tunisia, and translation in the Netherlands. Makaddam has lived in The Netherlands since the early 1990s, and has worked as a broadcast journalist for Radio Holland Worldwide since 2009.

Karen McNeil has an MA in Arabic from Georgetown University, with a speciality in Tunisian Arabic and Arabic linguistics. She was lead revising editor of the *Oxford Arabic Dictionary* (2014), and has translated Arabic poetry and short stories for *World Literature Today*, *Banipal*, and *al-Jadid*. She is co-creator of the Tunisian Arabic Corpus, www.tunisiya.org.

Hassouna Mosbahi is a Tunisian writer, literary critic and journalist, born in Kairouan. He lived and worked in Munich, Germany, from 1985 to 2005. He won the National Novel Prize (Tunisia) in 1986 and in 2000 the Munich Tukan Prize for the German translation of his novel *Tarshish Hallucination*. He has published, in Arabic and German, four volumes of short stories, four novels, a travel book and some non-fiction. His short story "The Tortoise" was short-listed for the Caine Prize for African Writing in 2001. *A Tunisian Tale* (AUC Press, 2011) is his first novel in English translation. He won the 2016 Mohamed Zefzef Prize, awarded by the Assilah Forum.

Suneela Mubayi has a PhD on the intersection of classical and modern Arabic poetry from New York University. She has translated poems and short stories between Arabic, English and Urdu, which have been published in *Banipal*, *Beirut39*, *Jadaliyya*, and elsewhere.

Widad Nabi is a Syrian Kurdish writer and poet, born in 1985 in the Syrian city of Kobani. She graduated from the College of Economics and Commerce, Aleppo University. She has two poetry collections, published in Aleppo, 2013, and in Beirut, 2016. Many of her poems have appeared in literary journals and in anthologies in German, French, Turkish, and English translation. She has participated in several German literary festivals, including the 2017 Berlin Poetry Festival. She lives in Berlin.

Margaret Obank is publisher, and founder of *Banipal* magazine and the Banipal Trust for Arab Literature. She has a BA in English and Philosophy from Leeds University and an MA in Applied Linguistics from Birkbeck London.

Youssef Rakha is an Egyptian journalist, author and essayist (the latter in both Arabic and English). He has a first class BA Hons in English and Philosophy (Hull University, UK, 1998) and was awarded the Larkin Prize for English and the Chris Ayers Prize for Philosophy. His first two novels came out in 2011 and 2012, and are translated into English – *The Book of the Sultan's Seal: Strange Incidents from History in the City of Mars* and *Crocodiles*. His third one, *Paolo* (2016), was longlisted for the 2017 IPAF.

CONTRIBUTORS

Clare Roberts has a BA in Arabic and Islamic Studies (Oxford University) and an MA in Arabic Poetry and Turkish Politics (SOAS, London). She works at a charity, and reviews for *Banipal*.

Safi Said is a Tunisian writer, journalist and novelist. He coined the term 'Arab Spring' in January 2011, inspired by his own encyclopaedic volume *Khareef al-Arab* (The Arabs' Autumn, Beirut, 2005). Said spent nearly 25 years away from home, travelling in different countries and continents and has authored over 20 books of biography, geopolitics, history, and futurology. Living now in Tunis, he ran for the Tunisian Presidency as an independent candidate in the 2014 elections and scored an advanced ranking.

Abdelaziz Baraka Sakin was born in Kassala, eastern Sudan, in 1963. He has published seven novels and four short story collections, most of which are banned in Sudan, but circulate online. He is lives now in Austria.

Randa Shaath is a photographer based in Cairo, Egypt. She teaches photography at the American University in Cairo and has worked as photo editor at *Al Shorouk* daily newspaper, as photographer for *Al-Ahram Weekly* and as a mentor for grantees of the Arab Documentary Photography Program. She has exhibited her work widely in Egypt and abroad, and represented Egypt at the Bienal de São Paulo in 2006. She has published three monographs: *Watani ala Marma Haggar* (1988), *Misr Umm el Dunia* (1990), and *Under the Same Sky; Cairo* (2003).

Adel El Siwi is an Egyptian painter and translator of Italian poetry into Arabic. Born in 1952 in Beheira, Egypt, he studied medicine at Cairo University (1970-1976) and also studied at the faculty of fine arts 1974-1975. He lived and worked in Milan during the 1980s decade before moving back permanently to Cairo, where he continues to live and work. He has had numerous solo shows in many different countries, and has participated in many group shows as well as in Biennales in Cairo, Sharjah and Venice. El Siwi has translated into Arabic many texts by artists such as Leonardo da Vinci and Paul Klee, as well as the complete works of Italian poet Guiseppe Ungaretti, for which he was awarded the Mediterranean Prize for Translation of the 2007 Cairo Book Fair.

Paul Starkey is Emeritus Professor of Arabic at Durham University and Vice-President of BRISMES. He has translated many works by contemporary Arab authors, and won the 2015 Saif Ghobash Banipal Prize for Youssef Rakha's *The Book of the Sultan's Seal* (Interlink, 2014). He is a contributing editor of *Banipal* and chair of the Banipal Trust.

Susannah Tarbush is a freelance journalist specialising in cultural affairs in the Middle East. She writes the Tanjara blog, and is a consulting editor of *Banipal* and regular reviewer.

Mahmoud El-Wardany, born in Cairo in 1950, is an Egyptian writer and journalist. Since 1984 he has published four collections of short stories, eight novels and an autobiographical work. He is the co-founder of Cairo's weekly literary journal *Akhbar al-Adab*. He has won the Sawiris cultural award twice, in 2008 for his short stories *al-Hafla al-Sabahi* (A Morning Party), and in 2011 for his novel *Bayt al-Nar* (House of Fire). His latest novel is *al-Bahth 'An Dina* (Looking for Dina).

Jonathan Wright is a prizewinning translator who worked for many years as a journalist in the Arab world. His translations include three IPAF winners, Ahmed Sadawi's *Frankenstein in Baghdad* (2014), Saud Alsanousi's *The Bamboo Stalk* (IPAF 2013 & 2016 Saif Ghobash Banipal Prize), and Youssef Ziedan's *Azazeel* (IPAF 2009 & 2013 Saif Ghobash Banipal Prize), and Hassan Blasim's *The Iraqi Christ* (2014 Independent Foreign Fiction Prize).

Nariman Youssef is an Egyptian translator. She has a BSc in computer science from the American University in Cairo, MAs from Birkbeck College London and the University of Edinburgh, and is currently a doctoral candidate at Manchester University. Her translations include *The American Granddaughter* by Iraqi writer Inaam Kachachi, shortlisted for the 2009 IPAF. In October 2011 her e-book *Summer of Unrest: Tahrir - 18 Days of Grace* came out with Vintage Books.

> For more information on all the authors in *Banipal 60* and all the translators, writers and book reviewers, please go to:
> www.banipal.co.uk/contributors/